Nellie Bly

Undercover
Reporting for *The New York World* 1887-1894

The Archive of American Journalism

Lincoln Steffens

Henry Stanley

Theodore Roosevelt

Richard Harding Davis

Ray Stannard Baker

Nellie Bly

H.L. Mencken

Stephen Crane

Jack London

Mark Twain

Ernest Hemingway

Horace Greeley

Ambrose Bierce

Ida Tarbell

Undercover

Reporting for
The New York World
1887 - 1894

The Archive ▲ St. Paul, Minnesota

Note on Sources

All articles are complete and unabridged, with headlines, subheads and formatting that match those of the original publication. Note that minor edits have been made to correct obsolete spelling and punctuation. Students and researchers: these are "public domain" texts that can be freely copied, reproduced and distributed without permission or cost. Please credit The Archive of American Journalism as your source.

The Archive LLC
9269 Troon Court
Woodbury, MN 55125.

Article selection and original Introduction Copyright ©2014 by Tom Streissguth

Cover Image: Lewis Hine, "Newsgirl, Park Row" (1910), from the Library of Congress, National Child Labor Committee Collection

Library of Congress Control Number: 2014949309
ISBN: 978-0-9907137-2-2
Manufactured in the United States of America

Acknowledgments
For their encouragement and suggestions, sincere thanks to Mark Lerner, Gordon Hagert, Pier Gustafson, Phil Gapp, Jonathan Peacock, John Hatch, Marian Streissguth and our original founding supporters:

William F. Zeman
Phil Gapp
Walter Crowley
Adele Streissguth
Richard Prosser
Abhilash Zarhadi
James McGrath Morris

Contents

Introduction

Behind Asylum Bars
The New York World/October 9, 1887
3

Inside the Madhouse
The New York World/October 16, 1887
36

Trying to Be A Servant
The New York World/October 30, 1887
69

What Becomes of Babies
The New York World/November 6, 1887
79

Wanted—A Few Husbands
The New York World/December 4, 1887
90

In the Magdalen's Home
The New York World/February 12, 1888
105

Nellie Bly on the Stage
The New York World/March 4, 1888
115

Nellie Bly as a Mesmerist
The New York World/March 25, 1888
121

The Infamy of the Park
The New York World/August 5, 1888
133

Exposed by Nellie Bly
The New York World/November 11, 1888
142

Visiting the Dispensaries
The New York World/December 2, 1888
155

Nellie Bly a Prisoner
The New York World/February 24, 1889
168

Shadowed by a Detective
The New York World/April 28, 1889
186

Nellie Bly as a Salvation Army Girl
The New York World/October 1, 1893
202

The Siren of the Coleman House
The New York World/February 18, 1894
228

A New Trick in "Bargains"
The New York World/March 18, 1894
248

Worked by the Hindoo Idol
The New York World/March 25, 1894
256

In the Biggest New York Tenement
The New York World/August 5, 1894
265

In Trinity's Tenements
The New York World/December 17, 1894
278

Sources

Further Reading

Online Collections

Introduction

Anyone with an interest in journalism, as a scholar, professional writer or casual reader, owes a heavy debt to Elizabeth Jane Cochran, aka "Nellie Bly." Among the countless newspaper and broadcast reporters who have gone undercover to get a story—of all those assuming a disguise of clothing, voice or mannerism to dig out and write up the truth—she was the first, and perhaps still the best.

Bly used no press releases, anonymous sources, or phone calls to "media relations" or marketing departments to pull together her stories for Joseph Pulitzer's *New York World*. She didn't use wire sources; she didn't dig deep into library catalogues or Google up her information on the Net. Nor did she attend official briefings, rush to crime scenes, or scribble down interviews with bystanders in a little notebook. Instead, she marched into New York's riskier neighborhoods, skillfully deceived her intended targets, heard their explanations and confessions, and then wrote them up in damning, fascinating detail. The *World* splashed her stories across five or six columns of microscopic type in the fat Sunday editions, and put her *nom de plume* right in the headline. She gave names, addresses, descriptions and direct quotes with, apparently, no fear whatsoever of legal, professional or physical retribution.

For a few years, this peculiar approach to journalism was hers alone; her gender made it easier for editors and the public to accept, with polite deference, her disguises and deceptions. She first claimed the public's attention in 1887 by playing an incoherent lunatic and getting herself committed to the city's dungeon asylum on Blackwell's (now Roosevelt) Island, where her medical treatment consisted of several forms of mental and physical torture. The result was a sensational public scandal in the most jaded city on earth, and a powerful outcry for reform of the system.

The Bly Method was born; taking the appropriate accents and clothing, she wandered into chaotic theater productions, eerie mesmerists' homes, depressing factory sweatshops, and awful downtown tenements. She tricked estate-sale ripoff artists, adoption scamsters, cut-rate surgeons, cat murderers, and a Central Park sex fiend, then took them down on the front page of the *World* with no deference and no mercy. Her friendly, familiar, and opinionated writing style, and her myriad details of New York street life and behind-doors shenanigans, can still get a modern reader deeply fascinated, even at the remove of more than a century.

There have been plenty of Nellie Bly biographies, but her articles are rarely reprinted in full and have never been properly collected. Reading her original pieces on the Internet means struggling through a blurry, migraine-inducing facsimile of the original *World* pages. This book is the first of three Bly compilations by The Archive that together will bring this author's complete, unedited newspaper writings to students, historians, journalists, and readers with an interest—all those with a debt to Nellie Bly.

T.S.

August, 2014.

Undercover:
Reporting for
The New York World
1887-1894

THE WORLD.  PAGES 21 TO 28.

NEW YORK, SUNDAY, AUGUST 5, 1894.

IN THE BIGGEST NEW YORK TENEMENT.

Nellie Bly Spends the Two Hottest Days of the Year in the Largest "Double-Decker" in Town.

3,632 PEOPLE IN THE BLOCK.

One Family Occupying Only Three Rooms Have Eight Boarders and Lodgers.

SLEEPING ON THE FIRE-ESCAPES.

No Scenes of Disturbance or Disorder Among the Throngs of Over-Crowded Tenants.

STRANGE PHASES OF LIFE IN A BIG CITY.

THE HOTTEST NIGHT OF THE YEAR IN NEW YORK'S BIGGEST "DOUBLE-DECKER" TENEMENT.

The New York World
October 9, 1887

Behind Asylum Bars

The Mystery of the Unknown Insane Girl

Remarkable Story of the Successful Impersonation of Insanity

How Nellie Brown Deceived Judges, Reporters and Medical Experts

She Tells Her Story of How She Passed at Bellevue Hospital

ON the 22d of September I was asked by *The World* if I could have myself committed to one of the Asylums for the Insane in New York, with a view to writing a plain and unvarnished narrative of the treatment of the patients therein and the methods of management, etc. Did I think I had the courage to go through such an ordeal as the mission would demand? Could I assume the characteristics of insanity to such a degree that I could pass the doctors, live for a week among the insane without the authorities there finding out that I was only a "chiel amang 'em takin' notes?" I said I believed I could. I had some faith in my own ability as an actress and thought I could assume insanity long enough to accomplish any mission intrusted to me. Could I pass a week in the insane ward at Blackwell's Island? I said I could and I would. And I did. My instructions were simply to go on with my work as soon as I felt that I was ready. I was to chronicle faithfully the experiences I underwent, and when once within the walls of the asylum to find out and describe its inside workings, which are always so effectually hidden by white-capped nurses, as well as by bolts and bars, from the knowledge of the public. "We do not ask you to go there for the purpose of making sensational revelations. Write up things as you find them, good or bad; give praise or blame as you think best, and the truth all the time. But I am afraid of that chronic smile of yours," said the editor. "I will smile no more," I said, and I went away to execute my delicate and, as I found out, difficult mission.

THE PRELIMINARIES

All the preliminary preparations for my ordeal were left to be planned by myself. Only one thing was decided upon, namely, that I should pass under the pseudonym of Nellie Brown, the initials of which would agree with my own name and my linen, so that there would be no difficulty in keeping track of my movements and assisting me out of any difficulties or dangers I might get into. There were ways of getting into the insane ward, but I did not know them. I might adopt one of two courses. Either I could feign insanity at the house of friends, and get myself committed on the decision of two competent physicians, or I could go to my goal by way of the police courts. On reflection I thought it wiser not to inflict myself upon my friends or to get any good-natured doctors to assist me in my purpose. Besides, to get to Blackwell's Island my friends would have had to feign poverty, and, unfortunately for the end I had in view, my acquaintance with the struggling poor, except my own self, was only very superficial. So I determined upon the plan which led me to the successful accomplishment of my mission and to which the bulk of the following narrative will be devoted. I succeeded in getting committed to the insane ward at Blackwell's Island, where I spent ten days and nights and had an experience which I shall never forget. I took upon myself to enact the part of a poor, unfortunate crazy girl, and felt it my duty not to shirk any of the disagreeable results that should follow. I became one of the city's insane wards for that length of time, experienced much, and saw and heard more of the treatment accorded to this helpless class of our population, and when I had seen and heard enough, my release was promptly secured. I left the insane ward with pleasure and regret–pleasure that I was once more able to enjoy the free breath of heaven; regret that I could not have brought with me some of the unfortunate women who lived and suffered with me, and who, I am convinced, are just as sane as I was and am now myself. But here let me say one thing: From the moment I entered the insane ward on the island I made no attempt to keep up the assumed role of insanity. I talked and acted just as I do in ordinary life. Yet strange to say, the more sanely I talked and acted, the crazier I was thought to be by all except one physician, whose kindness and gentle ways I shall not soon forget.

PREPARING FOR THE ORDEAL

But to return to my work and my mission. After receiving my instructions I returned to my boarding-house, and when evening came I began to practice the role in which I was to make my debut on the morrow. What a difficult task, I thought, to appear before a crowd of people and convince them that I was insane. I had never been near insane persons before in my life, and had not the faintest idea of what their actions were like. And then to be examined by a number of learned physicians who make insanity a specialty, and who daily come in contact with insane people! How could I hope to pass these doctors and convince them that I was crazy? I feared that they could not be deceived. I began to think my task a hopeless one; but it had to be done. So I flew to the mirror and examined my face. I remembered all I had read of the doings of crazy people, how first of all they have staring eyes, and so I opened mine as wide as possible and stared unblinkingly at my own reflection. I assure you the sight was not reassuring, even to myself, especially in the dead of night. I tried to turn the gas up higher in hopes that it would raise my courage. I succeeded only partially, but I consoled myself with the thought that in a few nights more I would not be there, but locked up in a cell with a lot of lunatics. The weather was not cold; but, nevertheless, when I thought of what was to come, wintery chills ran races up and down my back in very mockery of the perspiration which was slowly but surely taking the curl out of my bangs. Between times, practicing before the mirror and picturing my future as a lunatic, I read snatches of improbable and impossible ghost stories, so that when the dawn came to chase away the night, I felt that I was in a fit mood for my mission, yet hungry enough to feel keenly that I wanted my breakfast. Slowly and sadly I took my morning bath and quietly bade farewell to a few of the most precious articles known to modern civilization. Tenderly I put my tooth-brush aside, and, when taking a final rub of the soap, I murmured, "It may be for days, and it may be—for longer." Then I donned the old clothing I had selected for the occasion. I was in the mood to look at everything through very serious glasses. It's just as well to take a last "fond look," I mused, for who could tell but that the strain of playing crazy, and being shut up with a crowd of mad people, might turn my own brain, and I would never get back. But not once did I think of shirking my mission. Calmly, outwardly at least, I went out to my crazy business. I walked down Second Avenue. It had been arranged that I should enter one of the many temporary homes or shelters for females, and that once in I should do the best I could to get forwarded on my journey to Blackwell's Island. The place selected was the Temporary Home for Females, 84 Second Avenue.

IN THE TEMPORARY HOME.

II.

I was left to begin my career as Nellie Brown, the insane girl. As I walked down the avenue I tried to assume the look which maidens wear in pictures entitled "Dreaming." "Far-away" expressions have a crazy air. I passed through the little paved yard to the entrance of the Home. I pulled the bell, which sounded loud enough for a church chime, and nervously awaited the opening of the door to the Home, which I intended should ere long cast me forth and out upon the charity of the police. The door was thrown back with a vengeance, and a short, yellow-haired girl of some thirteen summers stood before me.

"Is the matron in?" I asked, faintly.

"Yes, she's in; she's busy. Go to the back parlor," answered the girl, in a loud voice, without one change in her peculiarly matured face.

I followed these not overkind or polite instructions and found myself in a dark, uncomfortable back-parlor. There I awaited the arrival of my hostess. I had been seated some twenty minutes at the least, when a slender woman, clad in a plain, dark dress entered and, stopping before me, ejaculated inquiringly, "Well?"

"Are you the matron?" I asked.

"No," she replied, "the matron is sick; I am her assistant. What do you want?"

"I want to stay here for a few days, if you can accommodate me."

"Well, I have no single rooms, we are so crowded; but if you will occupy a room with another girl, I shall do that much for you."

"I shall be glad of that," I answered. "How much do you charge?" I had brought only about seventy cents along with me, knowing full well that the sooner my funds were exhausted the sooner I should be put out, and to be put out was what I was working for.

"We charge thirty cents a night," was her reply to my question, and with that I paid her for one night's lodging, and she left me on the plea of having something else to look after. Left to amuse myself as best I could, I took a survey of my surroundings. By the time I had become familiar with my quarters a bell, which rivaled the door-bell in its loudness, began clanging in the basement, and simultaneously women went trooping down-stairs from all parts of the house. I imagined, from the obvious signs, that dinner was served, but as no one had said anything to me I made no effort to follow in the hungry train. Yet I did wish that some one would invite me down. It always produces such a lonely, homesick feeling to know others are eating, and we haven't a chance, even if we are not hungry. I was glad when the assistant matron came up and asked me if I did not want something to eat. I replied that I did, and then

I asked her what her name was. Mrs. Stanard, she said, and I immediately wrote it down in a notebook I had taken with me for the purpose of making memoranda, and in which I had written several pages of utter nonsense for inquisitive scientists. Thus equipped I awaited developments. But my dinner–well, I followed Mrs. Stanard down the uncarpeted stairs into the basement; where a large number of women were eating. She found room for me at a table with three other women. The short-haired slavey who had opened the door now put in an appearance as waiter. Placing her arms akimbo and staring me out of countenance she said:

"Boiled mutton, boiled beef, beans, potatoes, coffee or tea?"

"Beef, potatoes, coffee and bread," I responded.

"Bread goes in," she explained, as she made her way to the kitchen, which was in the rear. It was not very long before she returned with what I had ordered on a large, badly battered tray, which she banged down before me. I began my simple meal. It was not very enticing, so while making a feint of eating I watched the others. After dinner I went upstairs and resumed my former place in the back parlor. I was quite cold and uncomfortable, and had fully made up my mind that I could not endure that sort of business long, so the sooner I assumed my insane points the sooner I would be released from enforced idleness. Ah, that was indeed the longest day I had ever lived. I listlessly watched the women in the front parlor, where all sat except myself. One did nothing but read and scratch her head and occasionally call out mildly, "Georgie," without lifting her eyes from her book. "Georgie" was her over-frisky boy, who had more noise in him than any child I ever saw before. He did everything that was rude and unmannerly, I thought, and the mother never said a word unless she heard some one else yell at him. Another woman always kept going to sleep and waking herself up with her own snoring. I really felt wickedly thankful it was only herself she awakened. The majority of the women sat there doing nothing, but there were a few who made lace and knitted unceasingly. The enormous door-bell seemed to be going all the time, and so did the short-haired girl. The latter was, besides, one of those girls who sing all the time snatches of all the songs and hymns that have been composed for the last fifty years. There is such a thing as martyrdom in these days. The ringing of the bell brought more people who wanted shelter for the night. Excepting one woman, who was from the country on a day's shopping expedition, they were working women, some of them with children. As it drew toward evening Mrs. Stanard came to me and said:

SHE BEGINS TO SHOW SIGNS

"What is wrong with you? Have you some sorrow or trouble?"

"No," I said, almost stunned at the suggestion. "Why?"

"Oh, because," she said, womanlike, "I can see it in your face. It tells the story of a great trouble."

"Yes, everything is so sad," I said, in a haphazard way, which I had intended to reflect my craziness.

"But you must not allow that to worry you. We all have our troubles, but we get over them in good time. What kind of work are you trying to get?"

"I do not know; it's all so sad," I replied.

"Would you like to be a nurse for children and wear a nice white cap and apron?" she asked.

I put my handkerchief up to my face to hide a smile, and replied in a muffled tone, "I never worked; I don't know how."

"But you must learn," she urged; "all these women here work."

"Do they?" I said, in a low, thrilling whisper. "Why, they look horrible to me; just like crazy women. I am so afraid of them."

"They don't look very nice," she answered, assentingly, "but they are good, honest working women. We do not keep crazy people here."

I again used my handkerchief to hide a smile, as I thought that before morning she would at least think she had one crazy person among her flock.

"They all look crazy," I asserted again, "and I am afraid

of them. There are so many crazy people about, and one can
never tell what they will do. Then there are so many murders
committed, and the police never catch the murderers," and I
finished with a sob that would have broken up an audience of
blasé critics. She gave a sudden and convulsive start, and I knew
my first stroke had gone home. It was amusing to see what a
remarkably short time it took her to get up from her chair and
to whisper hurriedly: "I'll come back to talk with you after a
while." I knew she would not come back and she did not. When
the supper-bell rang I went along with the others to the basement
and partook of the evening meal, which was similar to dinner,
except that there was a smaller bill of fare and more people,
the women who are employed outside during the day having
returned. After the evening meal we all adjourned to the parlors,
where all sat, or stood, as there were not chairs enough to go
round. I watched two women, who seemed of all the crowd to
be the most sociable, and I selected them as the ones to work out
my salvation, or, more properly speaking, my condemnation and
conviction. Excusing myself and saying that I felt lonely, I asked
if I might join their company. They graciously consented, so with
my hat and gloves on, which no one had asked me to lay aside,
I sat down and listened to the rather wearisome conversation,
in which I took no part, merely keeping up my sad look, saying
"Yes," or "No," or "I can't say," to their observations. Several
times I told them I thought everybody in the house looked crazy,
but they were slow to catch on to my very original remark.
One said her name was Mrs. King and that she was a Southern
woman. Then she said that I had a Southern accent. She asked
me bluntly if I did not really come from the South. I said "Yes."
The other woman got to talking about the Boston boats and
asked me if I knew at what time they left. For a moment I forgot
my role of assumed insanity, and told her the correct hour of
departure. She then asked me what work I was going to do, or if
I had ever done any. I replied that I thought it very sad that there
were so many working people in the world. She said in reply
that she had been unfortunate and had come to New York, where
she had worked at correcting proofs on a medical dictionary for
some time, but that her health had given way under the task, and

that she was now going to Boston again. When the maid came to tell us to go to bed I remarked that I was afraid, and again ventured the assertion that all the women in the house seemed to be crazy. The nurse insisted on my going to bed. I asked if I could not sit on the stairs, but she said, decisively: "No; for every one in the house would think you were crazy." Finally I allowed them to take me to a room.

A KIND SOUL DISCOVERED

Here I must introduce a new personage by name into my narrative. It is the woman who had been a proofreader, and was about to return to Boston. She was a Mrs. Caine, who was as courageous as she was good-hearted. She came into my room, and sat and talked with me a long time, taking down my hair with gentle ways. She tried to persuade me to undress and go to bed, but I stubbornly refused to do so. During this time a number of the inmates of the house had gathered around us. They expressed themselves in various ways. "Poor loon!" they said. "Why, she's crazy enough!" "I am afraid to stay with such a crazy being in house." "She will murder us all before morning." One woman was for sending for a policeman to take me at once. They were all in a terrible and real state of fright. No one wanted to be responsible for me, and the woman who was to occupy the room with me declared that she would not stay with that "crazy woman" for all the money of the Vanderbilts. It was then that Mrs. Caine said she would stay with me. I told her I would like to have her do so. So she was left with me. She didn't undress, but lay down on the bed, watchful of my movements. She tried to induce me to lie down, but I was afraid to do this. I knew that if I once gave way I should fall asleep and dream as pleasantly and peacefully as a child. I should, to use a slang expression, be liable to "give myself dead away." So I insisted on sitting on the side of the bed and staring blankly at vacancy. My poor companion was put into a wretched state of unhappiness. Every few moments she would rise up to look at me. She told me that my eyes shone terribly brightly and then began to question me, asking me where I had lived, how long I had been in New

York, what I had been doing, and many things besides. To all her questionings I had but one response—I told her that I had forgotten everything, that ever since my headache had come on I could not remember.

Poor soul! How cruelly I tortured her, and what a kind heart she had! But how I tortured all of them! One of them dreamed of me—as a nightmare. After I had been in the room an hour or so, I was myself startled by hearing a woman screaming in the next room. I began to imagine that I was really in an insane asylum. Mrs. Caine woke up, looked around, frightened, and listened. She then went out and into the next room, and I heard her asking another woman some questions. When she came back she told me that the woman had had a hideous nightmare. She had been dreaming of me. She had seen me, she said, rushing at her with a knife in my hand, with the intention of killing her. In trying to escape me she had fortunately been able to scream, and so to awaken herself and scare off her nightmare. Then Mrs. Caine got into bed again, considerably agitated, but very sleepy. I was weary, too, but I had braced myself up to the work, and was determined to keep awake all night so as to carry on my work of impersonation to a successful end in the morning. I heard midnight. I had yet six hours to wait for daylight. The time passed with excruciating slowness. Minutes appeared hours. The noises in the house and on the avenue ceased. I kept thinking about the sad events of my life. I began at the beginning and, after living over again fifteen or twenty years of my existence, found I had only spanned over a space of five minutes. Failing to find anything more to think about of the past I turned my thoughts bravely to the future, wondering, first, what the next day would bring forth, then making plans for the carrying out of my project. I wondered if I should be able to pass over the river to the goal of my strange ambition, to become eventually an inmate of the halls inhabited by my mentally wrecked sisters. And then, once in, what would be my experience? And after? How to get out? Bah! I said, they will get me out.

I looked out toward the window and hailed with joy the slight shimmer of dawn. The light grew strong and gray, but the silence was strikingly still. My companion slept. I had still an hour or two to pass over. Fortunately I found some employment for my mental activity. Robert Bruce in his captivity had won confidence in the future, and passed his time as pleasantly as possible under the circumstances, by watching the celebrated spider building his web. I had less noble vermin to interest me. Yet I believe I made some valuable discoveries in natural history. I was about to drop off to sleep in spite of myself when I was suddenly startled to wakefulness. I thought I heard something crawl and fall down upon the counterpane with an almost inaudible thud. I had the opportunity of studying these interesting animals very thoroughly. They had evidently come for breakfast, and were not a little disappointed to find that their principal *plat* was not there. They scampered up and down the pillow, came together, seemed to hold interesting converse, and acted in every way as if they were puzzled by the absence of an appetizing breakfast. After one consultation of some length they finally disappeared, seeking victims elsewhere, and leaving me to pass the long minutes by giving my attention to cockroaches, whose size and agility were something of a surprise to me.

SYMPATHY IN TROUBLE

My room companion had been sound asleep for a long time, but she now woke up, and expressed surprise at seeing me still awake and apparently as lively as a cricket. She was as sympathetic as ever. She came to me and took my hands and tried her best to console me, and asked me if I did not want to go home. She kept me upstairs until nearly everybody was out of the house, and then took me down to the basement for coffee and a bun. After that, partaken in silence, I went back to my room, where I sat down, moping. Mrs. Caine grew more and more anxious. "What is to be done?" she kept exclaiming. "Where are your friends?" "No," I answered, "I have no friends, but I have some trunks. Where are they? I want them." The good woman tried to pacify me, saying that they would be found in good time. She believed that I was insane. Yet I forgive her. It is only after one is in trouble that one realizes how little sympathy and kindness there are in the world. The women in

the Home who were not afraid of me had wanted to have some
amusement at my expense, and so they had bothered me with
questions and remarks that had I been insane would have been
cruel and inhumane. Only this one woman among the crowd,
pretty and delicate Mrs. Caine, displayed true womanly feeling.
She compelled the others to cease teasing me and took the bed of
the woman who refused to sleep near me. She protested against
the suggestion to leave me alone and to have me locked up for
the night so that I could harm no one. She insisted on remaining
with me in order to administer aid should I need it. She smoothed
my hair and bathed my brow and talked as soothingly to me
as a mother would do to an ailing child. By every means she
tried to have me go to bed and rest, and when it drew toward
morning she got up and wrapped a blanket around me for fear I
might get cold; then she kissed me on the brow and whispered,
compassionately: "Poor child, poor child!" How much I admired
that little woman's courage and kindness. How I longed to
reassure her and whisper that I was not insane, and how I hoped
that, if any poor girl should ever be so unfortunate as to be what
I was pretending to be, she might meet with one who possessed
the same spirit of human kindness possessed by Mrs. Ruth
Caine.

THE ADVENT OF THE POLICE

III.

BUT to return to my story. I kept up my role until the
assistant matron, Mrs. Stanard, came in. She tried to persuade me
to be calm. I began to see clearly that she wanted to get me out of
the house at all hazards, quietly if possible. This I did not want.
I refused to move, but kept up ever the refrain of my lost trunks.
Finally someone suggested that an officer be sent for. After
awhile Mrs. Stanard put on her bonnet and went out. Then I knew
that I was making an advance toward the home of the insane.
Soon she returned, bringing with her two policemen–big, strong
men–who entered the room rather unceremoniously, evidently
expecting to meet with a person violently crazy. The name of one

of them was Tom Bockert. When they entered I pretended not to see them. "I want you to take her quietly," said Mrs. Stanard. "If she don't come along quietly," responded one of the men, "I will drag her through the streets." I still took no notice of them, but certainly wished to avoid raising a scandal outside. Fortunately Mrs. Caine came to my rescue. She told the officers about my outcries for my lost trunks, and together they made up a plan to get me to go along with them quietly by telling me they would go with me to look for my lost effects. They asked me if I would go. I said I was afraid to go alone. Mrs. Stanard then said she would accompany me, and she arranged that the two policemen should follow us at a respectful distance. She tied on my veil for me, and we left the house by the basement and started across town, the two officers following at some distance behind. We walked along very quietly and finally came to the station house, which the good woman assured me was the express office, and that there we should certainly find my missing effects. I went inside with fear and trembling, for good reason.

BEFORE CAPT. MCCULLAGH

I remembered the police station well because only ten days before I had been there and had seen Capt. McCullagh, from whom I had written as a reporter. If he were in, would he not recognize me? And then all would be lost so far as getting to the island was concerned. I pulled my sailor hat as low down over my face as I possibly could, and prepared for the ordeal. Sure enough there was sturdy Captain McCullagh standing near the desk. "Are you Nellie Brown?" he asked. I said I supposed I was. "Where do you come from?" he asked. I told him I did not know, and then Mrs. Stanard gave him a lot of information about me–told him how strangely I had acted at her home; how I had not slept a wink all night, and that in her opinion I was a poor unfortunate who had been driven crazy by inhuman treatment. There was some discussion between Mrs. Standard and the two officers, and Tom Bockert was told to take us down to the court in a car.

"Come along," Bockert said, "I will find your trunk for you." We all went together, Mrs. Stanard, Tom Bockert and his companion and myself. I said it was very kind of them to go with me, and I should not soon forget them. As we walked along I kept up my refrain about my trunks, injecting occasionally some remark about the dirty condition of the streets and the curious character of the people we met on the way. "I don't think I have ever seen such people before," I said. "Who are they?" I asked, and my companions looked upon me with expressions of pity, evidently believing I was a foreigner, an emigrant or something of the sort. They told me that the people around me were working people. I remarked once more that I thought there were too many working people in the world for the amount of work to be done, at which remark Policeman P. T. Bockert eyed me closely, evidently thinking that my mind was gone for good. We passed several other policemen, who generally asked my sturdy guardians what was the matter with me. By this time quite a number of ragged children were following us too, and they passed remarks about me that were to me original as well as amusing.

"What's she up for?" "Say, cop, where did ye get her?" "Where did yer pull 'er?" "She's a daisy!"

Poor Mrs. Stanard was more frightened than I was. The whole situation grew interesting, but I still had fears for my fate before the judge.

SEARCHING FOR LOST TRUNKS

At last we came to a low building, and Tom Bockert kindly volunteered the information: "Here's the express office. We shall soon find those trunks of yours."

I said that a great many people seemed to have lost their trunks. "Yes," he said, "nearly all these people are looking for trunks."

I said, "They all seem to be foreigners, too." "Yes," said Tom, "they are all foreigners just landed. They have all lost their trunks, and it takes most of our time to help find them for them."

We entered the courtroom. It was the Essex Market Police Courtroom. At last the question of my sanity or insanity was to be decided. Judge Duffy sat behind the high desk, wearing a look which seemed to indicate that he was dealing out the milk of human kindness by wholesale. I rather feared I would not get the fate I sought, because of the kindness I saw on every line of his face, and it was with rather a sinking heart that I followed Mrs. Stanard as she answered the summons to go up to the desk, where Tom Bockert had just given an account of the affair. "Come here," said an officer. "What is your name?"

"Nellie Brown," I replied, with a little accent. "I have lost my trunks, and would like if you could find them." "When did you come to New York?" he asked. "I did not come to New York," I replied (while I added, mentally, "because I have been here for some time.") "But you are in New York now," said the man. "No," I said, looking as incredulous as I thought a crazy person could, "I did not come to New York." "That girl is from the west," he said, in a tone that made me tremble. "She has a western accent." Some one else who had been listening to the brief dialogue here asserted that he had lived south and that my accent was southern, while another officer was positive it was eastern. I felt much relieved when the first spokesman turned to the judge and said, "Judge, here is a peculiar case of a young woman who doesn't know who she is or where she came from. You had better attend to it at once."

I commenced to shake with more than the cold, and I looked around at the strange crowd about me, composed of poorly dressed men and women with stories printed on their faces of hard lives, abuse and poverty. Some were consulting eagerly with friends, while others sat still with a look of utter hopelessness. Everywhere was a sprinkling of well-dressed, well-fed officers watching the scene passively and almost indifferently. It was only an old story with them. One more unfortunate added to a long list which had long since ceased to be of any interest or concern to them.

BEFORE JUDGE DUFFY

"Come here, girl, and lift your veil," called out Judge Duffy in tones which surprised me by a harshness which I did not expect, from the kindly face he possessed.

"Who are you speaking to?" I inquired, in my stateliest manner.

"Come here, my dear, and lift your veil. You know the Queen of England, if she were here, would have to lift her veil," he said, very kindly.

"That is much better," I replied. "I am not the Queen of England, but I'll lift my veil."

As I did so the little judge looked at me, and then, in a very kind and gentle tone, he said:

"My dear child, what is wrong?"

"Nothing is wrong except that I have lost my trunks, and this man," indicating Policeman Bockert, "promised to bring me where they could be found."

"What do you know about this child?" asked the judge, sternly, of Mrs. Stanard, who stood, pale and trembling, by my side.

"I know nothing of her except that she came to the home yesterday and asked to remain overnight."

"The home! What do you mean by the home?" asked Judge Duffy, quickly.

"It is a temporary home kept for working women at No. 84 Second Avenue."

"What is your position there?"

"I am assistant matron."

"Well, tell us all you know of the case."

"When I was going into the home yesterday I noticed her coming down the avenue. She was all alone. I had just got into the house when the bell rang and she came in. When I talked with her she wanted to know if she could stay all night, and I said she could. After awhile she said all the people in the house looked crazy, and she was afraid of them. Then she would not go to bed, but sat up all the night."

"Had she any money?"

"Yes," I replied, answering for her, "I paid her for everything, and the eating was the worst I ever tried."

There was a general smile at this, and some murmurs of "She's not so crazy on the food question."

"Poor child," said Judge Duffy, "she is well dressed, and

a lady. Her English is perfect, and I would stake everything on her being a good girl. I am positive she is somebody's darling."

At this announcement everybody laughed, and I put my handkerchief over my face and endeavored to choke the laughter that threatened to spoil my plans, in despite of my resolutions.

"I mean she is some woman's darling," hastily amended the judge. "I am sure some one is searching for her. Poor girl, I will be good to her, for she looks like my sister, who is dead."

There was a hush for a moment after this announcement, and the officers glanced at me more kindly, while I silently blessed the kind-hearted judge, and hoped that any poor creatures who might be afflicted as I pretended to be should have as kindly a man to deal with as Judge Duffy.

"I wish the reporters were here," he said at last. "They would be able to find out something about her."

I got very much frightened at this, for if there is any one who can ferret out a mystery it is a reporter. I felt that I would rather face a mass of expert doctors, policemen, and detectives than two bright specimens of my craft, so I said:

"I don't see why all this is needed to help me find my trunks. These men are impudent, and I do not want to be stared at. I will go away. I don't want to stay here."

So saying, I pulled down my veil and secretly hoped the reporters would be detained elsewhere until I was sent to the asylum.

"I don't know what to do with the poor child," said the worried judge. "She must be taken care of."

"Send her to the Island," suggested one of the officers.

"Oh, don't!" said Mrs. Stanard, in evident alarm. "Don't! She is a lady and it would kill her to be put on the Island."

For once I felt like shaking the good woman. To think the Island was just the place I wanted to reach and here she was trying to keep me from going there! It was very kind of her, but rather provoking under the circumstances.

"There has been some foul work here," said the judge. "I believe this child has been drugged and brought to this city. Make out the papers and we will send her to Bellevue for examination. Probably in a few days the effect of the drug will pass off and she will be able to tell us a story that will be startling. If the reporters would only come!"

I dreaded them, so I said something about not wishing to stay there any longer to be gazed at. Judge Duffy then told Policeman Bockert to take me to the back office. After we were seated there Judge Duffy came in and asked me if my home was in Cuba.

"Yes," I replied, with a smile. "How did you know?"

"Oh, I knew it, my dear. Now, tell me were was it? In what part of Cuba?"

"On the hacienda," I replied.

"Ah," said the judge, "on a farm. Do you remember Havana?"

"Si, señor," I answered; "it is near home. How did you know?"

"Oh, I knew all about it. Now, won't you tell me the name of your home?" he asked, persuasively.

"That's what I forget," I answered, sadly. "I have a headache all the time, and it makes me forget things. I don't want them to trouble me. Everybody is asking me questions, and it makes my head worse," and in truth it did.

"Well, no one shall trouble you any more. Sit down here and rest awhile," and the genial judge left me alone with Mrs. Stanard.

A REPORTER INTERVIEWS HER

Just then an officer came in with a reporter. I was so frightened, and thought I would be recognized as a journalist, so I turned my head away and said, "I don't want to see any reporters; I will not see any; the judge said I was not to be troubled."

"Well, there is no insanity in that," said the man who had brought the reporter, and together they left the room. Once again I had a fit of fear. Had I gone too far in not wanting to see a reporter, and was my sanity detected? If I had given the impression that I was sane, I was determined to undo it, so I jumped up and ran back and forward through the office, Mrs. Stanard clinging terrified to my arm.

"I won't stay here; I want my trunks! Why do they bother me with so many people?" and thus I kept on until the ambulance surgeon came in, accompanied by the judge.

THE AMBULANCE APPEARS

"HERE is a poor girl who has been drugged," explained the judge. "She looks like my sister, and any one can see she is a good girl. I am interested in the child, and I would do as much for her as if she were my own. I want you to be kind to her," he said to the ambulance surgeon. Then, turning to Mrs. Stanard, he asked her if she could not keep me for a few days until my case was inquired into. Fortunately, she said she could not, because all the women at the Home were afraid of me, and would leave if I were kept there. I was very much afraid she would keep me if the pay was assured her, and so I said something about the bad cooking and that I did not intend to go back to the Home. Then came the examination; the doctor looked clever and I had not one hope of deceiving him, but I determined to keep up the farce. "Put out your tongue," he ordered, briskly. I gave an inward chuckle at the thought. "Put out your tongue when I tell you," he said. "I don't want to," I answered, truthfully enough. "You must. You are sick, and I am a doctor." "I am not sick and never was. I only want my trunks." But I put out my tongue, which he looked at in a sagacious manner. Then he felt my pulse and listened to the beating of my heart. I had not the least idea how the heart of an insane person beat, so I held my breath all the while he listened, until, when he quit, I had to give a gasp to regain it. Then he tried the effect of the light on the pupils of my eyes. Holding his hand within a half inch of my face, he told me to look at it, then, jerking it hastily away, he would examine my eyes. I was puzzled to know what insanity was like in the eye, so I thought the best thing under the circumstances was to stare. This I did. I held my eyes riveted unblinkingly upon his hand, and when he removed it I exerted all my strength to still keep my eyes from blinking. "What drugs have you been taking?" he then asked me. "Drugs!" I repeated, wonderingly. "I do not know what drugs are." "The pupils of her eyes have been enlarged ever since she came to the Home. They have not changed once," explained Mrs. Stanard. I wondered how she knew whether they had or not, but I kept quiet. "I believe she has been using belladonna," said the doctor, and for the first time I was thankful that I was a little near-sighted, which of course answers for the enlargement of the pupils. I thought I might as well be truthful when I could without injuring my case, so I told him I was nearsighted, that I was not in the least ill, had never been sick, and that no one had a right to detain me when I wanted to find my trunks. I wanted to go home. He wrote a lot of things in a long, slender book, and then said he was going to take me home. The judge told him to take me and to be kind to me, and to tell the people at the hospital to be kind to me, and to do all they could for me. If we only had more such men as Judge Duffy, the poor unfortunates would not find life all darkness.

IN THE AMBULANCE WAGON

I began to have more confidence in my own ability now, since one judge, one doctor, and a mass of people had pronounced me insane, and I put on my veil quite gladly when I was told that I was to be taken in a carriage, and that afterward I could go home. "I am so glad to go with you," I said, and I meant it. I was very glad indeed. Once more, guarded by Policeman Brockert, I walked through the little, crowded courtroom. I felt quite proud of myself as I went out a side door into an alleyway, where the ambulance was waiting. Near the closed and barred gates was a small office occupied by several men and large books. We all went in there, and when they began to ask me questions the doctor interposed and said he had all the papers, and that it was useless to ask me anything further, because I was unable to answer questions. This was a great relief to me, for my nerves were already feeling the strain. A roughlooking man wanted to put me into the ambulance, but I refused his aid so decidedly that the doctor and policeman told him to desist, and they performed that gallant office themselves. I did not enter the ambulance without protest. I made the remark that I had never seen a carriage of that make before, and that I did not want to ride in it, but after awhile I let them persuade me, as I had right along intended to do. I shall never forget that ride. After I was put in flat on the yellow blanket, the doctor got in and sat near the door. The large gates were swung open, and the curious crowd which had collected swayed back to make way for the ambulance as it backed out. How they tried to get a glimpse at the supposed crazy girl! The doctor saw that I did not like the people gazing at me, and considerately put down the curtains, after asking my wishes in regard to it. Still that did not keep the people away. The children raced after us, yelling all sorts of slang expressions, and trying to get a peep under the curtains. It was quite an interesting drive, but I must say that it was an excruciatingly rough one. I held on, only there was not much to hold on to, and the driver drove as if he feared some one would catch up with us.

IN BELLEVUE HOSPITAL

IV.

AT last Bellevue was reached, the third station on my way to the island. I had passed through successfully the ordeals at the home and at Essex Market Police Court, and now felt confident that I should not fail. The ambulance stopped with a sudden jerk and the doctor jumped out. "How many have you?" I heard some one inquire. "Only one, for the pavilion," was the reply. A rough-looking man came forward, and catching hold of me attempted to drag me out as if I had the strength of an elephant and would resist. The doctor, seeing my look of disgust, ordered him to leave me alone, saying that he would take charge of me himself. He then lifted me carefully out and I walked with the grace of a queen past the crowd that had gathered curious to see the new unfortunate. Together with the doctor I entered a small dark office, where there were several men. The one behind the desk opened a book and began on the long string of questions which had been asked me so often. I refused to answer, and the doctor told him it was not necessary to trouble me further, as he had all the papers made out, and I was too insane to be able to tell anything that would be of consequence. I felt relieved that it was so easy here, as, though still undaunted, I had begun to feel faint for want of food. The order was then given to take me to the insane pavilion, and a muscular man came forward and caught me so tightly by the arm that a pain ran clear through me. It made me angry, and for a moment I forgot my role as I turned to him and said: "How dare you touch me?" At this he loosened his hold somewhat, and I shook him off with more strength than I thought I possessed. "I will go with no one but this man," I said, pointing to the ambulance-surgeon. "The judge said that he was to take care of me, and I will go with no one else." At this the surgeon said that he would take me, and so we went arm in arm, following the man who had at first been so rough with me. We passed through the well-cared-for grounds and finally reached the insane ward. A white-capped nurse was there to receive me. "This young girl is to wait here for the boat," said the surgeon, and then he started to leave me. I begged him not to go, or to take me with him, but he said he wanted to get his dinner first, and that I should wait there for him. When I insisted on accompanying him he claimed that he had to assist at an amputation, and it would not look well for me to be present. It was evident that he believed he was dealing with an insane person. Just then the most horrible insane cries came from a yard in the rear. With all my bravery I felt a chill at the prospect of being shut up with a fellow-creature who was really insane. The doctor evidently noticed my nervousness, for he said to the attendant: "What a noise the carpenters make." Turning to me he offered me explanation to the effect that new buildings were being erected, and that the noise came from some of the workmen engaged upon it. I told him I did not want to stay there without him, and to pacify me he promised soon to return. He left me and I found myself at last an occupant of an insane asylum.

SOME INTERIOR ARRANGEMENTS

I stood at the door and contemplated the scene before me. The long, uncarpeted hall was scrubbed to that peculiar whiteness seen only in public institutions. In the rear of the hall were large iron doors fastened by a padlock. Several stiff-looking benches and a number of willow chairs were the only articles of furniture. On either side of the hall were doors leading into what I supposed and what proved to be bedrooms. Near the entrance door, on the right-hand side, was a small sitting-room for the nurses, and opposite it was a room where dinner was dished out. A nurse in a black dress, white cap and apron and armed with a bunch of keys had charge of the hall. I soon learned her name, Miss Ball. An old Irishwoman was maid-of-all-work. I heard her called Mary, and I am glad to know that there is such a good-hearted woman in that place. I experienced only kindness and the utmost consideration from her. There were only three patients, as they are called. I made the fourth. I thought I might as well begin work at once, for I still expected that the very first doctor might declare me sane and send me out again into the wide, wide world. So I went down to the rear of the room and introduced myself to one of the women, and asked her all about herself. Her name, she said, was Miss Anne Neville, and she had been sick from overwork. She had been working as a chambermaid, and when her health gave way she was sent to some Sisters' Home to be treated. Her nephew, who was a waiter, was out of work, and, being unable to pay her expenses at the Home, had had her transferred to Bellevue.

"Is there anything wrong with you mentally as well?" I asked her.

"No," she said. "The doctors have been asking me many curious questions and confusing me as much as possible, but I have nothing wrong with my brain."

"Do you know that only insane people are sent to this pavilion?" I asked.

"Yes, I know; but I am unable to do anything. The doctors refuse to listen to me, and it is useless to say anything to the nurses."

AMONG THE INSANE PATIENTS

Satisfied from various reasons that Miss Neville was as sane as I was myself, I transferred my attentions to one of the other patients. I found her in need of medical aid and quite silly mentally, although I have seen many women in the lower walks of life, whose sanity was never questioned, who were not any brighter.

The third patient, Mrs. Fox, would not say much. She was very quiet, and after telling me that her case was hopeless refused to talk. I began now to feel surer of my position, and I determined that no doctor should convince me that I was sane so long as I had the hope of accomplishing my mission. A small, fair-complexioned nurse arrived, and, after putting on her cap, told Miss Ball to go to dinner. The new nurse, Miss Scott by name, came to me and said, rudely:

"Take off your hat."

"I shall not take off my hat," I answered. "I am waiting for the boat, and I shall not remove it."

"Well, you are not going on any boat. You might as well know it now as later. You are in an asylum for the insane."

Although fully aware of that fact, her unvarnished words gave me a shock. "I did not want to come here; I am not sick or insane, and I will not stay," I said.

"It will be a long time before you get out if you don't do as you are told," answered Miss Scott. "You might as well take off your hat, or I shall use force, and if I am not able to do it, I have but to touch a bell and I shall get assistance. Will you take it off?"

"No, I will not. I am cold, and I want my hat on, and you can't make me take it off."

"I shall give you a few more minutes, and if you don't take it off then I shall use force, and I warn you it will not be very gentle."

"If you take my hat off I shall take your cap off; so now."

Miss Scott was called to the door then, and as I feared that an exhibition of temper might show too much sanity I took off my hat and gloves and was sitting quietly looking into space when she returned. I was hungry, and was quite pleased to see Mary make preparations for dinner. The preparations were simple. She merely pulled a straight bench up along the side of a bare table and ordered the patients to gather 'round the feast; then she brought out a small tin plate on which was a piece of boiled meat and a potato. It could not have been colder had it been cooked the week before, and it had no chance to make acquaintance with salt or pepper. I would not go up to the table, so Mary came to where I sat in a corner, and while handing out the tin plate, asked:

"Have ye any pennies about ye, dearie?"

"What?" I said, in my surprise.

"Have ye any pennies, dearie, that ye could give me. They'll take them all from ye any way, dearie, so I might as well have them."

I understood it fully now, but I had no intention of feeing Mary so early in the game, fearing it would have an influence on her treatment of me, so I said I had lost my purse, which was quite true. But though I did not give Mary any money, she was none the less kind to me. When I objected to the tin plate in which she had brought my food she fetched a china one for me, and when I found it impossible to eat the food she presented she gave me a glass of milk and a soda cracker.

ONLY A CHARITY WARD

All the windows in the hall were open and the cold air began to tell on my Southern blood. It grew so cold indeed as to be almost unbearable, and I complained of it to Miss Scott and Miss Ball. But they answered curtly that as I was in a charity place I could not expect much else. All the other women were suffering from the cold, and the nurses themselves had to wear heavy garments to keep themselves warm. I asked if I could go to bed. They said "No!" At last Miss Scott got an old gray shawl, and shaking some of the moths out of it, told me to put it on. "It's rather a bad-looking shawl," I said. "Well, some people would get along better if they were not so proud," said Miss Scott. "People on charity should not expect anything and should not complain." So I put the moth-eaten shawl, with all its musty smell, around me, and sat down on a wicker chair, wondering what would come next, whether I should freeze to death or survive. My nose was very cold, so I covered up my head and was in a half doze, when the shawl was suddenly jerked from my face and a strange man and Miss Scott stood before me. The man proved to be a doctor, and his first greetings were, "I've seen that face before." "Then you know me?" I asked, with a great show of eagerness that I did not feel. "I think I do. Where did you come from?" "From home." "Where is home?" "Don't you know? Cuba." He then sat down beside me, felt my pulse, and examined my tongue, and at last said: "Tell Miss Scott all about yourself." "No, I will not. I will not talk with women." "What do you do in New York?" "Nothing." "Can you work?" "No, señor." "Tell me, are you a woman of the town?" "I do not understand you," I replied, heartily disgusted with him.

"I mean have you allowed the men to provide for you and keep you?"

I felt like slapping him in the face, but I had to maintain my composure, so I simply said: "I do not know what you are talking about. I always lived at home."

POSITIVELY DEMENTED

After many more questions, fully as useless and senseless, he left me and began to talk with the nurse. "Positively demented," he said. "I consider it a hopeless case. She needs to be put where some one will take care of her."

And so I passed my second medical expert.

After this, I began to have a smaller regard for the ability of doctors than I ever had before, and a greater one for myself. I felt sure now that no doctor could tell whether people were insane or not, so long as the case was not violent.

Later in the afternoon a boy and a woman came. The woman sat down on a bench, while the boy went in and talked with Miss Scott. In a short time he came out, and, just nodding good-bye to the woman, who was his mother, went away. She did not look insane, but as she was German I could not learn her story. Her name, however, was Mrs. Louise Schanz. She seemed quite lost, but when the nurses put her at some sewing she did her work well and quickly. At three in the afternoon all the patients were given a gruel broth, and at five a cup of tea and a piece of bread. I was favored; for when they saw that it was impossible for me to eat the bread or drink the stuff honored by the name of tea, they gave me a cup of milk and a cracker, the same as I had had at noon. Just as the gas was being lighted another patient was added. She was a young girl, twenty-five years old. She told me that she had just gotten up from a sick bed. Her appearance confirmed her story. She looked like one who had had a severe attack of fever. "I am now suffering from nervous debility," she said, "and my friends have sent me here to be treated for it." I did not tell her where she was, and she seemed quite satisfied. At 6.15 Miss Ball said that she wanted to go away, and so we would all have to go to bed. Then each of us—we now numbered six—were assigned a room and told to undress. I did so, and was given a short, cotton-flannel gown to wear during the night. Then she took every particle of the clothing I had worn during the day, and, making it up in a bundle, labeled it "Brown," and took it away. The iron-barred window was locked, and Miss Ball, after giving me an extra blanket, which, she said, was a favor rarely granted, went out and left me alone. The bed was not a comfortable one. It was so hard, indeed, that I could not make a dent in it; and the pillow was stuffed with straw. Under the sheet was an oilcloth spread. As the night grew colder I tried to warm that oilcloth. I kept on trying, but when morning dawned and it was still as cold as when I went to bed, and had reduced me to the temperature of an iceberg, I gave it up as an impossible task.

ANOTHER REPORTER TURNS UP

I had hoped to get some rest on this my first night in an insane asylum. But I was doomed to disappointment. When the night nurses came in they were curious to see me and to find out what I was like. No sooner had they left than I heard someone at my door inquiring for Nellie Brown, and I began to tremble, fearing always that my sanity would be discovered. By listening to the conversation I found it was a reporter in search of me, and I heard him ask for my clothing so that he might examine it. I listened quite anxiously to the talk about me, and was relieved to learn that I was considered hopelessly insane. That was encouraging. After the reporter left I heard new arrivals, and I learned that a doctor was there and intended to see me. For what purpose I knew not, and I imagined all sorts of horrible things, such as examinations and the rest of it, and when they got to my room I was shaking with more than fear. "Nellie Brown, here is the doctor; he wishes to speak with you," said the nurse. If that's all he wanted I thought I could endure it. I removed the blanket which I had put over my head in my sudden fright and looked up. The sight was reassuring.

A HANDSOME DOCTOR

He was a handsome young man. He had the air and address of a gentleman. Some people have since censured this action; but I feel sure, even if it was a little indiscreet, that the young doctor only meant kindness to me. He came forward, seated himself on the side of my bed, and put his arm soothingly around my shoulders. It was a terrible task to play insane before this young man, and only a girl can sympathize with me in my position.

"How do you feel tonight, Nellie?" he asked, easily.

"Oh, I feel all right."

"But you are sick, you know," he said.

"Oh, am I?" I replied, and I turned my head on the pillow and smiled.

"When did you leave Cuba, Nellie?"

"Oh, you know my home?" I asked.

"Yes, very well. Don't you remember me? I remember you."

"Do you?" and I mentally said I should not forget him. He was accompanied by a friend who never ventured a remark, but stood staring at me as I lay in bed. After a great many questions, to which I answered truthfully, he left me. Then came other troubles. All night long the nurses read one to the other aloud, and I know that the other patients, as well as myself, were unable to sleep. Every half-hour or hour they would walk heavily down the halls, their boot-heels resounding like the march of a private of dragoons, and take a look at every patient. Of course this helped to keep us awake. Then as it came toward morning, they began to beat eggs for breakfast, and the sound made me realize how horribly hungry I was. Occasional yells and cries came from the male department, and that did not aid in making the night pass more cheerfully. Then the ambulance-gong, as it brought in more unfortunates, sounded as a knell to life and liberty. Thus I passed my first night as an insane girl at Bellevue.

THE GOAL IN SIGHT

V.

AT 6 o'clock on Sunday morning, Sept. 25, the nurses pulled the covering from my bed. "Come, it's time for you to get out of bed," they said, and opened the window and let in the cold breeze. My clothing was then returned to me. After dressing I was shown to a washstand, where all the other patients were trying to rid their faces of all traces of sleep. At 7 o'clock we were given some horrible mess, which Mary told us was chicken broth. The cold, from which we had suffered enough the day previous, was bitter, and when I complained to the nurse she said it was one of the rules of the institution not to turn the heat on until October, and so we would have to endure it, as the steam-pipes had not even been put in order. The night nurses then, arming themselves with scissors, began to play manicure on the patients. They cut my nails to the quick, as they did those of several of the other patients. Shortly after this a handsome young doctor made his appearance and I was conducted into the sitting-room. "Who are you?" he asked. "Nellie Moreno," I replied. "Then why did you give the name of Brown?" he asked. "What is wrong with you?" "Nothing. I did not want to come here, but they brought me. I want to go away. Won't you let me out?"

WHO IS THIS MAN?

"If I take you out will you stay with me? Won't you run away from me when you get on the street?"

"I can't promise that I will not," I answered, with a smile and a sigh, for he was handsome.

He asked me many other questions. Did I ever see faces on the wall? Did I ever hear voices around? I answered him to the best of my ability. "Do you ever hear voices at night?" he asked. "Yes, there is so much talking I cannot sleep." "I thought so," he said to himself. Then turning to me, he asked: "What do these voices say?" "Well, I do not listen to them always. But sometimes, very often, they talk about Nellie Brown, and then on other subjects that do not interest me half so much," I answered, truthfully. "That will do," he said to Miss Scott, who was just on the outside. "Can I go away?" I asked. "Yes," he said, with a satisfied laugh, "we'll soon send you away." "It is so very cold here, I want to go out," I said. "That's true," he said to Miss Scott. "The cold is almost unbearable in here, and you will have some cases of pneumonia if you are not careful."

TESTS FOR INSANITY

With this I was led away and another patient was taken in. I sat right outside the door and waited to hear how he would test the sanity of the other patients. With little variation the examination was exactly the same as mine. All the patients were asked if they saw faces on the wall, heard voices, and what they said. I might also add each patient denied any such peculiar freaks of sight and hearing. At 10 o'clock we were given a cup of unsalted beef tea; at noon a bit of cold meat and a potato, at 3 o'clock a cup of oatmeal gruel and at 5.30 a cup of tea and a slice of unbuttered bread. We were all cold and hungry. After the physician left we were given shawls and told to walk up and down the halls in order to get warm. During the day the pavilion was visited by a number of people who were curious to see the crazy girl from Cuba. I kept my head covered, on the plea of being cold, for fear some of the reporters would recognize me. Some of the visitors were apparently in search of a missing girl, for I was made take down the shawl repeatedly, and after they looked at me they would say, "I don't know her," or "she is not the one," for which I was secretly thankful. Warden O'Rourke visited me, and tried his arts on an examination. Then he brought some well-dressed women and some gentlemen at different times to have a glance at the mysterious Nellie Brown.

PRAISE OF THE REPORTERS

The reporters were the most troublesome. Such a number of them! And they were all so bright and clever that I was terribly frightened lest they should see that I was sane. They were very kind and nice to me, and very gentle in all their questionings. My late visitor the night previous came to the window while some reporters were interviewing me in the sitting-room, and told the nurse to allow them to see me, as they would be of assistance in finding some clue as to my identity.

In the afternoon Dr. Field came and examined me. He asked me only a few questions, and one that had no bearing on such a case. The chief question was of my home and friends, and if I had any lovers or had ever been married. Then he made me stretch out my arms and move my fingers, which I did without the least hesitation, yet I heard him say my case was hopeless. The other patients were asked the same questions. As the doctor was about to leave the pavilion Miss Tillie Mayard discovered that she was in an insane ward. She went to Dr. Field and asked him why she had been sent there. "Have you just found out you are in an insane asylum?" asked the doctor. "Yes; my friends said they were sending me to a convalescent ward to be treated for nervous debility, from which I am suffering since my illness. I want to get out of this place immediately." "Well, you won't get out in a hurry," he said, with a quick laugh. "If you know anything at all," she responded, "you should be able to tell that I am perfectly sane. Why don't you test me?" "We know all we want to on that score," said the doctor, and he left the poor girl condemned to an insane asylum, probably for life, without giving her one feeble chance to prove her sanity.

Sunday night was but a repetition of Saturday. All night long we were kept awake by the talk of the nurses and their heavy walking through the uncarpeted halls. On Monday morning we were told that we should be taken away at 1.30.

The nurses questioned me unceasingly about my home, and all seemed to have an idea that I had a lover who had cast me forth on the world and wrecked my brain. The morning brought many reporters. How untiring they are in their efforts to get something new. Miss Scott refused to allow me to be seen, however, and for this I was thankful. Had they been given free access to me, I should probably not have been a mystery long, for many of them knew me by sight. Warden O'Rourke came for a final visit and had a short conversation with me. He wrote his name in my notebook, saying to the nurse that I would forget all about it in an hour. I smiled and thought I wasn't sure of that. Other people called to see me, but none knew me or could give any information about me.

LEAVING BELLEVUE

Noon came. I grew nervous as the time approached to leave for the Island. I dreaded every new arrival, fearful that my secret would be discovered at the last moment. Then I was given a shawl and my hat and gloves. I could hardly put them on, my nerves were so unstrung. At last the attendant arrived, and I bade good-bye to Mary as I slipped "a few pennies" into her hand. "God bless you," she said; "I shall pray for you. Cheer up, dearie. You are young, and will get over this." I told her I hoped so, and then I said good-bye to Miss Scott in Spanish. The rough-looking attendant twisted his arms around mine, and half-led, half-dragged me to an ambulance. A crowd of the students had assembled, and they watched us curiously. I put the shawl over my face, and sank thankfully into the wagon. Miss Neville, Miss Mayard, Mrs. Fox, and Mrs. Schanz were all put in after me, one at a time. A man got in with us, the doors were locked, and we were driven out of the gates in great style on toward the Insane Asylum and victory! The patients made no move to escape. The odor of the male attendant's breath was enough to make one's head swim.

When we reached the wharf such a mob of people crowded around the wagon that the police were called to put them away, so that we could reach the boat. I was the last of the procession. I was escorted down the plank, the fresh breeze blowing the attendant's whisky breath into my face until I staggered. I was taken into a dirty cabin, where I found my companions seated on a narrow bench. The small windows were closed, and, with the smell of the filthy room, the air was stifling. At one end of the cabin was a small bunk in such a condition that I had to hold my nose when I went near it. A sick girl was put on it. An old woman, with an enormous bonnet and a dirty basket filled with chunks of bread and bits of scrap meat, completed our company. The door was guarded by two female attendants. One was clad in a dress made of bed-ticking and the other was dressed with some attempt at style. They were coarse, massive women, and expectorated tobacco juice about on the floor in a manner more skillful than charming. One of these fearful creatures seemed to have much faith in the power of the glance on insane people, for, when any one of us would move or go to look out of the high window she would say "Sit down," and would lower her brows and glare in a way that was simply terrifying. While guarding the door they talked with some men on the outside. They discussed the number of patients and then their own affairs in a manner neither edifying nor refined.

The boat stopped and the old woman and the sick girl were taken off. The rest of us were told to sit still. At the next stop my companions were taken off, one at a time. I was last, and it seemed to require a man and a woman to lead me up the plank to reach the shore. An ambulance was standing there, and in it were the four other patients.

"What is this place?" I asked of the man, who had his fingers sunk into the flesh of my arm.

"Blackwell's Island, an insane place, where you'll never get out of."

With this I was shoved into the ambulance, the springboard was put up, an officer and a mail-carrier jumped on behind, and I was swiftly driven to the Insane Asylum on Blackwell's Island. Of my ten days' experience there I have yet to tell.

The New York World
October 16, 1887

Inside the Madhouse

Nellie Bly's Experience in the Blackwell's Island Asylum

Continuation of the Story of Ten Days With Lunatics

How the City's Unfortunate Wards Are Fed and Treated

The Terrors of Cold Baths and Cruel, Unsympathetic Nurses

Attendants Who Harass and Abuse Patients and Laugh at Their Miseries

AS the wagon was rapidly driven through the beautiful lawns up to the asylum my feelings of satisfaction at having attained the object of my work were greatly dampened by the look of distress on the faces of my companions. Poor women, they had no hopes of a speedy delivery! On the wagon sped, and I, as well as my comrades, gave a despairing farewell glance at freedom as we came in sight of the long stone buildings. We passed one low building, and the stench was so horrible that I was compelled to hold my breath, and I mentally decided that it was the kitchen. I afterward found I was correct in my surmise, and smiled at the signboard at the end of the walk: "Visitors are not allowed on this road." I don't think the sign would be necessary if they once tried the road, especially on a warm day.

The wagon stopped, and the nurse and officer in charge told us to get out. The nurse added: "Thank God! they came quietly." We obeyed orders to go ahead up a flight of narrow, stone steps, which had evidently been built for the accommodation of people who climb stairs three at a time. I wondered if my companions knew where we were, so I said to Miss Tillie Mayard: "Where are we?" "At the Blackwell's Island Lunatic Asylum," she answered, sadly. "Are you crazy?" I asked. "No," she replied; "but as we have been sent here we will have to be quiet until we find some means of escape. They will be few, though, if all the doctors, as Dr. Field, refuse to listen to me or give me a chance to prove my sanity." We were ushered into a narrow vestibule, and the door was locked behind us.

In spite of the knowledge of my sanity and the assurance that I would be released in a few days, my heart gave a sharp twinge. Pronounced insane by four expert doctors and shut up behind the unmerciful bolts and bars of a madhouse! Not to be confined alone, but to be a companion, day and night, of senseless, chattering lunatics; to sleep with them, to eat with them, to be considered one of them, was an uncomfortable position. Timidly we followed the nurse up the long uncarpeted hall to a room filled by so-called crazy women. We were told to sit down, and some of the patients kindly made room for us. They looked at us curiously, and one came up to me and asked: "Who sent you here?" "The doctors," I answered. "What for?" she persisted. "Well, they say I am insane," I admitted. "Insane!" she repeated, incredulously. "It cannot be seen in your face."

This woman was too clever, I concluded, and was glad to answer the roughly given orders to follow the nurse to see the doctor. This nurse, Miss Grupe, by the way, had a nice German face, and if I had not detected certain hard lines about the mouth I might have expected, as did my companions, to receive but kindness from her. She left us in a small waiting-room at the end of the hall, and left us alone while she went into a small office opening into the sitting or receiving-room. "I like to go down in the wagon," she said to the invisible party on the inside. "It helps to break up the day." He answered her that the open air improved her looks, and she again appeared before us all smiles and simpers.

"Come here, Tillie Mayard," she said. Miss Mayard obeyed, and, though I could not see into the office, I could hear her gently but firmly pleading her case. All her remarks were as rational as any I ever heard, and I thought no good physician could help but be impressed with her story. She told of her recent illness, that she was suffering from nervous debility. She begged that they try all their tests for insanity, if they had any, and give her justice. Poor girl, how my heart ached for her! I determined then and there that I would try by every means to make my mission of benefit to my suffering sisters; that I would show how they are committed without ample trial. Without one word of sympathy or encouragement she was brought back to where we sat.

Mrs. Louise Schanz was taken into the presence of Dr. Kinter, the medical man. "Your name?" he asked, loudly. She answered in German, saying she did not speak English nor could she understand it. However, when he said Mrs. Louise Schanz, she said "Yah, yah." Then he tried other questions, and when he found she could not understand one world of English, he said to Miss Grupe: "You are German; speak to her for me." Miss Grupe proved to be one of those people who are ashamed of their nationality, and she refused, saying she could understand but few worlds of her mother tongue. "You know you speak German. Ask this woman what her husband does," and they both laughed as if they were enjoying a joke. "I can't speak but a few words," she protested, but at last she managed to ascertain the occupation of Mr. Schanz. "Now, what was the use of lying to me?" asked the doctor, with a laugh which dispelled the rudeness. "I can't speak any more," she said, and she did not.

Thus was Mrs. Louise Schanz consigned to the asylum without a chance of making herself understood. Can such carelessness be excused, I wonder, when it is so easy to get an interpreter? If the confinement was but for a few days one might question the necessity. But here was a woman taken without her own consent from the free world to an asylum and there given no chance to prove her sanity. Confined most probably for life behind asylum bars, without even being told in her language the why and wherefore. Compare this with a criminal, who is given every chance to prove his innocence. Who would not rather be a murderer and take the chance for life than be declared insane, without hope of escape? Mrs. Schanz begged in German to know where she was, and pleaded for liberty. Her voice broken by sobs, she was led unheard out to us.

Mrs. Fox was then put through this weak, trifling examination and brought from the office, convicted. Miss Annie Neville took her turn, and I was again left to the last. I had by this time determined to act as I do when free, except that I would refuse to tell who I was or where my home was.

THEY EXAMINE HER AGAIN

But the Doctor Paid More Attention to the Nurse Than to His Patient

"NELLIE BROWN, the doctor wants you," said Miss Grupe. I went in and was told to sit down opposite Dr. Kinier at the desk. "What is your name?" he asked, without looking up. "Nellie Brown," I replied easily. "Where is your home?" writing what I had said down in a large book. "In Cuba." "Oh!" he ejaculated, with sudden understanding–then, addressing the nurse: "Did you see anything in the papers about her?" "Yes," she replied, "I saw a long account of this girl in the *Sun* on Sunday." Then the doctor said: "Keep her here until I go to the office and see the notice again." He left us, and I was relieved of my hat and shawl. On his return, he said he had been unable to find the paper, but he related the story of my debut, as he had read it, to the nurse. "What's the color of her eyes?" Miss Grupe looked, and answered "gray," although everybody had always said my eyes were brown or hazel. "What's your age?" he asked; and as I answered, "Nineteen last May," he turned to the nurse, and said, "When do you get your next pass?" This I ascertained was a leave of absence, or "a day off." "Next Saturday," she said, with a laugh. "You will go to town?" and they both laughed as she answered in the affirmative, and he said:

"Measure her." I was stood under a measure, and it was brought down tightly on my head. "What is it?" asked the doctor. "Now you know I can't tell," she said. "Yes, you can; go ahead. What height?" "I don't know; there are some figures there, but I can't tell." "Yes, you can. Now look and tell me." "I can't; do it yourself," and they laughed again as the doctor left his place at the desk and came forward to see for himself. "Five feet five inches; don't you see?" he said, taking her hand and touching the figures. By her voice I knew she did not understand yet, but that was no concern of mine, as the doctor seemed to find a pleasure in aiding her. Then I was put on the scales, and she worked around until she got them to balance. "How much?" asked the doctor, having resumed his position at the desk. "I don't know. You will have to see for yourself," she replied, calling him by his Christian name, which I have forgotten. He turned and also addressing her by her baptismal name, he said: "You are getting too fresh!" and they both laughed. I then told the weight–112 pounds–to the nurse, and she in turn told the doctor. "What time are you going to supper?" he asked, and she told him. He gave the nurse more attention than he did me, and asked her six questions to every one of me. Then he wrote my fate in the book before him. I said, "I am not sick and I do not want to stay here. No one has a right to shut me up in this manner." He took no notice of my remarks, and having completed his writings, as well as his talk with the nurse for the moment, he said that would do, and with my companions, I went back to the sitting-room.

"You play the piano?" they asked. "Oh, yes; ever since I was a child," I replied. Then they insisted that I should play, and they seated me on a wooden chair before an old-fashioned square. I struck a few notes, and the untuned response sent a grinding chill through me. "How horrible," I exclaimed, turning to a nurse, Miss McCarten, who stood at my side. "I never touched a piano as much out of tune." "It's a pity of you," she said, spitefully; "we'll have to get one made to order for you." I began to play the variations of "Home Sweet Home." The talking ceased and every patient sat silent, while my cold fingers moved slowly and stiffly over the keyboard. I finished in an aimless fashion and refused all requests to play more. Not seeing an available place to sit, I still occupied the chair in the front of the piano while I "sized up" my surroundings.

It was a long, bare room, with bare yellow benches encircling it. These benches, which were perfectly straight, and just as uncomfortable, would hold five people, although in almost every instance six were crowded on them. Barred windows, built about five feet from the floor, faced the two double doors which led into the hall. The bare white walls were somewhat relieved by three lithographs, one of Fritz Emmet and the others of negro minstrels. In the center of the room was a large table covered with a white bed-spread, and around it sat the nurses. Everything was spotlessly clean and I thought what good workers the nurses must be to keep such order. In a few days after how I laughed at my own stupidity to think the nurses would work. When they found I would not play any more, Miss McCarten came up to me saying, roughly: "Get away from here," and closed the piano with a bang.

"Brown, come here," was the next order I got from a rough, red-faced woman at the table. "What have you on?" "My clothing," I replied. She lifted my dress and skirts and wrote down one pair shoes, one pair stockings, one cloth dress, one straw sailor hat, and so on.

AT SUPPER

Rancid Butter, Weak Tea and Five Prunes Her Uninviting Portion

THIS examination over, we heard some one yell, "Go out into the hall." One of the patients kindly explained that this was an invitation to supper. We late comers tried to keep together, so we entered the hall and stood at the door where all the women had crowded. How we shivered as we stood there! The windows were open and the draught went whizzing through the hall. The patients looked blue with cold, and the minutes stretched into a quarter of an hour. At last one of the nurses went forward and unlocked a door, through which we all crowded to a landing of the stairway. Here again came a long halt directly before an open window. "How very imprudent for the attendants to keep these thinly clad women standing here in the cold," said Miss Neville. I looked at the poor crazy captives shivering, and added, emphatically, "It's horribly brutal." While they stood there I thought I would not relish supper that night. They looked so lost and hopeless. Some were chattering foolish nonsense to invisible persons, others were laughing or crying aimlessly, and one old, gray-haired woman was nudging me, and, with winks and sage noddings of the head and pitiful uplifting of the eyes and hands, was assuring me that I must not mind the poor creatures, as they were all mad. "Stop at the heater," was then ordered, "and get in line, two by two." "Mary, get a companion." "How many times must I tell you to keep in line?" "Stand still," and, as the orders were issued, a shove and a push were administered, and often a slap on the ears. After this third and final halt, we were marched into a long, narrow dining-room, where a rush was made for the table.

The table reached the length of the room and was uncovered and uninviting. Long benches without backs were put for the patients to sit on, and over these they had to crawl in order to face the table. Placed closed together all along the table were large dressing-bowls filled with a pinkish-looking stuff which the patients called tea. By each bowl was laid a piece of bread, cut thick and buttered. A small saucer containing five prunes accompanied the bread. One fat woman made a rush, and jerking up several saucers from those around her emptied their contents into her own saucer. Then while holding to her own bowl she lifted up another and drained its contents at one gulp. This she did to a second bowl in shorter time than it takes to tell it. Indeed, I was so amused at her successful grabbings that when I looked at my own share the woman opposite, without so much as by your leave, grabbed my bread and left me without any.

Another patient, seeing this, kindly offered me hers, but I declined with thanks and turned to the nurse and asked for more. As she flung a thick piece down on the table she made some remark about the fact that if I forgot where my home was I had not forgotten how to eat. I tried the bread, but the butter was so horrible that one could not eat it. A blue-eyed German girl on the opposite side of the table told me I could have bread unbuttered if I wished, and that very few were able to eat the butter. I turned my attention to the prunes and found that very few of them would be sufficient. A patient near asked me to give them to her. I did so. My bowl of tea was all that was left. I tasted, and one taste was enough. It had no sugar, and it tasted as if it had been made in copper. It was as weak as water. This was also transferred to a hungrier patient, in spite of the protest of Miss Neville. "You must force the food down," she said, "else you will be sick, and who know but what, with these surroundings, you may go crazy. To have a good brain the stomach must be cared for." "It is impossible for me to eat that stuff," I replied, and, despite all her urging, I ate nothing that night.

It did not require much time for the patients to consume all that was eatable on the table, and then we got our orders to form in line in the hall. When this was done the doors before us were unlocked and we were ordered to proceed back to the sitting-room. Many of the patients crowded near us, and I was again urged to play, both by them and by the nurses. To please the patients I promised to play and Miss Tillie Mayard was to sing. The first thing she asked me to play was "Rock-a-bye Baby," and I did so. She sang it beautifully.

IN THE BATH

Scrubbed with Soft Soap and Put to Bed in a Wet Gown

A few more songs and we were told to go with Miss Grupe. We were taken into a cold, wet bathroom, and I was ordered to undress. Did I protest? Well, I never grew so earnest in my life as when I tried to beg off. They said if I did not they would use force and that it would not be very gentle. At this I noticed one of the craziest women in the ward standing by the filled bathtub with a large, discolored rag in her hands. She was chattering away to herself and chuckling in a manner which seemed to me fiendish. I knew now what was to be done with me. I shivered. They began to undress me, and one by one they pulled off my clothes. At last everything was gone excepting one garment. "I will not remove it," I said vehemently, but they took it off. I gave one glance at the group of patients gathered at the door watching the scene, and I jumped into the bathtub with more energy than grace.

The water was ice-cold, and I again began to protest. How useless it all was! I begged, at least, that the patients be made to go away, but was ordered to shut up. The crazy woman began to scrub me. I can find no other word that will express it but scrubbing. From a small tin pan she took some soft soap and rubbed it all over me, even all over my face and my pretty hair. I was at last past seeing or speaking, although I had begged that my hair be left untouched. Rub, rub, rub, went the old woman, chattering to herself. My teeth chattered and my limbs were goose-fleshed and blue with cold. Suddenly I got, one after the other, three buckets of water over my head–ice-cold water, too–into my eyes, my ears, my nose and my mouth. I think I experienced some of the sensations of a drowning person as they dragged me, gasping, shivering and quaking, from the tub. For once I did look insane, as they put me, dripping wet, into a short canton flannel slip, labeled across the extreme end in large black letters, "Lunatic Asylum, B. I., H. 6." The letters meant Blackwell's Island, Hall 6.

By this time Miss Mayard had been undressed, and, much as I hated my recent bath, I would have taken another if by it I could have saved her the experience. Imagine plunging that sick girl into a cold bath when it made me, who has never been ill, shake as if with ague. I heard her explain to Miss Grupe that her head was still sore from her illness. Her hair was short and had mostly come out, and she asked that the crazy woman be made to rub more gently, but Miss Grupe said: "There isn't much fear of hurting you. Shut up, or you'll get it worse." Miss Mayard did shut up, and that was my last look at her for the night.

I was hurried into a room where there were six beds, and had been put into bed when some one came along and jerked me out again, saying: "Nellie Brown has to be put in a room alone tonight, for I suppose she's noisy." I was taken to Room 28 and left to try and make an impression on the bed. It was an impossible task. The bed had been made high in the center and sloping on either side. At the first touch my head flooded the pillow with water, and my wet slip transferred some of its dampness to the sheet. When Miss Grupe came in I asked if I could not have a night-gown. "We have not such things in this institution," she said. "I do not like to sleep without," I replied. "Well, I don't care about that," she said. "You are in a public institution now, and you can't expect to get anything. This is charity, and you should be thankful for what you get." "But the city pays to keep these places up," I urged, "and pays people to be kind to the unfortunates brought here." "Well, you don't need to expect any kindness here, for you won't get it," she said, and she went out and closed the door.

A sheet and an oilcloth were under me, and a sheet and black wool blanket above. I never felt anything so annoying as that wool blanket as I tried to keep it around my shoulders to stop the chills from getting underneath. When I pulled it up I left my feet bare, and when I pulled it down my shoulders were exposed. There was absolutely nothing in the room but the bed and myself. As the door had been locked I imagined I should be left alone for the night, but I heard the sound of the heavy tread of two women down the hall. They stopped at every door, unlocked it, and in a few moments I could hear them relock it. This they did without the least attempt at quietness down the whole length of the opposite side of the hall and up to my room. Here they paused. The key was inserted in the lock and turned. I watched those about to enter. In they came, dressed in brown and white striped dresses, fastened by brass buttons, large, white aprons, a heavy green cord about the waist, from which dangled a bunch of large keys, and small, white caps on their heads. Being dressed as were the attendants of the day, I knew they were nurses. The first one carried a lantern, and she flashed its light into my face while she said to her assistant: "This is Nellie Brown." Looking at her, I asked: "Who are you?" "The night nurse, my dear," she replied, and, wishing that I would sleep well, she went out and locked the door after her. Several times during the night they came into my room, and even had I been able to sleep, the unlocking of the heavy door, their loud talking, and heavy tread, would have awakened me.

THE HORROR OF FIRE

Escape Practically Impossible in Case the Building Should Burn

I could not sleep, so I lay in bed picturing to myself the horrors in case a fire should break out in the asylum. Every door is locked separately and the windows are heavily barred, so that escape is impossible. In the one building alone there are, I think Dr. Ingram told me, some 300 women. They are locked, one to ten to a room. It is impossible to get out unless these doors are unlocked. A fire is not improbable, but one of the most likely occurrences. Should the building burn, the jailers or nurses would never think of releasing their crazy patients. This I can prove to you later when I come to tell of their cruel treatment of the poor things entrusted to their care. As I say, in case of fire, not a dozen women could escape. All would be left to roast to death. Even if the nurses were kind, which they are not, it would require more presence of mind than women of their class possess to risk the flames and their own lives while they unlocked the hundred doors for the insane prisoners. Unless there is a change there will some day be a tale of horror never equaled.

In this connection is an amusing incident which happened just previous to my release. I was talking with Dr. Ingram about many things, and at last told him what I thought would be the result of a fire. "The nurses are expected to open the doors," he said. "But you know positively that they would not wait to do that," I said, "and these women would burn to death." He sat silent, unable to contradict my assertion. "Why don't you have it changed?" I asked. "What can I do?" he replied. "I offer suggestions until my brain is tired, but what good does it do? What would you do?" he asked, turning to me, the proclaimed insane girl. "Well, I should insist on them having locks put in, as I have seen in some places, that by turning a crank at the end of the hall you can lock or unlock every door on the one side. Then there would be some chance of escape. Now, every door being locked separately, there is absolutely none." Dr. Ingram turned to me with an anxious look on his kind face as he asked, slowly: "Nellie Brown, what institution have you been an inmate of before you came here?" "None. I never was confined in any institution, except boarding-school, in my life." "Where then did you see the locks you have described?" I had seen them in the new Western Penitentiary at Pittsburgh, Pa., but I did not dare say so. I merely answered: "Oh, I have seen them in a place I was in–I mean as a visitor." "There is only one place I know of where they have those locks," he said, sadly, "and that is at Sing Sing. The inference is conclusive." I laughed very heartily over the implied accusation, and tried to assure him that I had never, up to date, been an inmate of Sing Sing or even ever visited it.

Just as the morning began to dawn I went to sleep. It did not seem many moments until I was rudely awakened and told to get up, the window being opened and the clothing pulled off me. My hair was still wet and I had pains all through me, as if I had the rheumatism. Some clothing was flung on the floor and I was told to put it on. I asked for my own, but was told to take what I got and keep quiet by the apparently head nurse, Miss Grady. I looked at it. One underskirt made of coarse dark cotton goods and a cheap white calico dress with a black spot in it. I tied the strings of the skirt around me and put on the little dress. It was made, as are all those worn by the patients, into a straight tight waist sewed on to a straight skirt. As I buttoned the waist I noticed the underskirt was about six inches longer than the upper, and for a moment I sat down on the bed and laughed at my own appearance. No woman ever longed for a mirror more than I did at that moment.

I saw the other patients hurrying past in the hall, so I decided not to lose anything that might be going on. We numbered forty-five patients in Hall 6, and were sent to the bathroom, where there were two coarse towels. I watched crazy patients who had the most dangerous eruptions all over their faces dry on the towels and then saw women with clean skins turn to use them. I went to the bathtub and washed my face at the running faucet and my underskirt did duty for a towel.

THE FIRST MORNING

Combed with a Public Comb, the Breakfast and the Uniform

Before I had completed my ablutions a bench was brought into the bathroom. Miss Grupe and Miss McCarten came in with combs in their hands. We were told to sit down on the bench, and the hair of forty-five women was combed with one patient, two nurses, and six combs. As I saw some of the sore heads combed I thought this was another dose I had not bargained for. Miss Tillie Mayard had her own comb, but it was taken from her by Miss Grady. Oh, that combing! I never realized before what the expression "I'll give you a combing" meant, but I knew then. My hair, all matted and wet from the night previous, was pulled and jerked, and, after expostulating to no avail, I set my teeth and endured the pain. They refused to give me my hairpins, and my hair was arranged in one plait and tied with a red cotton rag. My curly bangs refused to stay back.

After this we went to the sitting-room and I looked for my companions. At first I looked vainly, unable to distinguish them from the other patients, but after awhile I recognized Miss Mayard by her short hair. "How did you sleep after your cold bath?" "I almost froze, and then the noise kept me awake. It's dreadful! My nerves were so unstrung before I came here, and I fear I shall not be able to stand the strain." I did the best I could to cheer her. I asked that we be given additional clothing, at least as much as custom says women shall wear, but they told me to shut up; that we had as much as they intended to give us.

We were compelled to get up at 5.30 o'clock, and at 7.15 we were told to collect in the hall, where the experience of waiting, as on the evening previous, was repeated. When we got into the dining-room at last we found a bowl of cold tea, a slice of buttered bread and a saucer of oatmeal, with molasses on it, for each patient. I was hungry, but the food would not down. I asked for unbuttered bread and was given it. I cannot tell you of anything which is the same dirty, black color. It was hard, and in places nothing more than dried dough. I found a spider in my slice, so I did not eat it. I tried the oatmeal and molasses, but it was wretched, and so I endeavored, but without much show of success, to choke down the tea.

After we were back to the sitting-room a number of women were ordered to make the beds, and some of the patients were put to scrubbing and others given different duties which covered all the work in the hall. It is not the attendants who keep the institution so nice for the poor patients, as I had always thought, but the patients, who do it all themselves—even to cleaning the nurses' bedrooms and caring for their clothing.

About 9.30 the new patients, of which I was one, were told to go out to see the doctor. I was taken in and my lungs and my heart were examined by the flirty young doctor who was the first to see us the day we entered. The one who made out the report, if I mistake not, was the Assistant Superintendent, Ingram. A few questions and I was allowed to return to the sitting-room.

I came in and saw Miss Grady with my note-book and long lead pencil, bought just for the occasion. "I want my book and pencil," I said, quite truthfully. "It helps me remember things." I was very anxious to get it to make notes in and was disappointed when she said: "You can't have it, so shut up." Some days after I asked Dr. Ingram if I could have it, and he promised to consider the matter. When I again referred to it, he said that Miss Grady said I only brought a book there; and that I had no pencil. I was provoked, and insisted that I had, whereupon I was advised to fight against the imaginations of my brain.

After the housework was completed by the patients, and as day was fine, but cold, we were told to go out in the hall and get on shawls and hats for a walk. Poor patients! How eager they were for a breath of air; how eager for a slight release from their prison. They went swiftly into the hall and there was a skirmish for hats. Such hats!

THE VIOLENT PATIENTS

Unspeakable Scenes in the Yard—The Evil of Enforced Idleness

We had not gone many paces when I saw, proceeding from every walk, long lines of women guarded by nurses. How many there were! Every way I looked I could see them in the queer dresses, comical straw hats and shawls, marching slowly around. I eagerly watched the passing lines and a thrill of horror crept over me at the sight. Vacant eyes and meaningless faces, and their tongues uttered meaningless nonsense. One crowd passed and I noted by nose as well as eyes, that they were fearfully dirty. "Who are they?" I asked of a patient near me. "They are considered the most violent on the island," she replied. "They are from the Lodge, the first building with the high steps." Some were yelling, some were cursing, others were singing or praying or preaching, as the fancy struck them, and they made up the most miserable collection of humanity I had ever seen. As the din of their passing faded in the distance there came another sight I can never forget:

A long cable rope fastened to wide leather belts, and these belts locked around the waists of fifty-two women. At the end of the rope was a heavy iron cart, and in it two women—one nursing a sore foot, another screaming at some nurse, saying: "You beat me and I shall not forget it. You want to kill me," and then she would sob and cry. The women "on the rope," as the patients call it, were each busy on their individual freaks. Some were yelling all the while. One who had blue eyes saw me look at her, and she turned as far as she could, talking and smiling, with that terrible, horrifying look of absolute insanity stamped on her. The doctors might safely judge on her case. The horror of that sight to one who had never been near an insane person before, was something unspeakable. "God help them!" breathed Miss Neville. "It is so dreadful I cannot look." On they passed, but for their places to be filled by more. Can you imagine the sight? According to one of the physicians there are 1600 insane women on Blackwell's Island.

I was annoyed a great deal by nurses who had heard my romantic story calling to those in charge of us to ask which one I was. I was pointed out repeatedly.

It was not long until the dinner hour arrived and I was so hungry that I felt I could eat anything. The same old story of standing for a half and three-quarters of an hour in the hall was repeated before we got down to our dinners. The bowls in which we had our tea were now filled with soup, and on a plate was one cold boiled potato and a chunk of beef, which on investigation, proved to be slightly spoiled. There were no knives or forks, and the patients looked fairly savage as they took the tough beef in their fingers and pulled in opposition to their teeth. Those toothless or with poor teeth could not eat it. One tablespoon was given for the soup, and a piece of bread was the final entree. Butter is never allowed at dinner nor coffee or tea. Miss Mayard could not eat, and I saw many of the sick ones turn away in disgust. I was getting very weak from the want of food and tried to eat a slice of bread. After the first few bites hunger asserted itself, and I was able to eat all but the crusts of the one slice.

Supt. Dent went through the sitting-room, giving an occasional "How do you do?" "How are you today?" here and there among the patients. His voice was as cold as the hall, and the patients made no movement to tell him of their sufferings. I asked some of them to tell how they were suffering from the cold and insufficiency of clothing, but they replied that the nurse would beat them if they told.

I was never so tired as I grew sitting on those benches. Several of the patients would sit on one foot or sideways to make a change, but they were always reproved and told to sit up straight. If they talked they were scolded and told to shut up; if they wanted to walk around in order to take the stiffness out of them, they were told to sit down and be still. What, excepting torture, would produce insanity quicker than this treatment? Here is a class of women sent to be cured? I would like the expert physicians who are condemning me for my action, which has proven their ability, to take a perfectly sane and healthy woman, shut her up and make her sit from 6 A. M. until 8 P. M. on straight-back benches, do not allow her to talk or move during these hours, give her no reading and let her know nothing of the world or its doings, give her bad food and harsh treatment, and see how long it will take to make her insane. Two months would make her a mental and physical wreck.

BAD FOOD AND WORSE HELP

When One Falls Ill the Natural Thing is to Simply Die

I have described my first day in the asylum, and as my other nine were exactly the same in the general run of things it would be tiresome to tell about each. In giving this story I expect to be contradicted by many who are exposed. I merely tell in common words, without exaggeration, of my life in a mad-house for ten days. The eating was one of the most horrible things. Excepting the first two days after I entered the asylum, there was no salt for the food. The hungry and even famishing women made an attempt to eat the horrible messes. Mustard and vinegar were put on meat and in soup to give it a taste, but it only helped to make it worse. Even that was all consumed after two days, and the patients had to try to choke down fresh fish, just boiled in water, without salt, pepper or butter; mutton, beef and potatoes without the faintest seasoning. The most insane refused to swallow the food and were threatened with punishment. In our short walks we passed the kitchen where food was prepared for the nurses and doctors. There we got glimpses of melons and grapes and all kinds of fruits, beautiful white bread and nice meats, and the hungry feeling would be increased tenfold. I spoke to some of the physicians, but it had no effect, and when I was taken away the food was yet unsalted.

My heart ached to see the sick patients grow sicker over the table. I saw Miss Tillie Mayard so suddenly overcome at a bite that she had to rush from the dining-room and then got a scolding for doing so. When the patients complained of the food they were told to shut up; that they would not have as good if they were at home, and that it was too good for charity patients.

A German girl, Louise–I have forgotten her last name–did not eat for several days and at last one morning she was missing. From the conversation of the nurses I found she was suffering from a high fever. Poor thing! She told me she unceasingly prayed for death. I watched the nurses make a patient carry such food as the well ones were refusing up to Louise's room. Think of that stuff for a fever patient! Of course, she refused it. Then I saw a nurse, Miss McCarten, go to test her temperature, and she returned with a report of it being some 150 degrees. I smiled at the report, and Miss Grupe, seeing it, asked me how high my temperature had ever run. I refused to answer. Miss Grady then decided to try her ability. She returned with the report of 99 degrees.

Miss Tillie Mayard suffered more than any of us from the cold, and yet she tried to follow my advice to be cheerful and try to keep up for a short time. Superintendent Dent brought in a man to see me. He felt my pulse and my head and examined my tongue. I told them how cold it was, and assured them that I did not need medical aid, but that Miss Mayard did, and they should transfer their attentions to her. They did not answer me, and I was pleased to see Miss Mayard leave her place and come forward to them. She spoke to the doctors and told them she was ill, but they paid no attention to her. The nurses came and dragged her back to the bench, and after the doctors left they said, "After awhile, when you see that the doctors will not notice you, you will quit running up to them." Before the doctors left me I heard one say—I cannot give it in his exact words—that my pulse and eyes were not that of an insane girl, but Supt. Dent assured him that in cases such as mine such tests failed. After watching me for awhile he said my face was the brightest he had ever seen for a lunatic. The nurses had on heavy undergarments and coats, but they refused to give us shawls.

Nearly all night long I listened to a woman cry about the cold and beg for God to let her die. Another one yelled "Murder!" at frequent intervals and "Police!" at others until my flesh felt creepy.

The second morning, after we had begun our endless "set" for the day, two of the nurses, assisted by some patients, brought the woman in who had begged the night previous for God to take her home. I was not surprised at her prayer. She appeared easily seventy years old, and she was blind. Although the halls were freezing cold, that old woman had no more clothing on than the rest of us, which I have described. When she was brought into the sitting-room and placed on the hard bench, she cried: "Oh, what are you doing with me? I am cold, so cold. Why can't I stay in bed or have a shawl?" and then she would get up and endeavor to feel her way to leave the room. Sometimes the attendants would jerk her back to the bench, and again they would let her walk and heartlessly laugh when she bumped against the table or the edge of the benches. At one time she said the heavy shoes which charity provides hurt her feet, and she took them off. The nurses made two patients put them on her again, and when she did it several times, and fought against having them on, I counted seven people at her at once trying to put the shoes on her. The old woman then tried to lie down on the bench, but they pulled her up again. It sounded so pitiful to hear her cry: "Oh, give me a pillow and pull the covers over me, I am so cold."

At this I saw Miss Grupe sit down on her and run her cold hands over the old woman's face and down inside the neck of her dress. At the old woman's cries she laughed savagely, as did the other nurses, and repeated her cruel action. That day the old woman was carried away to another ward.

MADE MAD BY SURROUNDINGS

The Tragic Case of Miss Tillie Mayard—Very Near to Detection

MISS TILLIE MAYARD suffered greatly from cold. One morning she sat on the bench next to me and was livid with the cold. Her limbs shook and her teeth chattered. I spoke to the three attendants who sat with coats on at the table in the center of the floor. "It is cruel to lock people up and then freeze them," I said. They replied she had on as much as any of the rest, and she would get no more. Just then Miss Mayard took a fit and every patient looked frightened. Miss Neville caught her in her arms and held her, although the nurses roughly said: "Let her fall on the floor and it will teach her a lesson." Miss Neville told them what she thought of their actions, and then I got orders to make my appearance in the office.

Just as I reached there Superintendent Dent came to the door and I told him how we were suffering from the cold, and of Miss Mayard's condition. Doubtless, I spoke incoherently, for I told of the state of the food, the treatment of the nurses and their refusal to give more clothing, the condition of Miss Mayard, and the nurses telling us, because the asylum was a public institution we could not expect even kindness. Assuring him that I needed no medical aid, I told him to go to Miss Mayard. He did so. From Miss Neville and other patients I learned what transpired. Miss Mayard was still in the fit, and he caught her roughly between the eyebrows or thereabouts, and pinched until her face was crimson from the rush of blood to the head, and her senses returned. All day afterward she suffered from terrible headache, and from that on she grew worse.

Insane? Yes, insane; and as I watched the insanity slowly creep over the mind that had appeared to be all right I secretly cursed the doctors, the nurses and all public institutions. Some one may say that she was insane at some time previous to her consignment to the asylum. Then if she were, was this the proper place to send a woman just convalescing, to be given cold baths, deprived of sufficient clothing and fed with horrible food?

On this morning I had a long conversation with Dr. Ingram, the assistant superintendent of the asylum. I found that he was kind to the helpless in his charge. I began my old complaint of the cold, and he called Miss Grady to the office and ordered more clothing given the patients. Miss Grady said if I made a practice of telling it would be a serious thing for me, she warned me in time.

Many visitors looking for missing girls came to see me. Miss Grady yelled in the door from the hall one day: "Nellie Brown, you're wanted." I went to the sitting-room at the end of the hall, and there sat a gentleman who had known me intimately for years. I saw by the sudden blanching of his face and his inability to speak that the sight of me was wholly unexpected and had shocked him terribly. In an instant I determined, if he betrayed me as Nellie Bly, to say I had never seen him before.

However, I had one card to play and I risked it. With Miss Grady within touching distance I whispered hurriedly to him, in language more expressive than elegant: "Don't give me away." I knew by the expression of his eye that he understood, so I said to Miss Grady: "I do not know this man." "Do you know her?" asked Miss Grady. "No; this is not the young lady I came in search of," he replied, in a strained voice. "If you do not know her you cannot stay here," she said, and she took him to the door. All at once a fear struck me that he would think I had been sent there through some mistake and would tell my friends and make an effort to have me released. So I waited until Miss Grady had the door unlocked. I knew that she would have to lock it before she could leave, and the time required to do so would give me opportunity to speak, so I called: "One moment, señor." He returned to me and I asked aloud: "Do you speak Spanish, senor?" and then whispered, "It's all right. I'm after an item. Keep still." "No," he said, with a peculiar emphasis, which I knew meant that he would keep my secret.

CHOKINGS AND BEATINGS

The Nurses Amuse Themselves by Worrying Their Helpless Charges

People in the world can never imagine the length of days to those in asylums. They seemed never ending, and we welcomed any event that might give us something to think about as well as talk of. Anxiously the hour was watched for when the boat arrived to see if there were any new unfortunates to be added to our ranks. When they came and were ushered into the sitting-room the patients would express sympathy to one another for them and were anxious to show them little marks of attention. Hall 6 was the receiving hall, so that was how we saw all newcomers.

Soon after my advent a girl called Urena Little-Page was brought in. She was, as she had been born, silly, and her tender spot was, as with many sensible women, her age. She claimed eighteen, and would grow very angry if told to the contrary. The nurses were not long in finding this out, and then they teased her. "Urena," said Miss Grady, "the doctors say that you are thirty-three instead of eighteen," and the other nurses laughed. They kept up this until the simple creature began to yell and cry, saying she wanted to go home and that everybody treated her badly. After they had gotten all the amusement out of her they wanted and she was crying, they began to scold and tell her to keep quiet. She grew more hysterical every moment until they pounced upon her and slapped her face and knocked her head in a lively fashion. This made the poor creature cry the more, and so they choked her. Yes, actually choked her. Then they dragged her out to the closet, and I heard her terrified cries hush into smothered ones. After several hours' absence she returned to the sitting-room, and I plainly saw the marks of their fingers on her throat for the entire day.

This punishment seemed to awaken their desire to administer more. They returned to the sitting-room and caught hold of an old gray-haired woman whom I have heard addressed both as Mrs. Grady and Mrs. O'Keefe. She was insane, and she talked almost continually to herself and to those near her. She never spoke very loud, and at the time I speak of was sitting harmlessly chattering to herself. They grabbed her, and my heart ached as she cried: "For God sake, ladies, don't let them beat me." "Shut up, you hussy!" said Miss Grady as she caught the woman by her gray hair and dragged her shrieking and pleading from the room. She was also taken to the closet, and her cries grew lower and lower, and then ceased.

The nurses returned to the room and Miss Grady remarked that she had "settled the old fool for awhile." I told some of the physicians of the occurrence, but they did not pay any attention to it.

One of the characters in Hall 6 was Matilda, a little old German woman, who, I believe, went insane over the loss of money. She was small, and had a pretty pink complexion. She was not much trouble, except at times. She would take spells, when she would talk into the steam-heaters or get up on a chair and talk out of the windows. In these conversations she railed at the lawyers who had taken her property. The nurses seemed to find a great deal of amusement in teasing the harmless old soul. One day I sat beside Miss Grady and Miss Grupe, and heard them tell her perfectly vile things to call Miss McCarten. After telling her to say these things they would send her to the other nurse, but Matilda proved that she, even in her state, had more sense than they. "I cannot tell you. It is private," was all she would say. I saw Miss Grady, on a pretense of whispering to her, spit in her ear. Matilda quietly wiped her ear and said nothing.

SOME UNFORTUNATE STORIES

A Few of the Apparently Sane Women Tell of Their Troubles

By this time I had made the acquaintance of the greater number of the forty-five women in Hall 6. Let me introduce a few. Louise, the pretty German girl whom I have spoken of formerly as being sick with fever, had the delusion that the spirits of her dead parents were with her. "I have gotten many beatings from Miss Grady and her assistants," she said, "and I am unable to eat the horrible food they give us. I ought not to be compelled to freeze for want of proper clothing. Oh! I pray nightly that I may be taken to my papa and mamma. One night when Dr. Field came I was in bed, and weary of the examination. At last I said: 'I am tired of this. I will talk no more.' 'Won't you?' he said, angrily. 'I'll see if I can't make you.' With this he laid his crutch on the side of the bed, and, getting up on it, he pinched me very severely in the ribs. I jumped up straight in bed, and said: 'What do you mean by this?' 'I want to teach you to obey when I speak to you,' he replied. If I could only die and go to papa!" When I left she was confined to bed with a fever, and maybe by this time she has her wish.

There is a Frenchwoman confined in Hall 6, or was during my stay, whom I firmly believe to be perfectly sane. I watched her and talked with her every day, excepting the last three, and I was unable to find any delusion or mania in her. Her name is Josephine Despreau, if that is spelled correctly, and her husband and all her friends are in France. Josephine feels her position keenly. Her lips tremble, and she breaks down crying when she talks of her helpless condition. "How did you get here?" I asked.

"One morning as I was trying to get breakfast I grew deathly sick, and two officers were called in by the woman of the house, and I was taken to the station-house. I was unable to understand their proceedings, and they paid little attention to my story. Doings in this country were new to me, and before I realized it I was lodged as an insane woman in this asylum. When I first came I cried that I was here without hope of release, and for crying Miss Grady and her assistants choked me until they hurt my throat, for it has been sore ever since."

A pretty young woman spoke so little English I could not get her story except as told by the nurses. They said her name is Sarah Fishbaum, and that her husband put her in the asylum because she had a fondness for other men than himself. Granting that Sarah was insane, and about men, let me tell you how the nurses tried to cure (?) her. They would call her up and say: "Sarah, wouldn't you like to have a nice young man?" "Oh, yes; a young man is all right," Sarah would reply in her few English words. "Well, Sarah, wouldn't you like us to speak a good word to some of the doctors for you? Wouldn't you like to have one of the doctors?" And then they would ask her which doctor she preferred, and advise her to make advances to him when he visited the hall, and so on.

I had been watching and talking with a fair-complexioned woman for several days, and I was at a loss to see why she had been sent there, she was so sane. "Why did you come here?" I asked her one day, after we had indulged in a long conversation. "I was sick," she replied. "Are you sick mentally?" I urged. "Oh, no; what gave you such an idea? I had been overworking myself, and I broke down. Having some family trouble, and being penniless and nowhere to go, I applied to the commissioners to be sent to the poorhouse until I would be able to go to work." "But they do not send poor people here unless they are insane," I said. "Don't you know there are only insane women, or those supposed to be so, sent here!" "I knew after I got here that the majority of these women were insane, but then I believed them when they told me this was the place they sent all the poor who applied for aid as I had done."

"How have you been treated?" I asked. "Well, so far I have escaped a beating, although I have been sickened at the sight of many and the recital of more. When I was brought here they went to give me a bath, and the very disease for which I needed doctoring and from which I was suffering made it necessary that I should not bathe. But they put me in, and my sufferings were increased greatly for weeks thereafter."

A Mrs. McCartney, whose husband is a tailor, seems perfectly rational and has not one fancy. Mary Hughes and Mrs. Louise Schanz showed no obvious traces of insanity.

NURSES WHO SWEAR

Patients Hurried Into the Asylum Without Sufficient Examination

One day two newcomers were added to our list. The one was an idiot, Carrie Glass, and the other was a nice-looking German girl—quite young, she seemed, and when she came in all the patients spoke of her nice appearance and apparent sanity. Her name was Gretchen. She told me she had been a cook, and was extremely neat. One day, after she had scrubbed the kitchen floor, the chambermaids came down and deliberately soiled it. Her temper was aroused and she began to quarrel with them; an officer was called and she was taken to an asylum. "How can they say I am insane, merely because I allowed my temper to run away with me?" she complained. "Other people are not shut up for crazy when they get angry. I suppose the only thing to do is to keep quiet and so avoid the beatings which I see others get. No one can say one word about me. I do everything I am told, and all the work they give me. I am obedient in every respect, and I do everything to prove to them that I am sane."

One day an insane woman was brought in. She was noisy, and Miss Grady gave her a beating and blacked her eye. When the doctors noticed it and asked if it was done before she came there the nurses said it was.

While I was in Hall 6 I never heard the nurses address the patients except to scold or yell at them, unless it was to tease them. They spent much of their time gossiping about the physicians and about the other nurses in a manner that was not elevating. Miss Grady nearly always interspersed her conversation with profane language, and generally began her sentences by calling on the name of the Lord. The names she called the patients were of the lowest and most profane type. One evening she quarreled with another nurse while we were at supper about the bread, and when the nurse had gone out she called her bad names and made ugly remarks about her.

In the evenings a woman, whom I supposed to be head cook for the doctors, used to come up and bring raisins, grapes, apples, and crackers to the nurses. Imagine the feelings of the hungry patients as they sat and watched the nurses eat what was to them a dream of luxury.

One afternoon, Dr. Dent was talking to a patient, Mrs. Turney, about some trouble she had had with a nurse or matron. A short time after we were taken down to supper and this woman who had beaten Mrs. Turney, and of whom Dr. Dent spoke, was sitting at the door of our dining-room. Suddenly Mrs. Turney picked up her bowl of tea, and, rushing out of the door flung it at the woman who had beat her. There was some loud screaming and Mrs. Turney was returned to her place. The next day she was transferred to the "rope gang," which is supposed to be composed of the most dangerous and most suicidal women on the island.

At first I could not sleep and did not want to so long as I could hear anything new. The night nurses may have complained of the fact. At any rate one night they came in and tried to make me take a dose of some mixture out of a glass "to make me sleep," they said. I told them I would do nothing of the sort and they left me, I hoped, for the night. My hopes were vain, for in a few minutes they returned with a doctor, the same that received us on our arrival. He insisted that I take it, but I was determined not to lose my wits even for a few hours. When he saw that I was not to be coaxed he grew rather rough, and said he had wasted too much time with me already. That if I did not take it he would put it into my arm with a needle. It occurred to me that if he put it into my arm I could not get rid of it, but if I swallowed it there was one hope, so I said I would take it. I smelt it and it smelt like laudanum, and it was a horrible dose. No sooner had they left the room and locked me in than I tried so see how far down my throat my finger would go.

LAST DAYS

One Good Nurse—Sitting Still for Five Days— Soap Only Once a Week

I want to say that the night nurse, Burns, in Hall 6, seemed very kind and patient to the poor, afflicted people. The other nurses made several attempts to talk to me about lovers, and asked me if I would not like to have one. They did not find me very communicative on the, to them, popular subject.

Once a week the patients are given a bath, and that is the only time they see soap. A patient handed me a piece of soap one day about the size of a thimble, I considered it a great compliment in her wanting to be kind, but I thought she would appreciate the cheap soap more than I, so I thanked her but refused to take it. On bathing day the tub is filled with water, and the patients are washed, one after the other, without a change of water. This is done until the water is really thick, and then it is allowed to run out and the tub is refilled without being washed. The same towels are used on all the women, those with eruptions as well as those without. The healthy patients fight for a change of water, but they are compelled to submit to the dictates of the lazy, tyrannical nurses. The dresses are seldom changed oftener than once a month. If the patient has a visitor, I have seen the nurses hurry her out and change her dress before the visitor comes in. This keeps up the appearance of careful and good management.

The patients who are not able to take care of themselves get into beastly conditions, and the nurses never look after them, but order some of the patients to do so.

For five days we were compelled to sit in the room all day. I never put in such a long time. Every patient was stiff and sore and tired. We would get in little groups on benches and torture our stomachs by conjuring up thoughts of what we would eat first when we got out. If I had not known how hungry they were and the pitiful side of it, the conversation would have been very amusing. As it was it only made me sad. When the subject of eating, which seemed to be the favorite one, was worn out, they used to give their opinions of the institution and its management. The condemnation of the nurses and the eatables was unanimous.

As the days passed Miss Tillie Mayard's condition grew worse. She was continually cold and unable to eat of the food provided. Day after day she sang in order to try to maintain her memory, but at last the nurse made her stop it. I talked with her daily, and I grieved to find her grow worse so rapidly. At last she got a delusion. She thought that I was trying to pass myself off for her, and that all the people who called to see Nellie Brown were friends in search of her, but that I, by some means, was trying to deceive them into the belief that I was the girl. I tried to reason with her, but found it impossible, so I kept away from her as much as possible, lest my presence should make her worse and feed the fancy.

TRANSFERRED TO ANOTHER WARD

She is Cursed Before She Leaves and Gets No Better Quarters

When Pauline Moser was brought to the asylum we heard the most horrible screams, and an Irish girl, only partly dressed, came staggering like a drunken person up the hall, yelling, "Hurrah! Three cheers! I have killed the devil! Lucifer, Lucifer, Lucifer," and so on, over and over again. Then she would pull a handful of hair out, while she exultingly cried, "How I deceived the devils. They always said God made hell, but he didn't." After she had been there an hour or so, Dr. Dent came in, and as he walked down the hall, Miss Grupe whispered to the demented girl, "Here is the devil coming, go for him." Surprised that she would give a mad woman such instructions, I fully expected to see the frenzied creature rush at the doctor. Luckily she did not, but commenced to repeat her refrain of "Oh, Lucifer." After the doctor left, Miss Grupe again tried to excite the woman by saying the pictured minstrel on the wall was the devil, and the poor creature began to scream, "You devil, I'll give it to you," so that two nurses had to sit on her to keep her down. The attendants seemed to find amusement and pleasure in exciting the violent patients to do their worst.

    I always made a point of telling the doctors I was sane and asking to be released, but the more I endeavored to assure them of my sanity the more they doubted it. "What are you doctors here for?" I asked one, whose name I cannot recall. "To take care of the patients and test their sanity," he replied. "Very well," I said. "There are sixteen doctors on this island, and excepting two, I have never seen them pay any attention to the patients. How can a doctor judge a woman's sanity by merely bidding her good morning and refusing to hear her pleas for release? Even the sick ones know it is useless to say anything, for the answer will be that it is their imagination." "Try every test on me," I have urged others, "and tell me am I sane or insane? Try my pulse, my heart, my eyes; ask me to stretch out my arm, to work my fingers, as Dr. Field did at Bellevue, and then tell me if I am sane." They would not heed me, for they thought I raved.

    Again I said to one, "You have no right to keep sane people here. I am sane, have always been so and I must insist on a thorough examination or be released. Several of the women here are also sane. Why can't they be free?" "They are all insane," was the reply, "and suffering from delusions."

    After a long talk with Dr. Ingram, he said, "I will transfer you to a quieter ward." An hour later Miss Grady called me into the hall, and, after calling me all the vile and profane names a woman could ever remember, she told me that it was a lucky thing for my "hide" that I was transferred, or else she would pay me for remembering so well to tell Dr. Ingram everything. "You d—n hussy, you forget all about yourself, but you never forget anything to tell the doctor." After calling Miss Neville, whom Dr. Ingram also kindly transferred, Miss Grady took us to the hall above, No. 7.

In Hall 7 there are Mrs. Kroener, Miss Fitzpatrick, Miss Finney, and Miss Hart. I did not see as cruel treatment as downstairs, but I heard them make ugly remarks and threats, twist the fingers and slap the faces of the unruly patients. The night nurse, Conway I believe her name is, is very cross. In Hall 7, if any of the patients possessed any modesty, they soon lost it. Every one was compelled to undress in the hall before their own door, and to fold their clothes and leave them there until morning. I asked to undress in my room, but Miss Conway told me if she ever caught me at such a trick she would give me cause not to want to repeat it.

The first doctor I saw here–Dr. Caldwell–chucked me under the chin, and as I was tired refusing to tell where my home was, I would only speak to him in Spanish.

THE "RETREAT" AND "ROPE GANG"

Some of the Cruel Atrocities Practiced There—
The Last Good-Bye

A Mrs. Coster told me that for speaking to a man she was sent to the Retreat. "The remembrances of that is enough to make me mad. For crying the nurses beat me with a broomhandle and jumped on me, injuring me internally so that I will never get over it. Then they tied my hands and feet and, throwing a sheet over my head, twisted it tightly around my throat, so I could not scream, and thus put me in a bathtub filled with cold water. They held me under until I gave up every hope and became senseless. At other times they took hold of my ears and beat my head on the door and against the wall. Then they pulled my hair out by the roots so that it will never grow in again."

Mrs. Cotter here showed me proofs of her story. The dent in the back of her head and the bare spots where the hair had been taken out by the handles give her story as plainly as possible. "My treatment was not as bad as I have seen others get in here, but it has ruined my health, and even if I do get out of here I will be a wreck. When my husband heard of the treatment given me he threatened to expose the place if I was not removed, so I was brought here. I am well mentally now. All that old fear has left me, and the doctor has promised to allow my husband to take me home."

I made the acquaintance of Bridget McGuinness, who seems to be sane at the present time. She said she was sent to Retreat 4, and put on the "Rope Gang." "The beatings I got there were something dreadful. I was pulled around by the hair, held under the water until I strangled, and I was choked and kicked. The nurses would always keep a quiet patient stationed at the window to tell them if any of the doctors were approaching. It was hopeless to complain to the doctors for they always said it was the imagination of our diseased brains, and besides we would get another testing for telling. They would hold patients under the water and threaten to leave them to die there if they did not promise not to tell the doctors. We would still promise because we know the doctors would not help us, and we would do anything to escape the punishment. After breaking a window I was transferred to the Lodge, the worst place on the island. It is dreadfully dirty in there, and the stench is awful. In the summer the flies swarm the place. The food is worse than we get in other wards and we are given only tin plates. Instead of the bars being on the outside, as in this ward, they are on the inside. There are many quiet patients there who have been there for years, but the nurses keep them to do the work. Among other beatings I got there, the nurses jumped on me once and broke two of my ribs.

"While I was there a pretty young girl was brought in. She had been sick and she fought about being put in that dirty place. One night the nurses took her and, after beating her, they held her naked in a cold bath, then they threw her on her bed. When morning came the girl was dead. The doctors said she died of convulsions, and that was all that was done about it.

"They inject so much morphine and chloral that the patients are made crazy. I have seen the patients wild for water from the effect of the drugs, and the nurses would refuse it to them. I have heard women beg for a whole night for one drop and it was not given them. I myself cried for water until my mouth was so parched and dry that I could not speak."

I saw the same thing myself in Hall 7. The patients would beg for a drink before retiring, but the nurses—Miss Hart and the others—refused to unlock the bathroom that they might quench their thirst.

Hall 7 looks rather nice to a casual visitor. It is hung with cheap pictures and has a piano, which is presided over by Miss Mattie Morgan, who formerly was in a music store in this city. She has been training several of the patients to sing, with some show of success. The artiste of the hall is Under, pronounced Wanda, a Polish girl. She is a gifted pianist when she chooses to display her ability. The most difficult music she reads at a glance, and her touch and expression are perfect.

On Sunday the quieter patients, whose names have been handed in by the attendants during the week, are allowed to go to church. A small Catholic chapel is on the island, and other services are also held.

A "commissioner" came one day, and made the rounds with Dr. Dent. In the basement they found half the nurses gone to dinner, leaving the other half in charge of us, as was always done. Immediately orders were given to bring the nurses back to their duties until after the patients had finished eating. Some of the patients wanted to speak about their having no salt, but were prevented.

The Insane Asylum on Blackwell's Island is a human rat-trap. It is easy to get in, but once there it is impossible to get out. I had intended to have myself committed to the violent wards, the Lodge and Retreat, but when I got the testimony of two sane women who could give it, I decided not to risk my health—and hair—so I did not get violent.

I had, toward the last, been shut off from all visitors, and so when the lawyer, Peter A. Hendricks, came and told me that friends of mine were willing to take charge of me if I would rather be with them than in the Asylum, I was only too glad to give my consent. I asked him to send me something to eat immediately on his arrival in the city, and then I waited anxiously for my release.

It came sooner than I had hoped. I was out "in line" taking a walk, and had just gotten interested in a poor woman who had fainted away while the nurses were trying to compel her to walk. "Good-bye; I am going home," I called to Pauline Moser, as she went past with a woman on either side of her. Sadly I said farewell to all I knew as I passed them on my way to freedom and life, while they were left behind to a fate worse than death. "Adios," I murmured to the Mexican woman. I kissed my fingers to her, and so I left my companions of Hall 7.

I had looked forward so eagerly to leaving the horrible place, yet when my release came and I knew that God's sunlight was to be free for me again, there was a certain pain in leaving. For ten days I had been one of them. Foolishly enough, it seemed intensely selfish to leave them to their sufferings. I felt a quixotic desire to help them by sympathy and presence. But only for a moment. The bars were down and freedom was sweeter to me than ever.

Soon I was crossing the river and nearing New York. Once again I was a free girl after ten days in the mad-house on Blackwell's Island.

The New York World
October 30, 1887

Trying to Be A Servant

Nellie Bly's Strange Experience at Two Employment Agencies

She Pays a Dollar to the Agent and is Guaranteed a Situation—She Has No References—The Agent Knows Nothing of Her Character—Nevertheless, He Declares to a Customer that She Possesses All the Virtues in the Calendar—Can a Common Thief Thus Recommended Get Service in New York Homes?—How Applicants Are Treated—The Agency Sure to Make Money Whether the Girls Get Places or Not—The Out-of-Town Trick—A Weary Waiting for Work—Queer Experiences

No one but the initiated know what a great question the servant question is and how many perplexing sides it has. The mistresses and servants, of course, fill the leading roles. Then, in the lesser, but still important parts, come the agencies, which, despite the many voices clamoring against them, declare themselves public benefactors. Even the "funny man" manages to fill a great deal of space with the subject. It is a serious question, since it affects all one holds dear in life—one's dinner, one's bed and one's linen. I had heard so many complaints from long-suffering mistresses, worked-out servants, agencies and lawyers that I determined to investigate the subject to my own satisfaction. There was only one way to do it. That was to impersonate a servant and apply for a situation. I knew that there might be such a thing as "references" required, and, as I had never tested my abilities in this line, I did not know how to furnish them. Still, it would not do to allow a little thing like a "reference" to stop me in my work, and I would not ask any friend to commit herself to further my efforts. Many girls must at one time be without references, I thought, and this encouraged me to make the risk.

On Monday afternoon a letter came to THE WORLD office from a lawyer complaining of an agency where, he claimed, a client of his had paid for a servant, and the agent then refused to produce a girl. This shop I decided to make my first essay. Dressed to look the character I wanted to represent, I walked up Fourth Avenue until I found No. 69, the place I wanted. It was a low frame building, which retained all the impressions of old age. The room on the first floor was filled with a conglomeration of articles which gave it the appearance of a second-hand store. By a side door, leaning against the wall, was a large sign which told the passing public that that was the entrance to the "Germania Servants' Agency." On a straight, blue board, fastened lengthwise to a second-story window, was in large, encouraging white letters, the ominous word, "Servants."

I entered the side door, and as there was nothing before me but the dirty, uncarpeted hall and a narrow, rickety looking staircase, I went on to my fate. I passed two closed doors on the first landing and on the third I saw the word "Office." I did not knock, but turned the knob of the door, and, as it stuck top and bottom, I pressed my shoulder against it. It gave way, so did I, and I entered on my career as a servant with a tumble. It was a small room with a low ceiling, a dusty ingrain carpet and cheaply papered walls. A heavy railing and a high desk and counter which divided the room gave it the appearances of a police court. Around the walls were hung colored advertisements of steamship lines and maps. Above the mantel, which was decorated with two plaster-paris busts, was a square sheet of white paper. I viewed the large black letters on this paper with a quaking heart. "References Investigated!!" with two exclamation points. Now, if it had only been put quietly and mildly, or even with one exclamation point, but two—dreadful. It was a death-warrant to the idea I had of writing my own references if any were demanded.

A young woman who was standing with a downcast head by the window turned to look at the abrupt newcomer. A man who had apparently been conversing with her, came hastily forward to the desk. He was a middle-sized man, with a sharp gray eye, a bald head, and a black frock coat buttoned up tightly, showing to disadvantage his rounded shoulders.

QUESTIONED IN THE AGENCY

"Well?" he said to me in a questioning manner, as he glanced quickly over my "get up."

"Are you the man who gets places for girls?" I asked, as if there were but one such man.

"Yes, I'm the man. Do you want a place?" he asked, with a decidedly German twang.

"Yes, I want a place," I replied.

"What did you work at last?"

"Oh, I was a chambermaid. Can you get me a position, do you think?"

"Yes, I can do that," he replied. "You're a nice-looking girl and I can soon get you a place. Just the other day I got a girl a place for $20 a month, just because she was nice-looking. Many gentlemen, and ladies also, will pay more if the girls are nice looking. Where did you work?"

"I worked in Atlantic City," I said, with a mental cry for forgiveness.

"Have you no city reference?" he asked.

"No, none whatever, but I prefer the city, that's why I came here."

"Well, I can get you a position," he said, "but some people are mighty particular about references."

"Have you no place you can send me to now?" I said, determined to get at my business as soon as possible.

"You have to pay to get your name entered on the book first," he said, opening a large ledger, as he asked, "What is your name?"

"How much do you charge?" I asked, in order to give me time to decide on a name.

"I charge you one dollar for the use of the bureau for a month, and if I get you a big salary you will have to pay more."

"How much more?"

"That depends entirely on your salary," he answered, non-committal. "Your name?"

SHE PAYS THE REQUIRED DOLLAR

"Now, if I give you a dollar you will assure me a situation?"

"Certainly; that's what I'm here for."

"And you guarantee me work in this city?" I urged.

"Oh, certainly, certainly; that's what this agency is for. I'll get you a place, sure enough."

"All right. I'll give you a dollar, which is a great deal for a girl out of work. My name is Sally Lees."

"What shall I put you down for?"

"Oh, anything," I replied, with a generosity that surprised myself.

"Then I shall put it chambermaid, waitress, nurse or seamstress." So my name, or the one assumed, was entered in the ledger and as I paid my dollar I ventured the information that if he gave me a situation directly I should be pleased to give him more money. He warmed up at this and told me he should advertise me in the morning.

"Then you have no one in want of help now?"

"We have plenty of people, but not just now. They all come in the morning. This is too late in the day. Where are you boarding?"

At this moment a woman clad in a blue dress, with a small, black shawl wrapped around her, entered from a room in the rear. She also looked me over sharply, as if I was an article for sale, as the man told her in German all that he knew about me.

"You can stay here," she said in broken, badly broken English, after she had learned that I was friendless in the city. "Where is your baggage?"

"I left my baggage where I paid for my lodging tonight," I answered. They tried to induce me to stop at their house. Only $2.50 a week, with board, or 20 cents a night for a bed. They urged that it was immaterial to them, only I had a better chance to secure work if I was always there; it was only for my own good they suggested it. I had one glance of the adjoining bedroom, and that sight made me firm in my determination to sleep elsewhere.

THE RECEIPT

As the evening drew on I felt that they would have no more applications for servants that afternoon, and after asking the hour that I should return in the morning, I requested a receipt for my money. "You don't need to be so particular," he said, crossly, but I told him I was, and insisted until he was forced to comply. It was not much of a receipt. He wrote on the blank side of the agency's advertising card:

Sally Lees has paid $1.
Good for one month use of bureau.
69 4th ave.

On the following morning, about 10.30, I made my appearance at the agency. Some eight or ten girls were in the room, and the man who had pocketed my fee on the previous afternoon still adorned the throne back of the desk. No one said good morning, or anything else for that matter, so I quietly slid onto a chair near the door. The girls were all comfortably dressed, and looked as if they had enjoyed hearty breakfasts. All sat silent, with a dreamy expression on their faces, except two who stood by the window watching the passing throng and conversing in whispers with one another. I wanted to be with or near them, so that I might hear what was said. After waiting for some time I decided to awake the man to the fact that I wanted work, not a rest.

"Have you no place to send me this morning?"

"No, but I advertised you in the paper," and he handed me the *Tribune* of Oct. 25 and pointed out the following notice:

NURSE, &c—By excellent, very neat English girl as nurse and seamstress, chambermaid and waitress or parlor maid. Call at 69 4th ave., no cards answered.

I choked down a laugh as I read myself advertised in this manner, and wondered what my role would be next time. I began to hope someone would soon call for the excellent girl, but when an aged gentleman entered I wished just as fervently that he was not after me. I was enjoying my position too much, and I fear I could not restrain my gravity if any one began to question me. Poor old gentleman? He looked around helplessly as if he was at a loss to know what to do. The agent did not leave him long in doubt. "You want a girl, sir?"

THE AGENT FURNISHES REFERENCES

"Yes, my wife read an advertisement in the *Tribune* this morning and she sent me here to see the girl."

"Yes, yes, excellent girl, sir, come right back here," opening the gates and giving the gentleman a chair behind the high counter. "You come here, Sally Lees," indicating a chair beside the visitor for me. I sat down with an inward chuckle and the agent leaned over the back of a chair. The visitor eyed me nervously, and after clearing his throat several times and making vain attempts at beginning he said:

"You are the girl who wants work?" And after I answered in the affirmative he said: "Of course you know how to do all these things—you know what is required of a girl?"

"Oh, yes, I know," I answered confidently.

"Yes—well, how much do you want a month?"

"Oh, anything," I answered, looking to the agent for aid. He understood the look, for he began hurriedly:

"Fourteen dollars a month, sir. She is an excellent girl, good, neat, quick and of an amiable disposition."

I was astonished at his knowledge of my good qualities, but I maintained a lofty silence.

"Yes, yes," the visitor said musingly. "My wife only

pays $10 a month, and then if the girl is all right she is willing to pay more, you know. I really couldn't, you know—"

"We have no ten-dollar girls here, sir," said the agent with dignity. "You can't get an honest, neat and respectable girl for that amount."

"H'm, yes; well, this girl has good references, I suppose."

"Oh, yes, I know all about her," said the agent, briskly and confidently. "She is an excellent girl, and I can give you the best personal reference—the best of references."

Here I was, unknown to the agent. So far as he knew, I might be a confidence woman, a thief or everything wicked, and yet the agent was vowing that he had good personal references.

"Well, I live in Bloomfield, N.J., and there are only four in the family. Of course you are a good washer and ironer?" he said, turning to me. Before I had time to assure him of my wonderful skill in the line the agent interposed: "This is not the girl you want. No, sir, this girl won't do general housework. This is the girl you are after," bringing up another. "She does general housework," and he went on with a long list of her virtues, which were similar to those he had professed to find in me. The visitor got very nervous and began to insist that he could not take a girl unless his wife saw her first. Then the agent, when he found it impossible to make him take a girl, tried to induce the gentleman to join the bureau. "It will only cost you $2 for the use of the bureau for a month," he urged, but the visitor began to get more nervous and to make his way to the door. I thought he was frightened because it was an agency, and it amused me to hear how earnestly he pleaded that really he dare not employ a girl without his wife's counsel.

SOME OF THE GIRLS' STORIES

After the escape of the visitor we all resumed our former positions and waited for another visitor. It came in the shape of a red-haired Irish girl.

"Well, you are back again?" was the greeting given her.

"Yes. That woman was horrible. She and her husband

fought all the time and the cook carried tales to the mistress. Sure and I wouldn't live at such a place. A splendid laundress, with a good 'karacter,' don't need to stay in such places, I told them. The lady of the house made me wash every other day; then she wanted me to be dressed like a lady sure and wear a cap while I was at work. Sure and it's no good laundress who can be dressed up while at work, so I left her."

The storm had scarcely passed when another girl with fiery locks entered. She had a good face and a bright one, and I watched her closely.

"So you are back, too. You are troublesome," said the agent. Her eyes flashed, as she replied.

"Oh, I'm troublesome, am I? Well, you can take a poor girl's money, anyway, and then you tell her she's troublesome. It wasn't troublesome when you took my money, and where is the position? I have walked all over the city, wearing out my shoes and spending my money in carfare. Now, is this how you treat poor girls?"

"I did not mean anything by saying you were troublesome. That was only my fun," the agent tried to explain, and after a while the girl quieted down.

THE OUT-OF-TOWN TRICK

Another girl came and was told that, as she had not made her appearance the day previous she could not expect to obtain a situation. He refused to send her word if there was any chance. Then a messenger boy called and said that Mrs. Vanderpool, of No. 88 West Thirty-ninth Street, wanted the girl advertised in the morning paper. Irish girl No. 1 was sent, and she returned, after several hours' absence, to say that Mrs. Vanderpool said, when she learned where the girl came from, that she knew all about agencies and their schemes and she did not propose to have a girl from them. The girl buttoned Mrs. Vanderpool's shoes and returned to the agency to take her post of waiting.

I succeeded at last in drawing one of the girls—Winifred Friel—into conversation. She said she had been waiting for several days and that she had no chance of a place yet. The agency had a place out of town to which they tried to force girls who declared they would not leave the city. Quite strange they never offered the place to girls who said they would work anywhere. Winifred Friel wanted it, but they would not allow her to go, yet they tried to insist on me accepting it.

"Well, now, if you won't take that I would like to see you get a place this winter," he said angrily, when he found that I would not go out of the city.

"Why, you promised that you would find me a situation in the city."

"That's no difference; if you won't take what I offer, you can do without," he said indifferently.

"Then give me my money," I said.

"No, you can't have your money. That goes into the bureau." I urged and insisted, to no avail, and so I left the agency to return no more.

AT ANOTHER AGENCY

My second day I decided to apply to another agency, so I went to Mrs. L. Seely's, No. 68 West Twenty-second Street. I paid my dollar fee and was taken to the third story and put in a small room which was packed as close with women as sardines in a box. After edging my way in I was unable to move, so packed were we. A woman came up, and, calling me "that tall girl," told me roughly as I was new it was useless for me to wait there. Some of the girls said Mrs. Seely was always cross to them, and that I should not mind it. How horribly sitting those rooms were! There were fifty-two in the room with me, and the two other rooms I could look into were equally crowded, while groups stood on the stairs and in the hallway. It was a novel insight I got of life. Some girls laughed, some were sad, some slept, some ate and others read, while all sat from morning till night waiting a chance to earn a living. They are long waits, too. One girl had been there two months, others for days and weeks. It was good to see the glad look when called out to see a lady, and sad to see them return saying that they did not suit because they wore banks, or their hair in the wrong style, or that they looked bilious, or that they were too tall, too short, too heavy or too slender. One poor woman could not obtain a place because she wore mourning and so the objections ran.

I got no chance the entire day and I decided that I could not endure a second day in that human pack for two situations, so I resolved to follow the resolution of several of the other girls and try answering the advertisements in the morning papers. How I succeeded in this I shall tell some other time.

The New York World
November 6, 1887

What Becomes of Babies

Hundreds and Hundreds of Little Ones Given Away Yearly

Not the Petted Darlings of the Rich, but the Infants Born to Shame—These Are the Ones that Are Given into Alien Hands—Regular Traffic in New-Born Babes—A Money-Making Trade in Humanity

What name awakens such universally tender feelings as that of "baby?" Last week some philanthropist wrote to THE WORLD to suggest that I try to find out what becomes of all the baby waifs in this great city. Not the little ones who are cordially welcomed by proud parents, happy grandparents and a large circle of loving relatives, but the many hundreds of babies whose coming is greeted with grief and whose unhappy mothers hide their little lives in shame. Unhappily there are hundreds and hundreds of them, but it is an impossible task to tell what their fate is.

However, here is a condensed account of my studious inquiries in this direction. I took several Sunday newspapers and made note of many of the medical and manicure advertisements. The following is the result: Dr. Hawker, of No. 21 West Thirteenth Street, has a suggestive advertisement. I thought from that he might know something on the subject I wished to investigate, so I called on him. The door opened in response to my knock, and a well-dressed, short man, with a bald head, looked out over his glasses at me. I saw a young man in the office, so I said, with a blush not at all assumed: "I want to speak with you privately, please."

"Oh, yes, yes," he said, stepping out into the hall and closing the office door; "step this way. Wait here, I will see you presently."

He opened the door and I entered a back room. It was already occupied by a man and a woman. From appearances, the bed-lounge, cupboard, table, kitchen-stove and bureau, I think that room answered the purpose of the entire house. No one spoke, so I sat down on the lounge and took in my surroundings.

The front office, into which I was soon ushered, was vastly different from the room in the rear. The floor was nicely carpeted, and the chairs, desks and medicine case all helped to lend the air of the office of a well-to-do physician. The doctor drew his chair close to mine in a confidential manner and waited, inquiringly, for me to begin. My position was a delicate one, and I knew it. So I said: "I read your advertisement, and as you say you give 'advice free,' I thought I would come to you for aid. There is a—a baby I want to dispose of. Can you help me?"

WHAT TO DO WITH IT

"Yes. How old is the child?"

"It was born on the 5th of May," I answered, with a gasp.

"Yes; pretty good child by this time. Boy or girl?"

"Oh, a girl!" (I hadn't thought of this before.) "A girl? Too bad. They are very hard to get rid of. Now, if it was only a boy you would have more chance." I got a little quaky by this time, and I almost felt like assuring him that it made no difference to me, that really if boys were easier to bargain for it might just as easily be said a boy. Luckily I kept still.

"The child is healthy?" I nodded my head. "What complexion?"

"Neither dark nor fair," I replied, as I couldn't tell the complexion of a babe I had never seen. "What shall I do with it?"

"The child is yours?" he asked.

I was almost stunned, for I feared next he would ask me questions I could not answer without any questions being asked. "Can it be done?"

"Yes, it is done daily. It is mostly done when the child is born. However, I can advertise for you. Will you make a full surrender?"

"What is that?"

"You give up the child and never know where it goes or anything more about it. I will do this for you for $25; you to pay advertising and all outside expenses."

This was soon agreed on. I did not hesitate at $25 when I was never going to pay it.

"Tell me something about such cases. It is all new to me. What becomes of the babies and how can the mothers tell whether they live or die or are treated well?" I asked, aiming for the news I was in search of.

"After a mother makes full surrender of a babe, which is done at the place it is born, she has no way to tell what becomes of it. Of course, it may be ill-treated or reared in the wrong manner, but it has to take the chance. We advertise and people reply. We never ask them who or what they are. I don't know as much about them as I do about you this moment. Many of the women come veiled and we never even see their faces. If satisfied they take the babe, pay their fee, jump into a carriage and drive no one knows where. The child has no chance ever to find out who it is. The ones who take it have not the faintest idea who or what the mother is; they have never even seen her.

"Of course there are some women who do not make full surrender, but get me to procure boarding places for the babies. I had a woman who lived in Fifty-second Street that did all this work for me, but she died a few weeks ago, and I have no one since. I can have your child boarded for $4 a week. No, the care is not what mothers would give. What is the death rate of such children? At the very least eighty out of one hundred. You think it horrible? Well, it's the way of the world. Women who do not want the expense of a child, and who do not wish to make full surrender, leave them at the Catholic Home in Sixtieth Street, near Lexington Avenue. When the home is not full, a basket is hung on the door-knob at night, and women drop their babies into it. If you are not a Catholic you won't want to do that. Others give them to the Commissioners, who send them to Ward's Island, where there are 800 children. If you dread bad treatment and large death rates you should see that place!"

I pretended that I had some love for the imaginary child, and really I did have, so I said I should take the night to think it over, and if I decided to relinquish it I would return on the morrow.

BOY BABIES BETTER THAN GIRLS

Mrs. Conradsen
Healing Medium. Hours, 9 to 9
West 15th St.

So read the next advertisement on my list. I had no idea who she was or what, but somehow the notice seemed to suggest that I would not apply to her in vain. She lived in a large, three-story brownstone house, which had the appearance, from the closed shutters and doors, of being unoccupied. I rang the bell repeatedly before I was shown into the presence of the woman, who was not ill-looking. My first story had been such a success that I decided to repeat it, with a slight difference. As the doctor said girls were hard to get rid of, I determined this time it should be a boy, and so have every chance there was.

"I have a child I want to get rid of, without being known or appearing in the case. Can you help me?"

She then asked the age, health and complexion of the baby boy. Apparently she was satisfied, for she said she could board him out at $4 a week for me. When I told her it was necessary that I cut off all connection with the child, she said for $10 she would get me someone to take it. She noticed my accent and she asked me how long I had been from France. I told her I was a Southerner and she said she knew I did not belong in New York or I would not have to ask so many questions on the subject.

"It seems odd for you to keep the child so long," she

said. "I always advertise them in about a day after they are born. I do not charge anything for placing babies when they are born here, but, as yours was not, I will have to charge you $10 for my trouble. That is little enough, and you must bear all other expenses, for I may not be able to place him for a month or so. How do I place them? Well, if the mother makes a full surrender, I advertise them and lots of people answer. Plenty come only through curiosity and many in hopes of getting a trace of news. Sometimes they imagine they can see resemblances in the baby's face to one they suspect. I always know such people, as they ask who the mother is, what she is like, where from, if I have any knowledge of the father, and what sort of a man visited the mother while she was here. I very quickly show them the door. Those who want babies never ask a single question."

WHAT BECOMES OF THEM

"What do they do with them? Ah, that is hard to say. I have known women to get babies repeatedly, but I don't know what for. Who are the mothers? They are never poor girls, but all come from the middle and higher classes. Not one out of a hundred is a working girl. Do they get rid of the children? Only occasionally. They generally tell me to get a home and they will pay for the keeping. I have a long list of people. They mostly live in flats, who keep themselves on the incomes derived from mothers. Sometimes the mothers know where their children are and visit them, but oftener all the business is done through me No, I do not suppose the best care is taken of babies. What can one expect of a woman who may have twelve to care for? When they die they are buried as the woman's child and no questions are asked."

"Are there many babies?"

"Why, my dear, there is no place that can equal New York. There is a doctor who runs a large place on Sixth Avenue for aristocrats alone, and his place is always filled. He keeps all the babies, but I can't say what he does with them. He never knows who his visitors are, and he only asks one question of them; that is, What should he do with them in case they die. I have had girls come to me whose homes were only a few blocks above here and no one was ever the wiser. It is seldom I know my guests. I have no desire to know. They do not see one another. I charge from $6 a week to $25. Do I have plenty? My house is never empty. I have only one room unoccupied now. In connection with this I am a doctor and I give massage and electric baths. There are free homes for children, but if you want the child to live you won't take the chances there. Yes, a number of children die at birth. The mothers are never here longer than two or three weeks."

    I had all the news I wanted from her and so I bade her a friendly good-by, promising to bring the babe and pay her $10 for its disposal in any manner, so that I was left entirely clear of all connections with it. She asked me no personal questions.

    In West Sixteenth Street I called at several manicure parlors, but they were found to be legitimate, as far as I could ascertain, although very few of them seemed at all surprised at the nature of my visit. From an advertisement of Mrs. Stone's I concluded she could give me some valuable information as to what became of all the babies. I asked the woman who made her appearance if she was Mrs. Stone. She said no, that the advertisement was put in for a regular practicing physician of Brooklyn. I wanted the address, but she said she was not allowed to give it, but if I would return in a few hours she would ascertain if I could see the party.

A BROOKLYN "HOME"

    I got the address on my return, and I went away over to Howard and Monroe streets, Brooklyn. A commodious frame house, surrounded by an ill-kept lawn, stood directly on the corner. It proved to be the one I wanted. From all indications the house was but recently occupied. To the woman who answered to the name of Mrs. Stone, I repeated my oft-told tale, and asked her prices. She could not think of having the child adopted for less than $50.

    "I presume you have plenty of this business to do," I suggested.

    "Plenty; why there is no business that can compare with it."

"It is a blessing there is someone to take charge of the babies, else it would be hard on them, I suppose," I suggested, in hopes she would venture some information.

"It would make me sick to try to tell you what is done many times by girls who have not enough money to pay for having their babies adopted. I knew one girl, the daughter of a clergyman in Jersey City, who ran away from home and came to New York. After all her expenses were paid she had not enough money to pay for having the child adopted. When she was able to return home, she rolled up a bundle of clothing and, taking her baby, started saying that she was going home. On the way she smothered the child. That was the last of it.

"What do I do with the babies? Well, I advertise one as soon as it is born. I never allow the mother to even see its face. Sometimes I know who takes the child, but more frequently I do not. Some people are particular and want the child born in wedlock, so I have several marriage certificates on hand to satisfy them. They never see the mother, or she them. We know nothing of the child after it is taken away. Oh, yes, the business pays, for it is only people of the higher classes who are our patients."

"Mrs. Stone, if babies die while in your care, is it difficult to obtain a burial permit?"

"No, it is very easy. We always retain a physician who never asks any questions, but writes out the burial permit according to our instructions. No, we never give the correct name, but assume any we wish. I seldom know who my patients are. If a patient dies she is buried under the name she gave me. In the Potter's Field? Certainly. It is as easy to get a burial permit for a woman as for a child."

I promised to take the baby to Mrs. Stone the next day, and to sign a paper to the effect that I would never inquire after the child after the time I gave her $50 to dispose of it.

A MONEY-MAKING TRAFFIC

The next advertisement was that of a man who proclaimed himself "ladies' physician," in Sixteenth Street. He advertised under the name of Morgan, but the plate on the door bore the name of Dr. Clarke. However, I asked for Dr. Morgan and was told that he was in. The general appearance of the house bespoke good business. Dr. Morgan grew very confidential when he found that I would not hesitate at any price, so the child was taken out of my hands. I had by this time a very tender feeling for this imaginary child. I had lessened his age, as most of them complained it was too old, and I had changed its complexion. I had long ceased to pretend it was my own. It now belonged to a friend of mine. This was a more comfortable position for us. My mind pictured it one of these handsome, dimpled baby boys we read about, and I occasionally felt a mild surprise that the mother could part with it. One's imagination is a wonderful thing when one once gives way to it.

"What becomes of all the babies?" I asked earnestly.

"Most of them die," he replied, "and those that live are given to women who advertise that they will take them. What becomes of them then, no one knows. They procure full surrender and so no one has the right to ask. Or it is very easy to say that someone adopted the child, but they don't know who. It all depends on the mother. If she is willing to spend money she can get a home for it."

Fully eight out of every ten who advertised medicated, vapor, electric or any sort of baths were in the habit of taking children for money considerations. What do they do with them? Is a question unanswerable. They all say that the entire year does not bring them a slack week. Of course the majority of children die, but is it supposable that there are rich families enough to be adopted daily without ceasing? Every one said that only the rich adopt the babies. If it is only the rich, then the supply must be greater than the demand.

The gentleman who wrote to THE WORLD said that his wife called on Mrs. Gray in Sixth Avenue, who advertises manicure and vapor baths, and while there she found that the house was filled with mothers and babies. I climbed two flights of narrow, dirty stairs and saw Mrs. Gray, who said she would take the baby on full surrender only, for $50. She said the mother could never know what became of the child afterwards.

AFRAID OF DISCOVERY

"I get lots of children; but one has to be careful, as there are so many schemes going around. I had a woman come here the other day that acted as if she were a detective. I gave her no information. One never knows when they will get caught up."

Mrs. Gray then brought an infant from an inner room and showed it to us. As I grew liberal with my price she grew more confidential, but throughout the interview she displayed a shrewdness and a fear of betraying something.

"I had a woman come to me one day and say that her husband threatened to leave her if she did not part with a child she had previous to the marriage. She got me to take the child and put it in a home. She paid me well and paid the child's board, visiting it every week, while the husband thought she did not know where it was. It is now seven years old. Burial permits are easy to get. I retain a reputable physician and he never asks any questions. Where do all the babies go? Why, rich people adopt them, of course." I promised her the baby and a fifty-dollar bill, and I was never to know anything of it afterwards.

DR. MAY—W. 24th, graduate of university, Phil., Pa; 25 years' experience, skillful, safe treatment; one interview sufficient, consultation strictly private.

I called on Dr. May and I really thought the man was insane. In order to inspire us with confidence he told of the most criminal actions. He readily consented to take charge of the child for the modest sum of $500, and he told us he could not be asked to do anything that he would refuse. He showed us diplomas from a New York and also a Philadelphia medical college. He also said he belonged to the Board of Health and was a member in good standing in the Masonic lodge. Notwithstanding all this, he confessed to the most criminal actions, and when we started to go he asked me if I had any money with me. I said no, and then he begged that I give him, if but 25 cents, to retain his services. I shudder when I think of what a horrible creature he is, according to his own confession, yet see the position that at least he claims to hold.

"A physician is bound not to reveal the secrets of his patients," he said. "Once I was taken to court in a divorce case. It was just another story of a jealous husband and pretty wife in love with her physician, but I refused to reveal anything, and the man lost his case. An insurance company also took me upon a case where a man died of hard drink. I treated him for it; but I would not tell, and so the company was the loser. Women always trust me. They know that once they pay me I'm bound not to tell on them."

CHILDREN ADOPTED FOR A PURPOSE

LADIES can confidently consult Mrs. K. Golias, ladies' physician, West 29th St.

Mrs. Golias was at home and ready to be consulted. She would take the child for $35. "I always have children taken away by the time they are a day old. It is a great deal of trouble to have several-months-old babies adopted. Why? Well, women want to pass the babies for their own and so they get them young. I have had women come from France and Germany to adopt a child. They have had property that depended on an heir, or they wanted to cheat other relatives out of it, and so buy a child. Customers always say what complexion they want the babe. I think they are all rich people who take the children, for what would poor people want with them? We never know anything about the child afterwards. The charitable homes where infants are taken are horrible places. Last summer at one asylum the babies died by the hundreds. I keep a physician who gives burial permits for infants or adults who die in my house. The mothers seldom, if ever, keep their children. A short time ago a woman gave up her babe, and the parties who adopted it told me accidentally that they had bought a home on Long Island and from whom I told the woman, and strange as it may seem, they had bought their home from her father who is a farmer, and would be her neighbor, though they never knew it. So you see the woman can see her child every day."

I visited the New York Foundling Asylum in Sixty-eighth Street, near Third Avenue. The Sister at the desk kept attending to her fingernails while I was talking to her. "I will only make arrangements with the mother. If she gives us the child, she never sees or hears from it again. We only take full surrender and no one can know where they go."

As I left the asylum I met sixty-two girls in blue dresses and 100 boys in line, crossing Lexington Avenue. I do not know where they were from, but their orphanage was stamped on them.

The New York World
December 4, 1887

Wanted—A Few Husbands

Nellie Bly's Strange Experience at a Noted Matrimonial Agency

Some of the Men Were Bashful, Some Were Bold, Some Poor and Some Rich, But All Were "The Favorites of Their Circle"—Queer Letters—Husbands That Cost $100—Quick Proposals—Meeting One's Fate.

The New York woman can hardly have a single desire that cannot be gratified through some bureau or agency of this town. Through them she can get a house, have it furnished, secure new wardrobe, a good form, a clear complexion, the latest shade of hair, and a loan to start the wheels of the concern in good running order. If she desires a husband, and a family warranted to have a marked resemblance, they can be had through the same channels at a nominal price. This husband-getting interested me. I did not want to marry but I was as curious as a little boy with a dynamite cartridge. I wanted to investigate. But how? A woman always hesitates about telling that she wants to marry. She would not confess to the lack of opportunity under any circumstances.

I saved the address of a matrimonial bureau which does business now in East Thirty-first Street, and late one evening I called. I was ushered into a parlor and was soon talking to a man and woman who professed to introduce congenial spirits. He was a small, nervous man, with light brown hair and blue eyes. His wife was a black-eyed, black-haired, pleasant-looking little woman, with persuasive conversational abilities that her husband fully recognized. I told them I had heard of the agency and was anxious to partake of the bliss of making fires and sewing on buttons. I wanted to try through them to give some lonely man a chance to find his ideal. Knowing absolutely nothing of the running of the concern, I made inquiries very carefully.

"You find plenty of people anxious to marry, I suppose?"

"Oh, yes. We have between five and seven thousand names on our books of matrimonial candidates."

"Not all in New York?"

"The majority live here, although our list covers the greater part of the United States. Who are the people? Well, we have one minister, several doctors and medical students, and all classes of business men down to the laborer. We have not the same variety among the women. They are mostly those who need a home or who are many days past a desirable marrying age. I should think that you would have plenty of proposals and would not need our assistance," he concluded, flatteringly.

"One tires of meeting friends always in the way endorsed by society," I answered, "and it seems possible that, by stepping aside from the ordinary way, I may meet some congenial one that I could never have known otherwise."

He rubbed his hands, smiled and showed me the mammoth album containing photographs of gentlemen. (I was not permitted to see the women.) Such a collection! The Rogues' Gallery is hardly more varied or interesting. By the side of a clerical-looking man, with quite hypocritical face, came an ancient Santa Claus, who looked as if, after all his years, he ought to know better. It was all very interesting, and I was longing to take the album away as a souvenir. It may be that these photographs were not all of would-be Benedicts, for I noticed over the mantel a large card announcing that orders would be taken there for photographs.

The woman wanted me to fill out a descriptive blank. I was at that moment in a very tight place. I dared not give my own address, lest they find out that I belonged to a newspaper, and I had no other. I said I was living with an aunt and that she was so conventional that if she ever heard of me doing such a thing she would do all sorts of harm to me. But I wanted a copy of the descriptive blank and had to invent something to get permission to take the blank home. Through a great many imaginary stories I got it and filled it out the next day. Here it is as I filled it up:

THE CATALOGUE OF VIRTUES
Lady's Description Blank No. 17,244
Registered in Book ----, Page ----.

When you have filled out this description blank plainly write your full address on a separate piece of paper; pin both together and return to us.

Your name will be given in confidence and no person whatever can obtain it from us. All others will know and address you (in our care) by a number only.

For $5 you are entitled to our services until you become engaged (or for $3 for three months) in assisting you to make selections from the description blanks and from the advertisements that may appear, also to the forwarding of post-paid letters and the insertion of a forty-word advertisement during the time for which you engage our services.

1. What is your age? Eighteen.
2. What is your weight? Varies; 120 pounds in sealskin.
3. What is your height? Five foot five inches, including French heels.
4. What is your complexion? Brunette.
5. What is your nationality? American.
6. What is your occupation? Killing time.
7. What is your religion? Very liberal.
8. What is your amount of real and personal property? (?)
9. What is your yearly income? $2,000.
10. What amount do you expect to inherit? $200,000 on the death of my grandparents.
11. Have you good health? Perfect.
12. Were you ever married? Left a widow two months after my marriage.
13. If so, how many children have you? None.

14. What are age and sex of children?----
15. What are your views and habits in regard to the use of tobacco and alcoholic drinks? Liberal, if not used to excess.
16. Are you accomplished in vocal or instrumental music? Yes, in both.
17. In what State or Territory do you reside? New York, at present, cosmopolitan.
18. Will you answer in some way all courteous letters we may forward to you from our patrons whom we believe to be sincere? With pleasure.
19. Between what ages must your correspondents be? Twenty-three and eighty years.
20. Do you object to one who has been married? No.
21. Do you object if your correspondent has one child? No.
22. Do you object if your correspondent has more than one child? No.
23. State what religion you prefer. Have no preference.
24. State what nationality you prefer. Have no preference.

Your photograph is a very valuable addition to the description, and will be held by us subject to such instructions as you send with it, and promptly returned when requested. In selecting correspondence from our lists, our patrons almost always prefer those of whom a photograph and the most complete description may be seen.

If you give good references it enables us to introduce you more promptly and often to a better class of our patrons. Inquiries are never addressed to your references over our own signature, or in a manner to give them an intimation of your business with us.

Any further description you may desire to give of yourself or correspondent must be written concisely and plainly, without your name or address, upon one side only of a sheet of paper containing no other matter. Names of references should be written on still another sheet of paper.

THE PRICE OF A HUSBAND

After I had filled out the blank and paid my fee I was requested to sign a check for the amount I would pay on the day I married. Then came the hitch. They wanted my address so as to insure them the money and I could not give it. I pleaded my aunt's displeasure, my disinheritance by my grandparents and at last said I would rather not come than have to give it. They had the $5, and they suggested that I try the agency for ten days and if, at the end of that time, I did not have enough confidence in them to give my address, we would arrange some other way. I was glad to get off so easily, so I signed the check with my assumed name. Here is the check:

$100   NEW YORK, Nov. 11, 1887

When I marry, or promise to marry a man whose acquaintance I have formed through the influence of, or to whom I have been in any manner introduced by .... either through the columns of ...., or otherwise, I promise to pay .... or order on demand, for value received, in above services rendered, the full sum of $100.

Signed, Mrs. JEAN HASTING THOMPSON.

"How do you get so many people?" I asked, for almost every time I went there I found the three-story house filled and the several clerks always kept busy.

"We advertise for many different things, and when we get the replies we send them our matrimonial paper. Then we have parties who send us names and addresses."

ANSWERS TO PERSONALS

About the same time a young friend who had more recklessness than discretion answered a "personal," and received the following reply from the agent I was patronizing:

Miss-----:

The advertisement which you answered by addressing Burnette, Box 20 Journal, uptown, we inserted for one of our patrons with whom we are personally acquainted. As you gave so brief a description of yourself, it is impossible for us to tell whether our client would be suited with your description or not.

If you will call we will give you a full description of him. If you cannot do this and will fill out and return to us enclosed description blank we can then give you more definite information, and if agreeable a personal introduction at our rooms. Respectfully,

H.B. WELLMAN (BARNARD)

This letter, if presented within two weeks from date, will entitle you to an introduction to the gentleman described. If you accept this invitation appoint your own time in the evening or Sunday.

I next bought a box at a downtown office where I could receive my letters. Shortly afterwards I got a little yellow envelope and in it was this strange missive:

A.No.1.986
MISS GYPSY HASTINGS: You are invited to be present at your rooms promptly at 8 o'clock P.M. Friday, Nov. 25, 1887. Hoping at that time to make you acquainted with an agreeable gentleman, we are, respectfully, H.B. WELLMAN.

NOTE—If you desire to be introduced by any other name than the one written above, plainly write it here..............................

Detach the part of this sheet marked B and return to us in enclosed envelope by return mail. If you accept the invitation, sign and date the printed form B; if you decline the invitation, or if you cannot be present at the time stated, and desire us to endeavor to make arrangements at some other time, state the time and write full particulars on the back of sheet marked B.

On arrival ring the bell nearest our name-plate at the door. You will be shown to a private reception room. Then present the portion of this letter marked A to the one who has admitted you, and you will be notified when the person arrives who is to meet you.

Should the interview continue longer than one hour after the time appointed, an additional charge will be made.

B.No 1.986

It is optional with our patrons to accept or decline these invitations, but if accepted and an unforeseen emergency should prevent your coming, you will notify us at once by telegraph or messenger. The failure to notify us in this manner subjects you to a fine of 50 cents, which must be paid before you can receive another introduction.

................1887

MR. H.B. WELLMAN: I will on the terms above stated accept your invitation to be present at your reception rooms at 8 o'clock P.M. on Friday, Nov. 25, 1887.

GYPSY HASTINGS.

THE TALKING CANDIDATE

It was raining that evening when I started out to meet a would-be husband. Husband-hunting did not appear a very congenial pursuit, as I waded through the mud to a Broadway car that stopped half a block above where I signaled it. Once at the house the agent took me into a small room and lectured me on the good qualities of the man.

"He is not a dude, but he is a good man and would make a first-class husband. He is president of two mining companies and is very rich and aristocratic, so you'll have to be nice. Come now."

With eager expectancy I followed on tip-toe, and French heels, to meet the paragon of perfection. I stopped at the door, took a long breath and put to death an amused chuckle, as the agent rapped gently with his knuckles. There was no response, but the agent went right in and I followed. He mumbled something meant for an introduction, and a great, long figure arose from the sofa at the end of the room. The door closed and I was left alone with him.

He was easily six feet two, loosely built. His clothes, while comfortable, would never make him a rival of the great Berry Wall. He had brown hair, side whiskers and mustache. His movements, except of the tongue, were slow and heavy. He was fully forty-two years old.

"I did not hear your name," I said, after a long pause.

"I was introduced as Mr. Hoage, but my name is Calvin A. Poage. I am president of two mining companies. Our office is 61 Broadway, and I live at the Hotel Barrett."

AN INTERESTING BIOGRAPHY

Mr. Poage then handed me two certificates in proof of what he had said. They read that they were to "certify that H.C. Gilbert had bought 100 shares in the --------- Mining Company," and were signed H.C. Gilbert, Secretary, and C.A. Poage, President. "I was born in Virginia," he continued, "and my father was a teacher. When I was yet a child he removed to Missouri. He was a very smart man, and master of thirty different musical instruments. I am master of very nearly as many. I was a prodigy when a child. People used to come from miles around to see me. When I was eight years old I cold speak and write Latin, and when I was ten I wrote Greek. At eighteen I graduated from Princeton. Yes, I was always wonderfully smart," with a self-satisfied air. "I have gotten all the glory I want in this life, and now I am working for money. I am an eloquent orator, and was owner and editor of a paper called the *Occident,* in San Francisco, for years. I am well known as a writer, and people urge me to sell them letters."

"How lovely to be a writer," I breathed rapturously, and I kicked the table to remind me that a story depended on my self-control. "What do you write for, these horrid daily papers or the dear, delightful magazines?"

"I write for the *Century* and a number of others. I'm very famous as a writer, as well as a lecturer, and if I wanted to devote myself to literature I could make lots of money," with pride.

"Oh, really! How lovely!" I exclaimed, with an accent of wonderment, and not wholly assumed. "How silly I am! I always thought writers got very little money."

"Oh, no," pompously; "there is John Howard, Jr.—he is now senior—he got $25,000 a year from one paper."

It was again necessary for me to exercise my self-control. The assumed knowledge of one he did not know even by his correct name was too much.

"Henry George and I are bosom friends. When he was unknown, out in California, his paper and mine got up the great land scheme. I helped him organize the Anti-Poverty Society, and my name is No. 18 on the list. I am a lion in society and that's why I've left it for this. The young ladies all make such a favorite of me that it bores me."

HIS FAMOUS FRIENDS

"Do you know Talmadge? Well, he and I are like brothers. When he came to San Francisco his first visit was a complete failure. I took him up and my paper made his success. I am the distinguished literary man he speaks of in his lecture as going with him through Chinatown. I went over to his church one Sunday after I came East. I did not intend to trouble him when the sermon was over but as I started out he called to me: 'Come here, California,' and began climbing over the pews and everything to me."

The minutes dragged into hours and yet he talked. I quit listening to him at last and began to think of other things. When my thoughts returned to earth he was still talking. I was weary and faint from the siege, so I suggested, with quivering lips and a trembling voice, that it was time for me to go home.

"Can't I see you again?" he asked.

"Not so long as oatmeal is cheap and Rough on Suicides only 15 cents a box." I began to mentally swear. Then aloud. "Well, I couldn't see you here again, and Aunt is so queer." That poor aunt!

"What church does your aunt attend?"

"Methodist," I replied, carelessly.

"Well, you tell me her minister and I will get him to introduce me. I know she will be glad to meet me. Everybody is."

"Oh!" I exclaimed, realizing that I was in deep water. I must do something to save myself. "You don't know my aunt's minister. He believes in mission work, and prayers, and sewing and asking blessings over chicken dinners. Indeed he's dreadful," and I gave a little shudder at my narrow escape and the eloquent picture.

He then said that he often met women on the cars, in art galleries, at church fairs and in music stores. I disclaimed all knowledge of how to flirt, and added that even if I did my aunt would never recognize such a man. He left me on the corner without lifting his hat, and so ended my first introduction to a would-be husband. I got on a car, rode several blocks, got off, and made a complete circuit in this way, so that if any one were following me I should know it.

HARD TO SUIT

On the pleas of wanting to make a selection, I got the description book one day and read of its applicants. Most of the men were decidedly original in spelling and grammar. Most of those belonging to New York were commonplace and monotonous, while those from the West possessed at least an amusing sparkle. One man wrote opposite to the questions as to having children or if he objected to a widow with children: "Know"; another, "Now." Very few objected to a widow or to one child, but almost every one objected to more than one child. Several said that if the child was a boy they would not object. One man wrote that he wanted a wife who had money enough to start a drug store. Another wrote: "I am an athlete, a dead shot, am handsome and have a magnificent figure. The girl must be my equal in this." Evidently one man had a better taste in religious matters, for he wrote: "My wife must have a neat, trim figure and lost of vim. She must not expect to turn the house into a Y.M.C.A. hall or a 'Clergyman's Rest.'"

HE WAS ALL FOR LOVE

The next candidate was a slim little man with black hair and mustache. He looked like an undertaker in costume. He wore a double-breasted black coat, highly polished shoes, a silk hat, light overcoat and carried a large-headed cane. The agent first told me that he did not know much about this man and that I would have to watch out for myself. I told him I felt quite capable of doing that. Mr. Holmes, Miss Hastings, and I was left with him. He sat at the opposite side of the room and appeared quite bashful and nervous.

"Do you think you would always love your husband, Miss Hastings?" he asked bashfully.

I had some doubts on the subject, but I answered confidently in the affirmative. He smiled a bashful smile and gave his chair a hitch.

"Would you marry for love, Miss Hastings, regardless of what the man was?" he queried plaintively.

Again I replied heartily in the affirmative, and he smiled and gave his chair another hitch.

"Do you admire dark men, Miss Hastings?" I looked at his brunette complexion, and, with a soul-stirring sidelong glance, I breathed the affirmative. Again he smiled and gave his chair a hitch.

GOOD AT QUESTIONS

He was quite an adept at asking questions, and at each favorable reply the chair was slightly moved until I began to see that it was gradually making its way across the room to where I sat. To break the monotony I asked him of those he had met before me.

"I was not much taken with them," he said. "The last one I saw was about forty-five years old, and she was dreadful. She talked all the time about dudes, and I felt offended." I laughed quite heartily, for I wondered if he thought himself a dude. He told me then how much I pleased him, and asked me to meet him again. He got the matrimonial paper and showed me this advertisement of himself:

1558. A gentleman of thirty, with $60,000, a fine position, a good character, good health, reputation and habits, wishes the acquaintance of ladies under twenty-eight, highly educated and of unblemished character and social rank. Money no object.

I promised to write to him, so we exchanged addresses His was B.W. Holmes, P.O. Box 3, 441, City. Before the hour was over his chair, quite strangely, had crossed the room by itself and was close to mine. This made me think of home, so I said "Aunt" did not allow me out late and I must go.

In a few days I received quite a thrilling letter from him. It has not yet been answered.

HER THIRD CANDIDATE

My next candidate was quite devoid of sentiment. When I arrived at the house the clerk told me all the reception rooms were full and so she put me into a little side closet, where there was one table, a chair and an oil lamp. I peeped through the door and saw a young woman, apparently a servant, taken into another room. This was the only time I ever saw any one, although the house was always filled. At last the agent called me and I was brought face to face with a tall, fair-complexioned, sharp-featured man. He was not badly dressed and his manners were short and decided.

"I haven't the least idea of marrying," he said almost instantly, as if he feared I would fall into his arms. "I only come here for the fun of the thing. What do you come for?"

Instantly I thought maybe he was one of the detectives set to find out my purpose, so I determined to balk him. Nothing could induce me to speak ill of the place.

"Of course, people cannot meet for good purposes here. Any one can have friends enough without coming here for more."

I talked softly of fate guiding our footsteps and leading us to our alter egos, and made my eyes look a sentiment my heart was far from feeling.

"Well, my name is J.E. Cassett. I live at No. 152 Lexington Avenue and have an insurance agency at No. 155 Broadway. I was born in Cincinnati, O. My people are the first in the place and they just run the town. When I came here I did not know any one, so I thought I would try this place. I think it is a money-making scheme."

"Have you met many here?"

"No, I did the most of it through corresponding, but the letters all slopped over with one idea, and that was marriage. Every one was crazy to marry. I was not, so I quit it."

"Did you meet any of your correspondence?"

"Yes, I met one. She lived in Philadelphia, in a nice three-story brown front. I sent my card up to her, and when she came down she said I must let her folks think that I met her at Asbury Park last summer. She wanted to be married by a minister. I think that most of the people who come here are matured and long past the day of sentiment. It is the matter of money or a home with them."

HE USED TO BE ONE OF THE BOYS

My next candidate for matrimony was a little fellow with black mustache and eyes and head of gray hair, of which he was quite proud. This time I was in a little hall room with a sofa, a chair, a stand and a badly smelling oil lamp. The little fellow put his light cape overcoat across the chair and sat down on it. He talked a great deal about himself. He said he was quite a noted singer and socially was in the best circles. He longed to find a wife.

"Lately I think of nothing but marriage," he said. "I used to be one of the boys, but now I want to settle down. I want a wife who will be satisfied to love me and me alone."

"As if your wife would ever wish to love another!" I sighed.

"I did not like any of the ladies I met here before," he chirruped sweetly, "but I should like to meet you again. My assumed name is Carl W. Vincent, and I receive all my letters care of Ditson & Co., 867 Broadway. If you would only let me know what evening I could meet you I would be so happy."

I told Carl he had better meet more women at the agency before he decided on one. I encouraged him in this laudable search for a wife, but I refused my personal aid. One similarity in all the candidates' stories impressed me. With one exception they belonged to the best of families, moved in the highest society and were the favorites of their circles.

HE WANTED A HOUSEKEEPER

One of the funniest candidates was a man who evidently thought to get a housekeeper for nothing by marrying her. His first questions were: Can you cook and sweep well; can you make beds nicely; are you a good washer and ironer; will you make the fires and carry the coal, and is your health perfect? Answered in the affirmative, he said: "If you can give me proof of all this I will marry you."

One of the most sensible men I met there was a young Englishman. Barring his lisp, he was nice.

"I want a wife who loves her home and who is of a cheerful disposition. I do not care if she has money or not. I would not marry a woman for money. I went to see a young lady and she asked me whether I would get up and make the fires. 'What's the use of living if one has to make fires?' I replied. So she said she would never marry a man who would not promise to do that. I don't care whether a woman can work or not, but I must have a sensible, amiable, neat, happy wife. I do not know a girl among my acquaintances that will answer my ideal, so I sought this agent's aid to help me find one."

AN OLD WIDOWER

Among the other candidates was a Mr. Williams, who has a drug store in Harlem. He has been a widower for thirteen years and has a daughter fifteen years old. He was rather timid.

"You are so good-natured and happy," he said, looking admiringly at me, while I laughed at some of his remarks. "I wouldn't be afraid of you. It would not take me long to ask you to marry me. I suppose you think I am old enough to be your grandfather?"

"No, oh no," I replied with a smile. I did not want to discourage him.

"You have such a way about you. I would not be timid if I knew you long."

I laughed at the doubtful compliment and he flushed with pleasure.

"I have a nice home and a greenhouse, and today I bought a $300 hot soda fountain. Do you like soda? Wouldn't you like to be a druggist or a druggist's wife?"

I thought he was getting along too rapidly for his own good, so I changed the conversation.

"Tell me of some of the women you have met here," I said.

"With one exception they were perfectly horrible."

"How horrible?"

"Every way; dress, appearance, manners and so anxious to marry. I never saw one a second time."

"You must be hard to please," I suggested with a little pout.

"Oh, no. Really now, don't think that. If I had only met someone like you—"

But I told him my aunt would miss me and left him, and that ended my experiences in a matrimonial agency. I am still in search of a husband, and Mr. Wellman has my $5.

The New York World
February 12, 1888

In the Magdalen's Home

Nellie Bly's Visit to an
Institution for Unfortunate Women

A Wicked Girl's Chances for Reformation—How Poor Creatures Abuse a Noble Charity—Matron Burr's Experiences—The Girl Who Befriended an Unlucky Cat—The Toboggan Slide of Sin

Quite recently the thought was forced upon me by an incident which I witnessed in the street. Do women who have started thoroughly on the downward path ever reform?

I could recall hundreds of cases where men had been pointed out to me as having "once been wild, but had now reformed," but I could not remember an instance of a woman spoken of as reformed. As one thought brings another, I began to speculate on a woman's chances of reforming. I must confess I could not see many, but I knew that in New York there must be some institutions devoted to the good cause. I made inquiries and I learned of several, among them one that had been in operation for fifty-four years. I immediately decided to learn more about it. I allude to the New York Magdalen Benevolent Home, 7 East Eighty-eighth Street.

Dressed to suit the character I wished to represent, I went late one evening to East Eighty-eighth street. I saw an old-fashioned building surrounded by a high brick wall, and I knew without looking for the number that it was the institution I wanted. The wall looked very formidable, and I felt rather homesick as I gave a strong pull at the bell-knob. I shivered slightly, as I thought they must surely have a big, brutal doorkeeper, and I wondered if I could ever get out when once inside. It is not so droll as it may appear, this being locked up of one's own accord without a surety as to how long it may last.

ENTERING THE HOME

I heard footsteps. A chain rattled heavily against the gates, a key was turned, and before me, candle in hand, stood a meek-looking, little, beat woman. She viewed me calmly, and I recovered from my amazement enough to say:

"Is this the Magdalen Home?"

"Yes," she answered, still holding the gate but not offering me admittance.

"Well, I came to see if I could stay a few days," I stammered.

"We don't take any one in here for a few days. They must stay six months. But you had better come in and see," she said, noticing my disappointed look.

I stepped inside and waited until she bolted and barred the gate; then I followed her up the steps into the house. She set the candle on a table in the hall, and knocking on a door, told me to enter. A woman and a man occupied the room, and the former rose and came towards me.

"Are you the matron?" I asked.

"No, the matron is out. I act in her absence," she replied.

"I want to see if I can stay here awhile," I said rather timidly.

"Every one who comes here stays for six months," she answered. "There are other homes you can go to for a shorter time."

"Six months is a good while," I said, determined not to hear anything about other homes.

"It is not very long to those who really wish to reform. Have you been doing wrong?"

"Well, I thought it might do me good to get out of the city a while," I answered, non-committal.

"You know, I suppose, that we have here only drunkards

and those who have sinned? You should know if it is well for you to be among them, if you have done enough to merit it."

I began to think that for once I had failed in my attempt to dress the character I wished to represent. I had even put whiskey on my coat to create the impression that the color of my nose was not just due to the weather.

"I think it is just as well for me to flee," I stammered by way of explanation when she asked me to sit down.

"We think six months is short enough time for a girl to break off from old associates and form new habits. Those that come here know what is before and those sent by parents or judges are kept whether they want it or not."

"But they always reform?" I asked.

"No, very seldom, I am sorry to say. They come here and what they did not know before others tell them."

"Any one can come here?" I asked.

"Yes, any girl who wishes to reform can come here and after she tells her story and it is decided that she is a fit inmate for the Home she remains for six months. Clothing and food are furnished free to all. We give them every chance to do right. It is a very discouraging work though. I have spent years at it and I find we make very few, indeed the very fewest reformations. If you do not think you would like to stay six months you can stay any way tonight and have a talk with the matron, Mrs. Burr, in the morning. She went to the Florence Mission tonight to attend the wedding of one of our girls."

"They do marry, then?" I said.

"Oh, yes. That girl was in here for six months and when she went out she fell in with bad company again. While intoxicated she met another girl who tried to induce her to go to some place. She replied that she was bad enough and she would not get any worse. The other girl then, who had been persuading her to go to this place, said 'The Florence Mission is the place for you,' and took her there. Just think of a bad girl taking any one to a mission! Well, the girl got converted, and tonight she is marrying a very good man. I will see if I can get you a room for tonight, and by morning you will know whether you want to stay or not."

She went into the hall, and I could hear her talking with the little jailer who admitted me. I think the jailer had taken a dislike to me, and was urging that I be sent elsewhere. At any rate, they talked a long while, and I began to feel weary. Again the bell rang, and I heard them say:

"What did you come back for?"

"I didn't like the place," said the newcomer. "It was in the country, so I wouldn't stay," and then they told her what had to take, and I heard her go heavily up the uncarpeted stairs. Once more the bell resounded, and this time warm greetings were exchanged. Then the door opened and a very pleasant, kindly faced woman came in. she looked at me with a smile as she said "Good evening," and then sat down on the sofa beside me. It was the matron. She rather urged me to tell her why I wanted to come in the home, but I replied that I would rather not speak on that subject just yet.

"What you tell me, my dear, no one else ever hears, but we must know your history before we can say you are a fit subject for the home; otherwise one might come here and learn more wickedness than they would ever forget."

"Is it unpleasant to meet all those girls?" I asked, to avoid discussing the first person singular.

"Well, they will pounce on you and want to know all your history, and tell you all theirs the first thing. But if a girl really wishes to reform we give her every opportunity. You can think it over and I will talk with you in the morning. We have seventy girls at present, and I will have to put you in with another girl. She is a very good girl. She has done wrong, but I believe she is truly converted."

I was again at the mercy of the little jailer. She walked in advance, carrying a lamp, along some narrow hallways. Fire may be my weak point. I know, anyway, the thought came that if the house caught fire I should never be able to find my way out those narrow passages. Entering a room she set the lamp down on a wash-stand as she called out: "Johann, I have brought you a bed-fellow."

The girl turned her face around and, opening her large black eyes, looked at me.

"You get ready for bed," she said to me, as she started to leave the room, "and I'll come back for the lamp."

HOW THE NIGHT WAS SPENT

This was not much like a prison or any asylum. There were no cold baths. What a difference in the treatment of women who have erred and of the poor creatures who are addicted through no fault of their own! The room in which I was to spend the night was of good size. A worn Brussels carpet covered the floor. The walls were nicely whitened, and along one side were books for clothing. Beside the bed there were two cheap bureaus, a wash-stand and two chairs.

"Were you sent in?" was Johann's first question as I began to undress.

"No; I came myself," I answered.

"Ah!" with satisfaction and relief. "Then there is hope for you."

"Six months is rather a long time to stay here," I suggested as I unbuttoned my boot.

"What is six months here to an eternity in hell?"

I dropped my boot in astonishment and looked at her. She raised herself to a sitting position in the bed. Her black hair was tossed, and her eyes gleamed unnaturally.

"I really couldn't say, you know," I stammered. "I never spent any time in either place."

At this moment my jailer came for the lamp. As she went out the door she gave this parting salutation:

"Johann, don't throw her out the window before morning."

"Oh, no," replied Johann; "she is a very nice little girl." The door closed and we were left in the dark. She asked me all about myself, and I in turn questioned her.

"I make artificial flowers. I learned the business when I was a child. I need to make $2 per day; now I can only earn $7 a week. We are paid by the amount of work we do."

"Where do you live?" I asked.

"I rent a small room on a top floor in the locality of

Hester Street for $1.50 a week. It has a single bed in it, and I buy an oil-stove, on which I do my cooking. No, I cannot save any money. By the time I pay rent and for fuel and buy my food I have but little left for clothing myself."

"Why do you not board in some of these charitable homes? I would imagine it pleasanter than to live as you do."

"I am tired seeing misery, and the only people who go to charitable homes are miserable. I want to get it out of my sight and hearing for a while, so I have a room. Cheap boarding-houses are generally nests of vice, so I would not patronize them."

"Have you been here long?"

"I have been here a year now. I had gone to every extent in sinfulness and, as a last remedy, I came here. I am so glad, for I have seen the folly of my former life and am just as anxious to live rightly as I was once to live wrongly. I wish I never had to go out in the world again, but then I am sick of seeing the misery in Homes."

A DAY IN THE MAGDALEN

I was about ready to go to sleep when the rising bell rang. I had passed the night in a restless manner and was glad to find it ended. Johann got up and sat on the edge of the bed, while I put on my gown. We soon were ready to go downstairs. I followed her along the narrow hall and into the sitting-room. It was a good-sized room with white walls, benches and a desk. It looked similar to a country school-room. A large stove occupied the center of the room, and clustered around it were some twenty girls. They wore plain calico dresses and some wore aprons. They looked at me as curiously as I looked at them. One of the number made room for us and we joined the circle.

"How many new ones came last night?" asked a girl.

"Three," responded several.

"Did she," indicating me, "come herself?" asked another of Johann, who replied in the affirmative.

"What other Homes have you been in?" someone asked me.

"None; this is my first," I replied.

"Hello, Minna!" they called out in chorus to a newcomer with a youthful face and short gray hair. "Why didn't you sleep all day?"

"Sleep! I haven't closed my eyes all the night; I haven't slept for a week, and if they don't soon give me something they'll have to send me to the crazy-house on Blackwell's Island," said Minna, complainingly.

Gradually the circle increased around the stove until the breakfast-bell rang, when all made a rush for the hall. There were no rules or regulations to be obeyed, and everyone rushed at will. I followed in the train down to the dining room, which is in the basement. The matron, Mrs. Burr, was there, and she gave me a place at an end table. When the room was filled the girls began to chant a hymn of thanks, after which they repeated a prayer, and then began on the simple meal before them. It consisted of bread, butter, molasses and a bowl of coffee. One woman who sat at our table would not eat her bread, which she broke in bits and pushed to someone else's plate. This raised a disturbance, and Mrs. Burr sent her from the table as one would dismiss a naughty child. Otherwise the breakfast passed very quietly. Mrs. Burr always spoke in the most gentle and quiet manner to the unruly ones.

HOW THE PLACE LOOKS

I made a survey of the place. The ceiling was low but nicely whitened. On the walls were mottoes that would not harm people to obey. The women interested me most. There were probably fifty in the room—the youngest a pretty peach-and-cream-complexioned miss of not more than sixteen years, and the eldest a feeble woman who looked not less than seventy.

As they finished eating they left the table without asking to be excused. They were all expected to go to the sitting-room, but I do not think they did. However, the majority went there. Mrs. Burr, Mrs. Hartley and Miss Henscher took their places behind the desk. Mrs. Bartley read a chapter from the Bible and then prayed, after which the girls repeated a prayer in unison. The matrons then went to their breakfast and we were left alone.

"How do you spend the day?" I asked a girl.

"Just as we please," she said. "We read or we can work on mosquito-netting or in the laundry. Some knit or crochet. We generally please ourselves."

"Girls must have it very nice here?" I remarked.

"My aunt says it is an encouragement to laziness and crime," interposed a girl who had been listening to us.

"Well, I would think some are reformed by being here," I said.

"Oh, yes," answered another; "there is one here now who has been here four times, and she says it has done her good every time."

"What makes her come back if it does her good?" I asked.

"Well, when she gets out she falls in bad company and goes back to her old ways; then she gets into trouble and comes back here."

I could not see how the Home benefited her if it did not last after she got out. From the conversation of some of the girls I learned that they had been making the rounds of the charitable homes since childhood, and I don't doubt that their mothers did the same before them. Two of them even spoke of being in Homes in other cities. Johann was the only one I found who had the least remorse for what she had done. The others were as indifferent about it as if it were an honor to them.

They were all very nice to me, and when they saw that I was not inclined to be communicative they did not bother me with questions. They used snuff liberally and offered to share with me. I declined their kindness. During the day several letters arrived and, after being read by the matron, they were given to those for whom they were intended.

At noon we were given fish, bread and tea, and in the evening bread, butter and tea. The food was plain, but there was plenty of it. Several times during the day the girls came into the sitting room with slices of bread, so that I knew they never suffered from hunger. A large space of ground surrounds the Home, inclosed, of course, by the high wall, where the girls can go as much as they wish. The laundry work is done for the neighbors by such girls as are willing to work. It is done at reduced prices in order that the inmates may have something to employ their time. Each girl does her own washing. They have perfect liberty in everything except to go out the gate. The Home is non-sectarian, although Protestant services are held every Sunday. The girls are offered every chance of reforming, but they seldom accept. This life is like a toboggan slide. Once they start, it is impossible to stop until they reach the end, which is death. They keep up the rounds—from the streets to the courts, to the island, to the Home and to the streets again—year after year.

In the afternoon of my day there the ambulance came to take a sick girl to the hospital. The girls rushed to the front of the house to get a "peep uv de dop on' his brass buttons," they sayd, and many were the remarks passed about him. One girl won the admiration of the crowd by asserting that she winked at him.

There are many peculiar characters at the Home. The most interesting one is probably a little homely creature whom the girls call Vanderbilt, because she imagines she runs the house. Vanderbilt gets herself up in a comical style, but she is withal good-humored. When she first came to the Home some painters who had been there had painted a white cat green. The poor cat seemed likely to die. It became Vanderbilt's charge. She nursed it and touched it until the paint wore off—and took the hair with it. Vanderbilt would often go to Mrs. Burr and ask for some Vaseline to rub on her sore face, when instead she would rub it on Tom Vanderbilt's (as the cat is known) back. Tom knows who is kind to him, and follows Vanderbilt from one end of the house to the other. When she sits down he jumps on her lap and displays more affection than I ever saw a cat manifest before. Tom looks pretty well now, and his tail gives bright promise of once again wearing fur.

I was rather amused to hear the superstitious girls tell what "sign" the most common occurrence conveyed to them. When spoke to about the absurdity of such beliefs, one said:

"Well, I know they are true. One day I spat on the door, and I said 'That for change of residence,' and the next morning I was in the Police Court." This was convincing.

THE MOTHERLY MATRON

Towards evening Mrs. Burr took me into the reception room. She asked if I had yet concluded that I would like to stay six months. I did not feel inclined to forfeit my liberty, especially as I had gotten all the information I could, even if I remained a month. I had but little sympathy for those women who do wrong and have no inclination to do otherwise. I determined to get out as soon as possible. I said the time was too long, and that instead of being benefited by returning there, I should learn more wickedness. She told me of other Homes I could go to and stay a shorter time.

"I told you the women here are bad," she said. "We get the very worst. A great number of them have served their terms in the penitentiary and workhouse. We offer shelter to any woman who wants to reform and we teach her all we can, but it is not encouraging work."

"Do they ever reform?" I asked.

"Well, even if they wish to reform they find it almost impossible. We had a woman here who was once of a very wealthy family. She was well educated, but she fell in love and it ruined her. She got to be of the very worst before we got her. She repented and wanted to do right, but she could get no chance. She had no recommendations, and at every place she applied for work we were compelled to tell her history. No one would have her after that. One charitable woman said she would have taken her for a nurse, but she had two sons coming home from college and she could not have the girl in the house. Girls often leave here with a desire to do better, but they have no money, no trade, no character, and in a while they get discouraged and go back to their old haunts. The majority of them do not care to reform. They come here because it offers them refuge when they have nowhere else to go. We endeavor to do all we can for them."

Promising to go to see the receiving committee of the Home or to some other mission I left the Magdalen. I tell you the path of sin is like a toboggan slide; once we start down there is no stopping until we reach the end.

The New York World
March 4, 1888

Nellie Bly on the Stage

She Wears a Scant Costume and Marches With the Amazons

It Isn't Very Hard to Get Such a Job—The Girls Earn $5 a Week—Tights that Did Not Fit—Dressing in a Crowded Room—How She Behaved on the Stage—A Bad Beginning

I made my debut as a chorus girl or stage Amazon last week. It was my first appearance on any stage and came about through reading among THE WORLD advertisements one that called for 100 girls for a spectacular pantomime, so I found myself one afternoon at the stage door of the Academy of Music. There were but two men there. I looked at them and they looked at me, and as nobody made any movement to speak, I asked:

"Where do I go in answer to the advertisement?"

"Mr. Kiralfy told me to say he had all the girls he wants," replied one of them. Then, probably noticing my look of disappointment, he added: "But you can step in on the stage and see him yourself."

The stage was bare and cold. A solitary gas jet only added to the dismal aspect of the place. The scenery even leaned up against itself as if it were tired. Near the front of the stage was a row of girls, twenty-four in number, watching the movements of a graceful little Frenchman, who twisted and danced before them. Standing around in rather forlorn groups were other girls, of all sizes, ages and appearances. Some were talking in a lively way, while others stood about silent and sad. A woman who received the least attention of all was a ballet dancer who was practicing.

    I saw no one to speak to, so I followed the example of the other girls—stood and watched the rehearsal. Every two girls in the magic circle had a small gilded chair of mythological design. The Frenchman was teaching the girls to jump on the chair, then down, then to run around it, and up again and so on. It looked very uninteresting and simple, and yet the girls often made mistakes. The little master seemed to have unlimited patience, and at every false move gently showed the correct way. There was a remarkable absence of the "brutality" displayed against the poorly paid ballet girls which one hears so much about. The girls seemed to enjoy the exercise and the man was kind.

    At last I saw a man emerge from the gloomy portals at the far side of the stage and come towards me, where I stood on one foot, holding the other, like an elephant, or a goose, as you please, up to rest.

    "To whom shall I apply for a situation?" I asked.

    "For what?" he questioned, looking at me with a kindly smile.

    "In answer to the advertisement in today's WORLD."

    "Will you please sit down and wait? I'll see you in a moment," he said, and he left me.

    I looked around. I could see nothing but the perpendicular scenery and the stage door. My feelings were rather shocked. I remained standing.

    "Do you like the chorus?" I asked, turning to a slender girl, with a shabby dress, a careworn face and mournful eyes enclosed in dark rings.

    "Yes, I like it. It's as easy as anything a girl can do."

    "Does it pay well?"

    "I think as well as anything else. Girls in factories and stores work from 7 in the morning until 6 in the evening. They get from $1.50 up to $4. The very fewest number get $5. On the stage we work a few hours every night, and we have two matinees and two rehearsals a week, and we get $5. This is the best place."

"I would like to have that job," said another girl, indicating a woman with a towel around her head dusting the orchestra chairs. "She gets $6 a week, and then when she cleans the actresses' rooms they give her lace and old dresses, and sometimes a five-dollar bill."

"Come with me; I want your names," said the man who had spoken to me, and we followed him.

"I want to know how much you pay, first."

"Five dollars a week," he replied, while he suspended the pen.

"Well, then, we (indicating her companions) won't come."

"All right. Good day. Next!"

"They expected to get $25 a week," explained a girl.

We all gave our names and four of us were told to report for duty at the stage door at 7 o'clock that evening. It was only the rehearsals I wanted, but I decided, as this was all that offered, to see what it amounted to.

At 7 o'clock I walked past the crowd of men who surrounded the stage door into the Academy. I secretly wondered if they were the "eligibles" I had read so much of who swarmed about stage doors with their hearts and fortunes, flowers and diamonds to lay at the feet of their chosen idols. I did not see any evidence of any of these articles, but the crowd was there nevertheless.

There was no one on the stage or anywhere to be seen. The solitary gas jet was yet solitary. I could not find any one, so I took up my stand and stood. Presently from some mysterious part of the stage came the girls who had been engaged at the time I was. They began to complain because they had been informed that there were no extra suits for the extra girls—us.

"Are we to go on without any knowledge of the play?" I asked.

"Yes, we'll have to try to get beside some girls who will be good enough to help us."

I did not see how we could do it and not break up the show, but as I was bent on having fun I did not much care what form it took. The performers began to arrive. Almost all the girls carried little parcels of baskets. These I found contained their "make up." At last, Mr. Kiralfry came and seeing us he came up and spoke.

"There is nothing to do until after the first set so you can go up and watch the play."

He left us and then I saw a long string of men coming in, one after the other. They were making a noise like a cat, and I recognized them as being the men at the entrance whom I mistook for devoted lovers. They disappeared under the stage.

At last I and my friend were called to prepare for the stage. A few garments were given us and we were shown a room to dress in. It was already well filled with girls in all stages of dress and undress. "This room is full enough. Go somewhere else," cried one girl, crossly, and with the exception of the three prettiest girls, they were all angry because we crowded in with them. I spoke to two of three, but they did not reply—simply looked at me with quiet scorn. I had some idea of the dressing but my luckless companion had none.

"How do you get these things on?" she asked, in surprised disgust.

I looked at her. She was trying to get her thin silver tights on over her shoes and undergarments.

"You must take off your shoes," I explained, as no one else offered to.

"Indeed I will not," she said, vehemently. "It's very rude; I will not do it." But in a while she did take off her shoes.

"How do you get the tights on?" she cried again.

"You cannot get them on over all your undergarments," I told her, and even the angry girls laughed as they looked at her. I forgot my own appearance in laughing at hers. She got the tights half on, then she got the little short waist around her shoulders and the shoulder scarf around her waist. She put the band of white hair, which only encircles the head, on, and had no helmet. This allowed her black hair to show and make a queer picture. She got a spear and a shield, and so she made her way down to the stage looking like an Amazon who had been badly whipped in a fight.

I fared but little better. My garments were too large, my ballet slippers were easily four sizes too long. I put the rouge on my face and found I had forgotten my powder. The white wig was too small and would show my black hair underneath. My helmet was too large and would slip back. I was a sad sight.

"You will be too late. The curtain is up," cried someone, and I rushed after a girl down the stairs and to the wing. I was only conscious that there was a crowd of people going out and I was among them, giving a hitch every now and then to my armor. A blaze of light, a crash of music and with an inward laugh at my own boldness in attempting something I know nothing of, I was facing a New York audience in the Amazon march. I did not feel like an Amazon. Down we swept towards the footlights, while I wondered what our next move was to be.

"You started with the wrong foot," said a girl at my side. I did not know which foot I started with, so I said, "Which foot is it?"

"Oh, any one will do for you," was the satisfactory answer, while I mused on how funny it must look from the front to see one brave Amazon out of step with the whole army. Backwards we went, and my helmet slipped on the back of my neck.

"Your black hair is showing," whispered another girl. This was not reassuring, and did not tend to give me courage to try to do better. I gave a jerk to my helmet while the horrible thought struck me. What should I do if my helmet fell off on the stage and I was left with my sham wig and black crown before the audience? Once again we went to the front, and I congratulated myself on being in step when a girl in a very emphatic manner whispered:

"You have your shield on the wrong arm!" That reduced me again, and I resolved to change it in face of the audience, when she whispered:

"Face about."

I turned my face to her and found every girl had her face turned the other way, and if I kept on I would have to march backward while the rest went forward. I would not do this, so I simply took my time and turned in the right direction. I began mildly to wonder why the gallery gods did not notice my strange action. As we marched in a circle around the stage I changed my shield and poised my spear lightly on my side. (I had been carrying it under my arm.) Again we went to the footlights. A girl whispered for me to "stand at D," and I obeyed. I heard a voice from the wing cry:

"My ---- ----! What is wrong?"

I look with a smile to see what is wrong, and I see that the other girls are marching to one side; they have divided and I, being in the center, am left alone in front! I followed with more haste than grace after the nearest girl. Then we did movements which I had not the least knowledge of, so I was more than a little relieved when they marched to the wing. I was glad to get off. I found my poor companion still in a state of undress. Together we sought the dressing-room, and I forgot my own discomfort in laughing at her remarks. I am out of a stage engagement at present.

The New York World
March 25, 1888

Nellie Bly as a Mesmerist

The Strange and Awful Experience of a Certain Mr. Gray

He Consents to Allow the Learner of Mesmerism to Practice on Him and Undergoes Horrible Torture—The Professor Believes Nellie Bly to be a Kind of Feminine Fiend—How She Got Even with Him—Secrets of the Black Art

For what car fare costs, added to the price of a shave, I can become one of the greatest mesmerizers in the world. This is how I know. An advertisement in a Sunday newspaper a week or so ago attracted my attention. Under the name of "Mesmer" the advertiser offered to teach the art of mesmerism, with satisfactory tests at the completion of the lessons. In a day or two I had exchanged letters with "Mesmer" and had received his price for lessons and minute directions how to reach his place of residence. "From 3 to 6 or 7 to 9 I can see you any day," he wrote, so without advising him I went to Brooklyn. I found his home, No. 227 Court Street, to be about fifteen minutes' ride from the bridge. His name was Thompson and his place was on the top floor, rather bare and uninviting. His big wife was the only one at home, so I agreed to climb three flights of stairs again. The next day a little girl of six let me in and took me to her papa.

Mr. Thompson, besides being tall and thin, had long gray hair, combed back from his long, pale face. His eyes were a sharp black. A drooping mustache covered his mouth completely.

"Do I think you can learn to mesmerize?" he repeated, in answer to my question. "Yes, I assure you I can make you a first-class operator. My price is $10 in advance and $40 with the final test. What is the test? Well, after I give you two lessons I get a subject and allow you to operate on him. If you mesmerize him you are perfect in the art."

"I am afraid I cannot learn, and then I shall have given my money to no purpose," I urged.

"Oh, you can't help but learn," he reassured me. "I can see that you will make a splendid operator. Everybody does who learns from me. I impart to them some of my power, which, I think, some are born with. I've had men come to me and say that they understood mesmerism perfectly, but could not operate. Yet after a few lessons they could operate as well as I can. I am also a clairvoyant," he went on. "I'll teach you that after you learn mesmerism. It is very easy. One can soon learn how to throw one's self into a trance. There is lots of money in it for a clever person."

After making him guarantee that he would make a good operator of me I paid him the $10 fee and began my first lesson. He sat down on a sofa, facing me, and told me to do everything just as he did.

HOW IT IS DONE

"When you tell your subject to sit down see that he gets an easy position, for he has to sit perfectly still for ten minutes. Always see that he does not cross his knees or wear overshoes. Why? Because it detracts from the influence you get over him. I want first to tell you always to say 'please' to your subjects and have command in your voice. Repeat what I say and watch every word closely. 'Now, sir, please put the right thumb on the left pulse, press hard enough to feel the beating and think only of that.' All right; you did that well.

"The first lesson is to teach you to get control of the muscular power. In the second lesson, I teach you mental control. When you have the man in this position, with the right thumb on the left pulse, you must close his eyes, so, making a pass with your right hand down in front of his face, the fingertips almost touching him. You say 'Now, sir, please close your eyes.' When you once get a man's eyes closed so that he is unable to open them you can have him in your power.

"When you have the subject's eyes closed," he continued, going back to the lesson, "and he thinks of nothing but the pulse beatings, you go up to him about three times in ten minutes and make passes over him, three passes each time, in this way." He got up and, bringing his arms above my head, passed his hands slowly before my face close without touching, The movement was made as though he was sweeping some invisible thing from before my face. Then he told me to make the passes over him. I did so until it was done to his satisfaction.

"After the ten minutes have passed you take the subject's hands and place them gently one on each knee. Then with your left hand you take his and run your thumb close up between the joints of the little and ring finger and press very hard."

"What do you do that for?" I asked.

"I don't always tell, but I don't mind telling you. There is a nerve called the nerve of sensation between those fingers. You press hard on it and it communicates with the brain. At the same time you place the fingers of your right hand on the subject's head, and with the right thumb you press hard directly between the eyebrows. Then you are touching and controlling the organ of individuality. The nerve in the hand and this nerve connect, and this places the man in your power. While holding him so you say firmly, 'Now, sir, I am going to make you so that you can't open your eyes. Try hard! Open your eyes! Try hard!' And then he cannot open his eyes. After you remove your hold you snap your fingers close to his ears and say, 'All right, sir,' and he opens his eyes."

IN CASE OF FAILURE

"Yes, but what if he does open his eyes when I say he can't?" I urged.

"Well, then you try it over."

"Yes; but he might open his eyes every time, and I wouldn't like that."

"You must not try him more than three times. If you do not have him under the influence the third time, say 'You are partially under the influence, and at another sitting I can mesmerize you.' Be sure to add a remark about his strong will power. This has the effect of making him more susceptible to your influence the next time."

"Why cannot he open his eyes when I say 'Try hard?'"

"Because you are pressing hard on the organ of individuality. When you say 'Try hard,' which you must always do, he makes a great effort and tries to open his eyes by raising his brows. Your thumb prevents him. If he simply tried to unclose his eyes, which he would do if you did not urge him to 'try hard,' he would have no difficulty in so doing. When you remove your hand and say 'All right,' he quits trying hard and opens his eyes. Once you have done this you have the man in your power. I have sewed together with a needle whole rows of people while they were in this state."

"Beautiful!" I exclaimed, pleased with the idea which brought a vision to me of sewing all objectionable people on one thread. "Can I sew people?" "Yes, I will teach you that. Now, you know how to control the muscular movements and you can make the subject do just as you please, and he can't help himself. You have merely to catch his eye. 'Now, sir, please look at me.' He looks. Hold up your right index finger and move it. He will do the same. Say: 'Faster, sir, faster. Now, sir, you can't stop,' and you suddenly stop and point your finger at him. He can't stop, but keeps on until you snap your fingers and repeat, 'All right, sir.'"

"Yes, but what if he can stop?" I urged. The flesh was willing, but the spirit was very weak.

"Then you will have to try him again."

THE MENTAL POWERS

The next evening found me ready for another lesson. In this I was to learn the art of controlling the mental faculties of another. Did I learn? Well, just see what a wonderful test-show I had. "These are very precious secrets," he said, "and so the young girl [referring to the one who accompanied me] had better go somewhere and wait for you."

"To control the mental powers you tell the subject to stand up and face you. You take his hand in the same way as when you closed his eyes, then passing your open hand close to his face, letting it rest for a second before his eyes, you say, 'Now, sir, I am going to take away your name.' Of course you have asked him previously what his name is. You remove your hand and you say, 'Now, sir, what is your name?' and he can't tell you. Ha, ha!"

"Can't he?" I said, dubiously. "What would you do if he could?"

"Try it over. If you want to give an exhibition for your friends I can get you all the subjects you want for a car fare and a shave."

"Can you really?" I asked innocently. "That would be lovely. How can you get them?"

"Oh, I have a number of young men you can operate on, and they are glad to do it for a car fare and a shave. Then, you know, you generally have a supper. I used to give parlor entertainments at a house in Twenty-third Street. I once mesmerized the wife of the editor of the *Scientific American* there. It made a big excitement."

"Will you give me the addresses of your subjects?"

"When you have given the final test I will," he replied, warily. "One is a young travelling man, and another is in a store over in the city."

THE TEST

The young woman and I arrived a little late the next evening, but fully prepared for the donkey party. Mr. Thompson looked like a valentine, attired in a swallow-tail coat of the cut of forty years ago. He greeted us with a triumphant smile.

"Ah, ladies, let me introduce you to Mr. Gray," he said, as I began in a business-like way to take off my hat and coat.

"He is my subject?" I asked, and after their affirmative reply turned to Mr. Gray and said: "Are you ready to be butchered?"

MAKING PASSES ON HER SUBJECT

I knew that this subject was going to be mesmerized, even if I did not touch him. I immediately decided to do things contrary to what I had been taught and to prove to myself that the subject was shamming. Consequently I merely took hold of his hand and did not press the nerve, as instructed, and placed my right hand on his brow—without any pressure, however.

"Now, sir, you can't open your eyes. Try hard! Open your eyes! Try hard!" I said.

The subject pulled and twisted and jerked at his eyes, which still remained closed. I snapped my fingers, called "All right!" and he opened his eyes, rubbed them, and like the angelic heroine in the novel coming out of a sham fainting fit, exclaimed: "Where am I? What were you doing with me?"

I told him to sit on a chair and, after making passes over him, I told him he was unable to get up. He squirmed all around, but he sat there. I placed his hand on the wall and made passes over it and he pulled and twisted, apparently unable to release himself. Then I ran him all over the room, sometimes on his knees, then bent double and again straining his neck to view my finger as it was held above my head. Mr. Thompson protested that I was not treating the subject fairly, but I said that if he were mesmerized he could not feel it, and kept on. At last, when his face grew red from the violent exercise, I rested my hand on the edge of the piano. He put his head close down beside it. I jerked my hand quickly away and left him standing there.

"Don't leave him in that position too long," urged Mr. Thompson, ever watchful for the subject's comfort.

"I do not intend to take him out of it until tomorrow," I replied firmly. Mr. Thompson looked at me in surprise, and his wife, who had been witnessing the performance through a half-opened door, entered the room.

"Poor fellow! It's too bad to keep him in that position so long."

"Oh, you know," I said sweetly, "he can't feel uncomfortable so long as he is mesmerized. I'll be back tomorrow evening to bring him out."

HAVING FUN WITH A SUBJECT

After a great deal of urging, Mr. Thompson suggested that I would have more fun to make my subject see things, so I consented to remove him from his cramped position. A sigh of relief swept through the room when I changed my resolution. Then he went through another sham performance, in which I made him see snakes, pretty girls and rats. It would be tiresome to tell all the paces I put him through, but be assured I gave that young man more exercise than he would have had in breaking a bucking horse. Once I told him that he was Robert Ingersoll, and he began to address an imaginary audience. Then I made him try to imitate Bill Nye.

"Is there anything you can suggest?" asked Mr. Thompson.

"Yes, I will make him stand on his head," I answered.

"Oh, no; you must not do that," he answered, greatly alarmed, "he might hurt himself."

"Nonsense. As long as he is so thoroughly mesmerized he can't hurt himself," but Mr. Thompson urged me to put the young man in a cataleptic state, so I gave up my scheme of making him stand on his head and leaving him so.

I stood him up, put his feet close together, his hands by his sides and made several passes over him, while I whispered in his year, "You're a fraud." I gave him a gentle shove, and he fell back right into Mr. Thompson's arms, who lowered him to the floor.

"Now is he just like one dead?" I asked as if I were frightened.

"Just exactly," was the reply.

"Could I do anything to him and he would not know?" I asked again.

"Yes; he is paralyzed—he is in the state of death."

I made a sudden movement and went down on my knees by the subject's side. My movements were noted with surprise and alarm. "Why, his heart beats," I said, as I felt it throbbing.

"Yes," said Mr. Thompson, nervously, "of course his heart beats."

"But you said he would be just the same as dead. I can see him breathe. No one would ever bury him for a dead man."

"Do you want to paralyze his heart?" he asked, sternly.

"Certainly," I replied. "I want to put him in the state you said could not be told from death. This is nothing like it."

"Do you want to kill the man?" said Mrs. Thompson, rushing like a tigress up to me.

SHE DID NOT MIND KILLING HIM

"Oh, I don't object in the least," I replied, coolly. "Will he stay in this position until I take him out?"

"Certainly," replied Mr. Thompson, making an effort to regain his courage. "No one can do anything with him but you."

"Very well," I said with quiet determination. "I intend to go home now and when I return, a week from tonight, if he is just as I left him I shall believe in mesmerism."

"Oh, no; we can't do that," said Mr. Thompson, but I was deaf to all pleadings and protests.

"I never saw any one act like you," yelled Mrs. Thompson. "That man has a wife and two children, and I won't be responsible to them. I believe you would like to kill a man. I won't have it—now! It's getting late; this has to stop."

I did not answer, but quietly amused myself by pulling the subject's hair and pinching his ears and nose. He stood it bravely, never for an instant moving. Once I moved away and he turned his eyes to see what I was doing.

"Strange to see a dead man move his eyes," I said with a laugh. Mr. Thompson said I was mistaken, and his wife kept up her growl about me.

"I guess I might as well sew him now," I remarked with quiet calm.

"Oh, you must not do that; you'll kill the man. What do you mean, anyhow?" yelled Mrs. Thompson, while her husband joined in urging me to desist.

"I might as well learn to sew men now," I said, taking a needle from my dress, which I had brought along for the purpose, and deliberately trying to point on my thumbnail.

"I won't allow that to be done in my house," yelled the wife, and the little girl, seeing such a turmoil, began to cry. Even the young girl with me said I had better wait, but I was determined to test my subject.

"Say miss, wouldn't you rather sew him when you have him singing?" asked my instructor, coaxingly. "It's much more effective."

By this time I had tried the point several times on the subjects ear, and observed a slight twitch every time. I had no desire to butcher him in cold blood. I knew that if I ran it through the muscles of his ear he would be compelled to yell, but really my heart failed me, much as I despised him for his fraud. I stuck my needle back in my dress and, taking his head between my hands, thumped it up and down on the floor. Again Mrs. Thompson protested, and Mr. Thompson protested he could not have his subjects treated so badly. I must say that the subject filled his position to perfection. I put the needle through the lobe of his ear twice, and he sang on. Of course those who have had their ears pierced know that the pain is comparatively nothing, so I did not regard it as a sure test. Mr. Thompson looked at me in triumph, but I had one more card to play against him.

"I have a final test to make," I said, and going to my coat I took from the pocket a small bottle I had brought along just for this purpose.

A HORRIBLE TEST

"What is it?" asked Thompson, eyeing me in a frightened manner.

"Asafoetida," I replied, shortly.

"What is that?" he asked in a hushed whisper, as the color left his face. I turned to my subject, who had stopped singing, and saw him watching me intently.

With deliberation I pulled the cork from the bottle. The odor of the beastly stuff filled the room, sickening even me. I slowly poured about two tablespoonfuls into a glass. Placing one hand on the shoulder of my subject and holding the glass outstretched in my right hand I said, in a most determined and solemn voice:

"This, Mr. Thompson, is the terrible drug known to scientists as asafoetida. It is composed by mixing several deadly drugs together. You notice its odor? (I was almost choked and the young girl was buried in her handkerchief up to her eyes.) Well, if this man is mesmerized and I give him this drug, it can do him no harm; if he is not—"

"What will it do?" asked Mr. Thompson, as I made the impressive pause.

"What will it do?" I repeated, as I shrugged my shoulder slightly, "Well, if he is not mesmerized the effects will be fatal."

The door burst open as he sank limp and helpless into a chair, and Mrs Thompson came in like a detained tornado. "Don't let her give it to him," she yelled excitedly.

"I won't," he answered in a shaking voice, trying to re-assert himself. "I can't allow my subjects to be treated in this manner." But he continued to sit there gazing at me in a helpless, bewildered way A quiet reigned for a moment and the subject began to sing, which he had left off when I was relating my fairy tale about asafoetida.

"Would you take that drug?" asked Mr. Thompson of me in an insinuating manner.

"This fatal drug? (the subject quieted his song to listen.) No, sir; nothing on earth could compel me to. This drug? Asafoetida? Why, if I were bound hand and foot I would die before I would swallow it."

Mr. Thompson again became limp and helpless, but Mrs. Thompson sprang at me like a tigress.

"What sort of woman are you, anyhow? You would do anything. Give me that poison," and she made a rush for the bottle. I quietly took both bottle and glass in my hand, remarking that the deadly (?) drug was my property. I looked at my subject and he quickly turned his eyes from me and began to sing.

"When I'm dead let Tom go free; papa, promise this to me." I smiled slightly and resumed my dramatic discourse.

"Now, Mr. Thompson, this man's life is in your hands. If you say he is mesmerized, I will give him this terrible drug—(Little Eva's song is cut short)—and, if you have told me an untruth, then he will die."

"Stop," he pleaded. (Little Eva's song is resumed.) Turning to his wife he asked, sadly, "Did you ever hear of asafoetida?"

"Yes, I have, but I don't know what it is. Don't allow her to give it to him. She would murder; she will do anything. What are you?" she cried, turning to me. "Have you no feeling?"

I made no reply, but gently held the glass close to my subjects nose. He moved his head from side to side to escape the odor. The room was filled with it and I felt that I must soon close the scene or smother.

"Your decision, Mr. Thompson. I can wait no longer," I said impatiently. The order was more than I bargained for and the young girl whispered:

"I can't stand this smell. Give it to him and let's go."

"Won't you just taste it?" pleaded Mr. Thompson.

"Taste asafoetida?" I asked in surprise. "Mr. Thompson, it is easily seen that you don't know anything about the fatal drug you speak of. (Singing ceases.) I tell you honestly. I would die before I would allow any one to give it to me."

"You'll be responsible for his death," he almost sobbed.

"Oh, no; on you rests the responsibility. I do not ask you to tell me if this man is playing the fraud or not. I merely show this fatal drug—asafoetida—and tell you its effect. If Mr. Gray is mesmerized it will not hurt him; if he is not it will kill him. (The singing ceases in a little quaver and he pretends to arrange the imaginary strings on the banjo. He is past singing.) "Shall I give it, Mr. Thompson? Yes or no?" and I held the glass out as a handkerchief is held at an execution.

"No," he gasped. I had conquered. I snapped my fingers lightly in disgust and Mr. Gray dropped the cane and flung himself on the sofa.

"I won't take any drugs, only what is mixed and given by a physician," he said.

I laughed, satisfied with my test. Here was my subject, who was supposed to have been unconscious, disclosing the fact that he knew what we had been talking about. Mr. Thompson was unable to speak, so Mr. Gray continued: "I'll stand anything but drugs or burning."

"Mr. Gray, I admire your nerve. I have all evening, else I should have been rougher with you."

Mr. Thompson refused to give me the names and address of any of his subjects. He did not even ask for the $10 to be given after the satisfactory test.

The New York World
August 5, 1888

The Infamy of the Park

Nellie Bly Unearths a Scoundrel Favored by the Police

Charles Cleveland, a Man of Leisure, Debauches Central Park to His Own Vile Uses—He Drives There Daily and Invites Young Girls to Ride—The Police Smile at Him and Assist in Getting His Prey

There is one man in this city who, with the sanction of the Park Police, debauches Central Park to his own infamous uses.

Many complaints have come, from time to time, to THE WORLD touching Park policemen. Women complain that they dare not go to the Park alone because of the familiar and offensive manner of these officers—those paid guardians of propriety and quietness. Young men complain that if they stay in the Park after dark these same guardians blackmail them, and that rather than be subjected to the disgrace of taking their companions before a magistrate, they accept the officers' offer to compromise and give up their money.

A few days ago a young married woman sent THE WORLD a letter, the startling contents of which suggested the necessity for an investigation. She said she went to Central Park every morning for a walk and she had noticed particularly the peculiar actions of one man. Regularly every morning he drove through the Park. Whenever he saw a girl sitting alone on a bench he would draw up and ask her to take a drive. One morning he asked a girl—who was to all appearances a working girl—to take a spin with him around the Park. She did so and when he brought her back the young married woman went to the same bench and, sitting down, began to talk to the girl. First they talked about the weather and then the girl, yielding to the subtle inquiries, told the story of her drive.

The man, while driving around, spoke to every officer and in return received familiar salutes. Several times he drew up and spoke in a whisper to some, who would continue on their beat with a smile, while he resumed his drive. He told the girl that every policeman knew him, and that they would solicit girls for him to take driving. Every day between 10 and 11 A.M. he took to the officers their beer, which they drank behind the trees. This insured his safety, and he could do anything he wished, from robbing a man to cutting down a tree or stealing flowers, and they would not molest him. He repeatedly referred to the "madam" who he said owned the team which he drove.

This was about the substance of the letter, which, in addition, contained a description of the man and his turnout, so I decided to see if the Park policemen, who are paid to protect, were capable of abetting crime. I dressed myself like a country girl and went to the Park. I sat down on a bench fronting the drive which leads from the Fifty-ninth Street entrance to the Seventy-second. I opened a book and awaited developments. I had not long to wait. Among all those driving I saw only one who answered the description of the man I wanted, and it required but a few moments to be convinced by his actions that I had made no mistake.

When he saw me sitting alone he endeavored to attract my attention. Although he never once glanced at the other women around who were accompanied by escorts. Four times he drove past me, coming within a few yards and repeating. He gave little whistles, coughs and smacking of his lips to make me look, but I still gazed at the top line in my book, which allowed me, without raising my eyes, to see all that was going on before me.

THE MEETING WITH THE SCOUNDREL

When he passed the fifth time, going towards Seventy-second Street, I lifted my head and gazed at him. He nodded his head for me to follow him, and though I made no move and did not look pleasant, he kept on making motions with his head for me to come after. An officer on the path, who could not but see the man's performances, merely looked at me lazily. I walked down along the path, going in the direction he had driven, and I saw him a few yards distant talking to a woman. He held his team close by the path and she stood on the green sward bordering the path and the drive, talking to him. A guard was standing beside his horse, on the opposite side of the road. I sat down on a bench facing the guard and pretended to read.

Just then the man and woman saw me. She laughed and went back to a bench, while he drove direct to me. He drove as closely to where I sat as the road would allow and then stopped.

"Good morning," he said. I made no reply, but kept my eyes fastened on my book.

"I would like to take you for a drive," he said, "if you will go down the path while I turn."

I got up without replying and looked at the officer. He was watching us.

"Which way?" I asked the man.

"Down towards Seventy-second Street," he replied. I walked past the officer, who turned his face, on which rested a broad smile, towards his horse, presenting his back to us. I passed the woman with whom the man had been talking and she looked at me in an amused way. I stopped where the first path crossed the drive and the man came up.

SOLID WITH THE POLICE

"Aren't you afraid to do this?" I asked as I got into the vehicle with him.

"Why, there's nothin' to be afraid of," he answered, as he arranged the lap robe.

"The officers," I suggested, "aren't you afraid they will arrest you?"

"No, I'm solid with them," he answered, laughing, as if the idea was a good joke. "They wouldn't touch me, no difference what I do."

"You are sure of that?" I asked. "Then they allow men to do such things in this park?"

"They wouldn't allow everybody," he answered, "but there are men who come out every day just to pick up girls and the police never bother them. They are only too glad to do something for me," he added. "Just notice how respectfully they salute me when I drive past them."

That's just what I intended to do, so I kept my eyes open. His boast was not a vain one. Every officer we met or passed, on foot or mounted, spoke to him, and in every instance smiled. Whether the smile was but pleasantness or had a meaning I do not know.

"This is a handsome team you drive," I said, "Yours, I suppose?"

"Oh, yes, they're mine; I've got lots more. I own a livery stable," he replied.

"Oh indeed. Then you come to the Park frequently, I presume," I insinuated.

"About four times a day."

"What do you call your horses?" I asked.

This seemed to stagger him, for he was silent some time; then he answered that he had no names for them. I smiled and said that seemed strange, as I never knew any one who owned horses to have them unnamed. He then asked me if I liked to drive and if I could ride. When I gave him an affirmative reply he said he had a phaeton he would allow me to drive, and he had a good saddle-horse I could have any time. I told him his kindness was overwhelming.

REGULARLY HUNTING FOR GIRLS

"Do you often get acquainted with girls this way?" I asked.

"Every day," he replied.

While we drove around he asked me all about myself. I told him that I was a country girl and had come to New York as a governess. He told me it was lucky that all my relatives were dead, and asked me if I would not like to go on the stage. He could easily get me on, as he had lots of friends among the profession. Lest the man be given to telling untruths I shall not publish the names of the managers whose friendship he claims; however, he told very strange stories concerning their treatment of the girls. He said he received lots of complimentary tickets and asked me to go with him to the theatre.

"Who was the woman you were talking to in the Park?" I asked him.

"She's a friend of mine," he answered.

"Why didn't you take her driving, then, instead of a stranger?" I inquired.

"Oh, I never take her driving," he said, with a laugh. "She understands it."

"Understands what?" I asked, but he would not answer.

"Does she often come to the Park?" I asked, and he answered that he talked with her there every day—of what I could not learn.

"I go away in a short time to visit all the summer resorts," he said. "I always take several horses along and I have a good time driving. Will you come along?"

"I?" I exclaimed, in my simple, country manner. "Oh, that would be impossible. Is your livery-stable far away?" I asked, artlessly.

URGING HER TO GO WITH HIM

"Down on West Fifty-eight Street, and I live on West Fifty-seventh Street," said he; "and where do you live?"

I named a street—the first one I thought of—and refused to give a number simply because I was afraid of giving wide of the mark, which he would find out. I endeavored to tell the avenues it lay between but got mixed up in that, which was due, I explained, to my country simplicity.

"You will go with me, then, to the summer resorts," he urged.

"Oh, you shouldn't ask me so soon; wait until we are better acquainted. Maybe we will not like each other then," I said evasively. "What is your name?" I asked coaxingly.

"If you meet me tomorrow I tell you my name," he said cunningly. "You can call me Charles until then."

Determined to hunt him down, I made an engagement to meet him the next morning at 10 o'clock, at the corner of Seventy-second street and the Boulevard. If it rained I should not come until the following morning.

WHAT HE LOOKS LIKE

The man, who is about 5 feet, 8 inches, usually wears a gray pongee duster, which is buttoned up closely to his chin, hiding his clothes entirely. He wears a white straw hat of cheap grade with a black band around it. His gloves are a snuff-brown lisle thread with brown leather inside, rather the worse for wear. His entire clothing is cheap and coarse. His face does not bespeak refinement or culture. His black eyes, deep set and rather close together, are overhung with heavy black brown. His nose is long and very red, the redness which looks more the work of the sun than drink. His drooping black mustache, in which are many gray streaks, covers his mouth completely. His chin and cheeks wore the stubbled beard of many day's growth. His collar, which accidentally got above his gray ulster, was a straight band, very much soiled. His hair is rather white on the temples and above his ears. His conversation is conducted without regard for any grammatical rules. The team he drove was above reproach. One was a bobtail sorrel and the other a bay whose tail almost touched the ground.

A reporter was instructed to follow me the next morning and to track the man to his house, while a photographer was waiting in the Park to get a picture of the man and his rig. Although it rained we were all on the watch for Mr. "Charles." I had found a place where I could watch without being seen. A few minutes before 10 the rain ceased and the sun came out—so did the man. He drove to the place where I was to meet him and round and round, as though expecting that I would yet come. At last he gave up in despair, and about 10.30 went to the Park, closely followed by the reporter. Here he met and talked with the woman he had met the day previous, and, after a consultation of some length, he resumed his drive. The woman went down a side path, and though the reporter followed after as quickly as he dared, she was lost to sight, and he was unable to again find her.

HIS NAME AND ADDRESS

A photographer from THE WORLD office got a view of the man and his team and the reporter followed him to the stable. There it was learned that his name is Charles Cleveland, and that he is said to be foreman of Lovell's boarding stable, No. 230 West Fifty-eighth Street. The team he was driving is said to be the property of Judge Hilton, who is boarding it there during the summer.

In hopes that he would throw some light on the business with the woman and his "pull" with the policemen, I was to meet him the next morning. It was a bright, sunny morning. I was there at the hour named, and Mr. Cleveland came a few moments afterwards. He wanted to go to the Riverside Drive, but I insisted on going to Central Park, where I knew a reporter was waiting for us. He refused to drive over the road where he found me the first morning; why, I do not know. He wanted to go out on the road, but I told him I was to go downtown with a woman and I must return in a few moments. He roughly told me the story was manufactured and kept on his way. He spoke to all the officers, as he had the other day.

Driving out the road on the occasion of our first meeting, he proffered the information that he intended to stop at a road house kept by a widow, a particular friend of his—for drinks. I told him I never drank and insisted on his returning. It made no difference, he drove up to a one-story frame house on One Hundred and Sixteenth Street, speaking to the two mounted guardians on the corner, and we got out. The horses were taken around to the stable, and he came into the reception-room, pulling off his gray ulster. He had on a clean collar, and his hair couldn't have been slicked tighter to his head. His trousers were the worst bagged at the knee I ever saw and were quite short, plainly showing the new heavy shoes he wore. After removing his ulster he looked at me in a self-satisfied way, as if he felt sure in all this "get-up" he would completely capture, as well as awe, the simple country girl.

IN THE ROAD HOUSE

He told me to "sit down and give us a tune," and when I declined he said: "I see my friend ---, of Wallack's Theatre, and he sez he'll take you on, so I want to hear your voice. Come, give us a tune!"

Finding that I would not he went out to order drinks. I had at last consented to drinking a lemonade. The waiter, in white jacket and apron, followed Mr. Cleveland in with two glasses, which he placed on the table. The lemonade was a deep amber shade to the depth of an inch on top.

"That doesn't look like country lemonade," I said, as I stirred it around with the straws until it all became an amber tinge. "What is in it?"

"I only had him put some sherry in it," he said. "Go ahead and drink it; it won't hurt you; it will brace you up."

"I don't want to drink it," I said.

"Drink it; it won't hurt you; you're mighty particular," he growled.

"All right, I don't intend to drink it," I said, firmly.

"You drink it, now. I have to pay for it," Mr. Cleveland said, coarsely. "You think I put something in it, don't you? That's why you won't drink; you're afraid."

"Probably I am," I answered slowly. "I could not trust a man who has done as you have."

THE SCOUNDREL'S PLAN

"I've been better to you than most men would be," he hurled at me. "When they bring girls out and they refuse to do what the men say they put them out and they have to get back to the city as best they can."

I gave him a gentle hint that it would save him trouble to take me where he got me, and so he made me go to the back of the house to where the team was standing beneath a shed. We drove back to the Park.

"You will get into trouble if you go around hunting up girls in the Park all the time," I said, after a long silence.

"Will I? I'm safe enough. I ask the girls to take a drive and if they make any fuss the police will pull them in. They wouldn't touch me. I'm solid."

"How do you get solid?" I ask.

"That doesn't make any difference. It's only the girls that get into fusses," he said. "I never ask regulars to get in; I always take girls who are strangers. Now, I knew you were a stranger the first moment I saw you."

"How did you know?"

"Well, I'm in the Park all the time, and I know everybody by sight who comes there. The moment a strange girl comes in I can pick her out. I'm no fool. I'm not picking up the ones that know the town. Anyway, you can't say that I used you badly."

"It's according to what we call badly," I said. "Any man who will try to entrap a girl because she looks innocent deserves harsh treatment."

"I don't want to talk about it. You can get out here," he said, gruffly.

I refused to get out because it was too far from any station, and compelled him to drive me nearer to Seventy-second Street. Mr. Cleveland let me get out, and whipped up the borrowed horses without a word of farewell—almost before my foot reached the ground.

The New York World
November 11, 1888

Exposed by Nellie Bly

A Swindling Magnetic "Doctor" Caught at His Tricks

He Has Advertised to Give a Big Free Exhibition To-Night, but "The World's" Active Reporter Discovered Him Just in Time—His Ingeniously Secreted Electric Wires by Which He Demonstrates his "Personal Magnetism"—A Long Criminal Career in Half a Dozen Big Cities—Convicted of Forgery at New Orleans—His Brilliant Advertising Schemes.

BROOKLYN ATHENAEUM
Cor. Atlantic Ave. and Clinton St., Brooklyn
ON SUNDAY EVENING, NOV. 11
Admission Free.

Orchestra in attendance. Doors open at 7.30 P.M.
Commence at 8

THE PUBLIC IN GENERAL IS CORDIALLY INVITED. The AFFLICTED and CHRONIC CRIPPLES are especially invited. No objectionable persons or children admitted to this REFINED lecture and exhibition.

PROF. ERNEST DE BLANC
The Famous Chevalier Electrician of Paris

Will exhibit HIS SKILL and
TREAT THE AFFLICTED FREE on the stage
IN VIEW OF THE AUDIENCE.

Specialist: Diseases, Deformity, Paralysis, Rheumatism, Consumption, Dyspepsia, Fits, Catarrh, Neuralgia, Nervous Diseases, Blindness, Deafness, Diseases of Indiscretion, and
FEMALE DISEASES TREATED SUCCESSFULLY.
STRICTLY CONFIDENTIAL,
GUARANTEED IN ALL CASES

PATIENTS DESIRING TO BE TREATED BY MEDICINE OR SURGERY ARE NOT ACCEPTED. NO CORRESPONDENCE ANSWERED UNLESS STAMP ENCLOSED.

Prof. Ernest de Blanc, in order to establish his fame among the WEALTHY CLASS, as well as Working Class Patients, would TREAT FREE a WEALTHY LADY AFFLICTED WITH ANY OF THE ABOVE DISEASE. On application state nature of case, if MARRIED, SPINSTER, WIDOW and AGE.

CIRCULARS MAILED FREE to any part of the United States.
OFFICE CONSULTATION FREE.
Daily from 8.30 A.M. to 3 P.M. and 6 to 8.30 P.M.
Sunday 9 A.M. to 3 P.M.

Prof. Ernest de Blanc is now permanently located at No. 84 Ashland Place, near Fulton St., Brooklyn, N.Y.

    I made up my mind to call on this remarkable person, as the advertisement seemed to bear on its face the evidence of fraud. Friday was a bad day for thin boots and Friday night was worse. I had had a long and tiresome day, but I could not rest until I investigated the schemes of the magnetic doctor.
    "What will you charge to take me to No. 84 Ashland Place?" I asked a cabby, who was leaning against his coupe as if asleep.
    "Two dollars," he said, straightening up.

THE "DOCTOR" AT HOME.

We arrived at Ashland Place in a little more than ten minutes. The street, like the night, was dark and dreary. From what I could distinguish I decided that it was a residence street and a respectable neighborhood.

After much hunting about in the darkness I found the right number and, pulling the bell, asked the man who opened the door if I was right.

"Zees is 84," replied the man, stepping inside the door as the driver returned to me.

"Good evening, good evening," said the man, as he held the door open for me to enter; "I was just about to close my house."

"Are you Doctor Ernest De Blanc?" I asked, entering the parlor.

"Yes, lady," he replied, with a pleasing accent. A woman, of medium height, with dark eyes and hair, flitted noiselessly out of sight.

"I saw your advertisement in the papers," I said, "and as I am tired taking medicine I concluded to come and try your treatments; you advertise 'no medicine given.'"

"That is right," he said, with a most agreeable smile. "I give no medicine. I cure entirely wizout zat."

"How do you treat patients?" I asked.

"Wiz personal magnetism, wiz animal electricity," he said, spreading out his hands, palms upward, and slightly elevating his shoulders. "Ze electricity all comes from me—from my body, I transmit it to ze patient. I give him treatments. I always cure him."

"Have you been here long?" I asked innocently.

"No. You see my house is yet not in good order," he said, with a sweep of his hands. "I have just moved in. What is wrong with you?"

"I am suffering from sick headaches," I utter plaintively.

"Ah! Are they frequent?"

"Yes, every week at the very least, and I am very stupid while they last."

"How long do they last?"

"Usually twenty-four hours at a time."

"Will you come here until I examine you?"

He stepped beneath the chandelier and I went to him. With both hands he pulled the lid of my eye down easily and examined it with a look which rivaled an owl's—in solemnity at least.

"Ah!" he said, with a great deal of force. "Ah! I must test your blood. It is greatly impoverished. Remove your rubbers, please, and your gloves."

While I obeyed orders he went out into the hall, and during his absence I will describe his rooms. The parlor, which I entered first from the hallway, is neatly but not luxuriously furnished. Everything is new. Long crimson portieres of flannel hide the back parlor from view. This was the room in which the examination took place, and bears the evidence of just coming out of a furniture store. It contains, besides several chairs, a desk and some sketches on the walls. The floor is carpeted, and lace curtains hang at the windows. In one corner, between the window and the mantel, is a red Brussels bed-lounge. In the midst of it lies a red Brussels rug, bound in gray. This rug is the only article in the two rooms that shows any evidence of wear, and from its appearance I should judge that it had been in the family for a long time.

THE DIAGNOSIS

Prof. De Blanc placed me on this rug and he stood before me. He touched my wrists and my cheek very daintily with the tips of his fingers.

"You will have to take off your shoes," he said at last.

I sat down and unbuttoned my boot while he went out into the hall again and returned. I stuck my boot under a chair and went—two inches higher on one side than the other, thanks to Louis Quinze heels—hobbling across the room to my former position on the rug. The Professor returned and took my arm caressingly in his two hands. My arm tingled at every touch. He touched my face, my eyelids, and his fingers seemed almost to stick to my flesh, so strong was the sensation which communicated itself from him to me.

"It's neuralgia," he exclaimed triumphantly as he led me back to a chair. "A very bad case of neuralgia, and needs immediate treatment."

"Are your treatments similar to this?" I asked.

"Yes, only more exhaustive; each treatment requires about fifteen minutes. You felt me?"

"Yes, very strongly," I replied, still pretending innocence. "What was it?"

"That is my power—my personal electricity."

"Does that electricity all come from you?" I asked.

"Oh, yes it does, it all comes from me—from my body," he said, earnestly. "My cures are marvelous. I cure cripples who never walked; I make the blind see. I heal every known thing, and all by my personal magnetism. On Sunday night I will give a big exhibition at the Athenaeum, the aristocratic hall. There I will in public perform my miracles. I will make the paralyzed walk, the deaf hear, the dumb speak. There will be hundreds of reporters—who have never seen me but heard of me---there to write it up, and if you look in THE WORLD on Monday morning you will see a long account of my exhibition."

I just thought if he looked in THE WORLD Sunday morning that he would see a long account of himself, but I held my peace.

"I have two assistants, surgeons from London," he said; "and I have calls from thousands of people."

"Where are you from?" I asked.

"I am from Paris," he said, looking at me sharply and taking up the more decided accent which unconsciously he drops at times.

"You speak very good English for that," I said slowly.

"Oh, I just come from Australia here," he said, with a startled look. "I want to locate here."

"How much will you charge to care for me?" I asked at length.

"Ah, lady," with a sweet smile and outward movement of the hands. "I will be honest wiz you. It ez a little case. I will then only charge you twenty-five dollar in advance for five treatments. After ze first one you have no more a headache."

"How lovely it would be to be rid of these horrible aches," I uttered, with a deep sigh.

"Do ze head aches ever; did you ever have fits?" he asked.

"No, but you can't know how many times I have felt that I would have them," I replied, choking a laugh.

"Ah, ze headaches should make you fear an inflammation of ze brain. It ez threatened," he said. He was working for the $25 in advance, and I knew it.

"What security have I that you will cure me if I give you the money?" I asked.

"I give you a written paper that I will cure you."

"But if you don't" I urged.

"But I say I will. And when I am so sure of my own power you should not be afraid to trust it," he said very sweetly, but I was not convinced.

THE SWINDLER'S CAREER

Prof. Ernest De Blanc, as he calls himself, is about five feet four and a half inches in height. He is of rather heavy build—that is, he is not thin. His black eyes are mounted with rather heavy eyebrows. His hair, black in color, grows very thick on the head and is slightly parted in the centre, and his nose is flat. His hands are large and he wore a standing collar, a white waistcoat and black coat and trousers. He talks with a French accent, which is not so marked when he forgets himself.

Ernest De Blanc has not half as much personal electricity as my cat, "Tippecanoe," has on a cold night. I knew his little scheme the moment he took me into his little parlor. It's the most simple thing imaginable. There is an electric battery concealed in the back hall, and a nickel-plated spring at the door by which he turns the electricity off and on. In the much worn rug which lies by the bed lounge are some connecting wires, very badly concealed, I must say. The rug is bound with rubber to make it non-conductive, to prevent the electricity from being transmitted to anything else. The rug is divided directly in the centre with a broad band of rubber. Very well, so far. Electricity is positive and negative. The Professor stands the patient on the side of the rug charged with the negative electricity. He goes into the hall, sees that his battery is all right, stops at the door, and in the face of his patient turns the nickel-plated knob, then plants himself directly on the side of the rug charged with the positive current. The patient feels the tingle of a slight shock, which he has the impudence and boldness to claim comes from his own body. It was such a glaring fraud that it made me disgusted. When people will deceive, why don't they do something well, so that it gives one some work to solve the trick?

This is not Prof. Ernest De Blanc's first effort in this line. A little of the history of his eventful career in America may prove interesting. The first account I could find of him was when he practiced his arts in Portland, Ore., under the name of Dr. Gelamardo. While there he assaulted one of his woman patients and was imprisoned. Next I find he appeared in San Jose, Cal., where he suddenly left town with the money advanced for treatments which people never received.

HIS ESCAPE AT TOLEDO

He was next heard of in Toledo, O., where he billed the town announcing his lecture and entertainment, but for some reason never appeared. He next worked Detroit, Mich., but his success was of short duration, as shown by the following clipping from the Detroit *Free Press:*

It will probably be remembered that a man calling himself "Dr. A. E. Gelamardo, the world-renowned electricity and magnetic healer," some time since advertised in this city that he would, with a talented company, present a play, written by himself, depicting his experience as a condemned felon and convict in the Oregon Penitentiary. He filled a brilliant engagement of one consecutive night at the Detroit Opera-House and then departed for fields and pastures new. On the 1st of this month he was lucky enough to marry at Chicago Mrs. Eva La Gay, a wealthy widow with one child. He immediately went on the road with his alleged drama and was forced to disband his company a day or two ago at Aurora, Ill. There are any number of suits against him, and he has disappeared, leaving no trace behind.

HE TURNS UP AT BUFFALO

No longer ago than July 7 he made his appearance in Buffalo under the name of Prof. Albert Le Grand. His record there is briefly told in the following telegram clipped from the Chicago *Herald*. The substance of it appeared in the New York newspapers at the same time:

BUFFALO, July 7,--Dr. Edward Storck, Chairman of the Erie County Medical Censors, today gave "Prof." Albert Le Grand notice to leave town or be arrested for practicing without a diploma. Le Grand gave free lectures in Music Hall and claimed to cure the lame, halt and blind in Biblical fashion. Dr. Storck said: "Prof. Le Grand has decided to leave the city within twenty-four hours. He admitted to me that he had no diploma, and that he was no physician, but a healer. When I asked him if he did not take fees he said that he did. Then, after a good deal of bluster, he gave in. I have learned some of his history. He was a Dr. Galamardo in Portland, Ore., and claimed to be a member of the Society of Sciences of Paris. He also exhibited a decoration, which he claimed to be a cross of the Legion of Honor. He left that city under a cloud, as he was arrested for criminally assaulting a woman patient. He then turned up in Denver, St. Louis, Kansas City, Baltimore and Boston. He was also arrested in Milwaukee. The society could prosecute him here if it wished so, but if he leaves the city that will be enough. Le Grand speaks French fluently and owned up to me that his magnetic touch was caused by an electric belt concealed in the palm of his hand. He had three or four dummies traveling with him who came upon the platform and were cured by him.

In a surprisingly short time afterwards Dr. Gelamardo, alias Dr. Albert Le Grand, turned up in New Orleans and advertised himself extensively in the local papers. This was on

July 20. He found little mercy there, and after he had spent some $300 in advertising, renting the St. Charles Theatre and paying for rooms and board in advance for himself and his wife, he had to flee the town to escape imprisonment for swindling a New Orleans man some fourteen years before.

SWINDLE IN NEW ORLEANS

Mr. Chas. D. Lafferranderie, a reputable business man, of New Orleans, says that in January, 1874, there arrived in New Orleans, from Antwerp, a person calling himself Aaron Gelamar. Through a common friend Mr. Lafferanderie became acquainted with Gelamar. Gelamar pretended to be the only child of very wealthy parents, his father being engaged in the ship-chandlery business at Antwerp. He had had a disagreement with his father, so he said, and for that reason had left home, but was given a large allowance by his indulgent parents. Gelamar's card contained a full-rigged ship and was printed in both French and English. The latter was:

Aaron Gelamar. To office Quai du Rhin 46 warehouses and store. Digal de Terre, street 81 next to water police, Antwerp. Dealer in old rags, chokens, and old hemp, rop, manila rope, canvas and old sails, etc., of all kinds paper stock. They beyst price will be payt for it.

So winning and persuasive did Gelamar prove himself that when he proposed a partnership in the ship-chandler's business in that city between himself and Mr. Lafferanderie it was gladly accepted. It was agreed, by reason of Gelamar's long apprenticeship in his father's shop, that he should come to New York to make the necessary purchases. As a proof of good faith, Lafferanderie was to advance Gelamar $100 before his departure, and on receipt of the invoices and the policy of insurance upon the merchandise, forwarded by a reliable New York firm, Gelamar would receive a draft of $400.

The result of that transaction I find in the New Orleans *Times-Democrat:*

In the course of time a receipted bill was received by Lafferanderie, made out to Gelamar & Lafferanderie, New Orleans, from Messrs. Baldwin, Hought & Co., No. 66 Sixth Avenue, New York, for $1,154.75. The bill was dated New York, Feb. 9, 1874, and stated on its face, "less received for cash on account, $754.75," leaving a balance due of $400.

This was followed by a policy of insurance of the Atlantic and Mutual Insurance Company, No. 55,153, made to Geistner & Lafferanderie, and was stated to cover a shipment of horseshoe nails and other goods shipped upon the steamer Western Metropolis. The policy was signed by J.H. Chapman, Secretary, and W.U.U. Moore, President.

Upon the back was indorsed as follows:

Insurance for $1,150 at 1-1/2............ ....$14.37
Policy... ... ...   1.25

Record 58, folio 17.

It was signed Feb. 9, 1874. On receipt of these documents Mr. Lafferanderie sent $400 by wire Feb. 14, the receipt for which was shown to the reporter, and bore the signature of J.T. Alleyn, cashier, for manager.

Mr. Lafferanderie then bided the arrival of the goods, which he has been doing ever since.

They never came to hand, and subsequent investigations revealed the fact that the letters purporting to have come from the New York firms were forgeries, as were also the invoices and the policy of insurance. They had all emanated from the brain of Aron Geismar, who had violated the trust and confidence placed within his hands by a too-confiding fellow-countryman.

FOLLOWING UP THE SCOUNDREL

Mr. Lafferanderie saw a picture of the "Professor" in the Toledo *Bee,* and recognized it as the face of the man who had swindled him. The picture in the newspaper was compared with the photograph in his possession, and though it had been taken years before, they were identical. Mr. Lafferanderie had made an effort to trace the swindling Gelamar, and while doing so he learned that he was practicing medicine out West. This was conclusive.

Yet, in order to make no mistake Mr. Lafferanderie called on Prof. Albert Le Grand, pretending he wished to be doctored. The recognition was mutual. Prof. Albert Le Grand, alias Dr. Gelamardo and Aron Geismar were one and the same. Mr. Lafferanderie went to make out an affidavit, but before his return Prof. Albert Le Grand had fled the town. He did not even wait to take his electric battery along, but his wife, who professed ignorance as to this place of abode, took it in charge. Thus there was no exhibition at the St. Charles Theatre and numbers of poor people escaped being swindled.

Aron Geismar, alias Dr. Gelamardo, alias Prof. Albert Le Grand, alias Prof. Ernest De Blank, is not an over clever swindler. Notice these peculiar wordings in his advertisement for Brooklyn and that for New Orleans.

HIS ADVERTISING SCHEMES

First: "Admission Free!" appears conspicuously in both.

Second: "No objectionable person, boys or children admitted to this refined lecture and exhibition." Brooklyn advertisement.
"No objectionable person, nor boys nor children admitted to this refined exhibition." New Orleans advertisement.

Third: "Prof. Ernest De Blanc, the famous chevalier electrician of Paris." Brooklyn advertisement.
"Prof. Albert Le Grand, the famous world-renowned Healer and Electrician of Paris, France." New Orleans advertisement.

The following are samples of his advertisements:

EXHIBITION AND LECTURE
By Prof. ERNEST DE BLANC
On SUNDAY EVENING, NOV. 11, 1888
At the
BROOKLYN ATHENAEUM

Admission Free!

Orchestra in attendance.	Doors open 7.30 P.M.
Commencing at 8 Sharp.
The public in general is cordially invited. The Afflicted with Chronic Diseases are specially invited.
No objectionable persons, boys or children admitted to this Refined Lecture and Exhibition.

Electricity is Life! Health is Happiness and Wealth combined!

Prof. ERNEST De BLANC
The Famous Chevalier and Electrician of Paris,

Will exhibit his Unrivalled Skill and Treat the Afflicted in view of the audience Free of Charge!
Patients daring to be treated by medicine or surgery not accepted.
Diseases treated without medicine and without surgery.

Prof. ERNEST De BLANC
is now permanently located at No. 87 Ashland place
(formerly Raymond street), near Fulton street,
Brooklyn, N.Y.

At New Orleans this was his method of advertising, and is just about the same thing he had adopted for Brooklyn:

ST. CHARLES THEATRE, NEW ORLEANS
ON SUNDAY, JULY 22, 1888

ADMISSION FREE
Come One! Come All! Free!
Commencing 8 P.M. sharp. Doors open 7.30 P.M.

PROF. ALBERT LE GRAND
THE FAMOUS WORLD-RENOWNED HEALER AND
ELECTRICIAN OF PARIS, FRANCE.

CONSULTATION FREE!
Diseases Cured Without Medicine and Without Any Surgery.
SPECIAL TERMS FOR THE WORKING-CLASS PATIENTS.

THE POOL OF SILOAM.

THE LAME WALK, THE BLIND SEE AND THE DEAF
HEAR AT TREMONT TEMPLE.

Prof. Albert Le Grand is now located for sixty days at No. 14 University Place, formerly Dryades street, New Orleans.

I think I have given enough to show that Prof. De Blanc is a swindler, and of the meanest kind, inasmuch as his victims are among the sick and ignorant. If this exposure saves one such person from expending his hard earned money on Galamar's quackery I shall feel that my work has not been in vain.

The New York World
December 2, 1888

Visiting the Dispensaries

Nellie Bly Narrowly Escapes Having Her Tonsils Removed

Treated as a Charity Patient in the Throat, Skin and Ear Infirmaries

She Joins the Throng of Poor Invalids and Finds Out How Free Medical Aid is Dispensed—One Brusque Old Doctor Probes Her Throat and Nose and Wants to Perform an Operation—A Young Physician Tells Her Never to Wash Her Face with Soap—The Druggists' Big Profits—What She Saw and Heard

    I started out the other day to investigate some of the New York dispensaries and see for myself how the poor girls fare who are really sick and have to seek charity. Naturally I concluded before I started that only the very poor were the recipients of free medical aid, so I spent some time over my make-up. When it was completed I flattered myself that I looked as poor as any of them.
    My first visit was to the Metropolitan Throat Hospital, 351 West Thirty-fourth Street. As I read the words, "Open the Door," on a big silver plate, and was obeying the order, I heard the most heartrending cries from an inside room. I stood holding the door for a moment and heard again those dreadful cries of pain:
    "Ow! Ow! Doctor! Ow!"

My bangs curled at these sounds, yet I stretched my eardrums lest I should miss one.

"I won't hurt you. I won't hurt you, my good woman. Keep perfectly still one moment," came the answer in a sharp, metallic voice. Then in lecture style, slow, with many impressive pauses, it continued:

"This, causes the tonsils, to turn, outward, and, so allows, a—a better view, of the—of the throat."

"O-w!!" a prolonged cry.

"Don't move; I am doing that on purpose." Then resuming the discourse: "You see, in this way"—

"Ow! My! Doctor!"

"Keep still. I am only spraying your throat." A strong whistling sound like a stage storm, then the lecture goes on. "The object, is, to make them, wear away, gradually, not to, make them burst, as was, formerly the practice. By this method, they come away, in white, or opaque chunks. It is as well—"

By this time I had come to the conclusion that some poor girl had called to have her throat attended to and had been taken into the operating room as an illustration for a lecture. Closing the door, I entered and quietly set down beside a women who occupied one end of a long bench in the hall. She was better clad than I, which made me feel quakish on my ability to "make up" appropriately, A woman with a very small waist and extra large shoulders came out of the first room and looked me over.

"Do you wish to see the doctor?" she asked.

"Yes," I replied, curtly.

"Throat?"

"Yes."

"Come in here," she said, leading the way into the room she had just left. It was a small, uncarpeted hall room, with long benches on one end. The front end, cut off with an iron fence, held a desk and a small apothecary shop. Over the mantel was a black table inscribed in commemoration of John D. Jones, Esquire's gift of the building in 1886. Below it sat a small box, whose plain face bore the words: "Charity Fund for the Hospital."

"What is your name?" asked the girl behind the railing.

THE PRELIMINARY EXAMINATION

"Norah Simpson," I replied modestly, as she dipped her pen in the ink preparatory to recording my answers.
"Where were you born?"
"Rhinebeck."
"New York State?"
"Yes."
"Where do you live?"
"At 110 West Twenty-fifth Street."
"Married or single?"
"Single."
"Present occupation."
"Making scarfs."
"Ever been here before?"
"No."

All these questions were printed in a small book in which she wrote my answers. Then marking my copy "9,585," she gave it to me with this card, one side of which was printed in German.

METROPOLITAN THROAT HOSPITAL
831 West Thirty-fourth Street.

Dr. CLINTON WAGNER's patient
NORAH SIMPSON   No. 9,585
Will attend on
MONDAY AND TUESDAY, at 2 o'clock

Medical staff:
Clinton Wagner, M.D., 34 West Fifty-first Street.
William J. Swift, M.D., 40 East Thirtieth Street.
G. B. Hope, M.D., 34 West Fifth-first Street.
Clinical Assistant:
J.D. Aspinwall, M.D.   J.H. Billings, M.D.
Medical Superintendent, Clinton Wagner, M.D.

"Sit out in the hall, and when the doctor is ready for you I will tell you," she said.

"They have had her in there for an hour," whispered the woman beside me on the bench. "They're experimenting on her so as to teach a young doctor. I wish the old doctor won't go away afore my turn. I hate young doctors to learn on me."

I echoed her sentiments.

"What is wrong with the woman?" I asked, her "ouches!" occasionally punctuating our conversation.

"She thinks she has cancer," she whispered. "It's all down here," indicating the middle of the collarbone, "and it's hard to get at. She suffers awful with it. Hear how bad they have made her voice. It wasn't so husky at first."

"How are the doctors, kind?" I asked.

"Oh, yes, they're kind enough. Then it doesn't cost anything unless you let 'em know your man gets good wages; then they'd want ter visit your house an' be paid."

More patients were coming. First came a young man, who I should judge from his clothing was in comfortable circumstances. Then a young woman came whose gown was so neat that I thought she had mistaken the place; but no, she sat down on the bench opposite. Two more young men, likewise well clad, joined the group. I was the poorest dressed in the hall.

A bell tapped twice and the young woman came from the room to say that the doctor wished to see the new patient first. It was I.

A HORRIBLE SITUATION

Stepping suddenly into the room from the dark hall made the brilliancy of the gas and reflectors dazzle me. Only for an instant, though; then I saw a doctor sitting at one side of the table motion to me. I sat down facing him and glanced about. The walls were covered with pictures of the throat in all conditions. The table was strewn with all sorts of gleaming instruments. Large reflectors made an unusual brilliancy. On the opposite side of the table, trying to make a young man open his mouth wider than nature had most liberally made it, was another doctor. Standing near by, intently watching every move, was a bald-headed pupil. Both of the doctors had glass reflectors bound over their right eyes. It looked so much like an engine headlight in a snow-storm that when it was turned on me I had a lively impulse to laugh.

"What is wrong?" he asked, curtly, taking my book and glancing through it.

"My throat," I replied, with ebbing spirits.

"Let me see," he said, taking a small instrument out of a finger bowl. "Open your mouth wide."

I opened it. I did not want to, but I knew I was in for it. He caught my chin firmly and ran the instrument down my throat. Just then the horrible thought came that with the same thing he had looked into the other woman's throat. And she had cancer! Ugh!

"What's wrong? What's wrong?" he asked sharply as I involuntarily jerked away and held my breath to prevent my disgust from materializing.

"I'm sick, that's all," I replied, faintly.

"Well, if you're going to pull away in that manner I can't do anything for you. Open again. Now say ah—ah."

"Ug—ng," I grunted, he meanwhile holding my tongue down.

"Ee—ee," he commanded.

"Iok—e--! I'em thiek," I pleaded.

"Very well. I want you to be," unfeelingly. "If you get sick it won't hurt you. I am making you that way on purpose."

The thing goes away down my throat again. My stomach rocks most frightfully. I know it is useless to beg off. I have half an inclination to laugh and half to box the doctor's ears.

"That tonsil needs a piece cut off," he said, dropping the probing instrument and taking up another whose bright gleam gave me a chill.

I'll do a great deal, I think pathologically, to get a story, but I won't give up half a tonsil. But how to get away? I can't run for the door, and if I object to giving up all claim to a useless tonsil, he will discover that I am not a bona fide patient.

I look at him in fear and alarm. He takes up a piece of linen. He throws his headlight into my eyes. I am blinded! With a quick movement he catches my tongue and wraps the linen tightly around it. I am by force speechless! Mercy, mercy, will he cut a tonsil out and not allow me a word of explanation?

Many warnings, which my acquaintances have hurled at me, time after time, about some day getting caught in my own trap flash like a specter before me. It's an agonizing thing to be able to think and not to speak in moments like these. Upon disagreeable realizations one always thinks of unpleasant things, instead of comedies, the latest jokes and the last minstrel show. I couldn't keep my mind off the doctor and the silver knife, try as I would.

He turns, still holding my tongue—more than I can do myself. I see again; he reaches for the dreaded instrument. I wildly catch his hands with both mine and pull my tongue free.

"I won't be cut," I cried. "I am too nervous, don't you know. I—I will come again when—when my nerves are better."

"That's all foolishness," he answered, shortly. "You must not give way to your nerves."

"But, somehow, I do lately," I pleaded, eagerly. "I am run down. My nerves are very bad today. I will come again."

"That's very foolish" (rubbing the knife). "They are no worse today than they will be any day."

"Oh, but I sat out there and heard that woman yell, and that has shattered me," I explained.

"I did not hurt that woman. Let me make one more examination." He took a piece of cotton, and wrapping it around a probe, dipped the end into a bottle of dark fluid. He held my head back and ran this up my nose until I could almost feel it touch my brain. It left a burning sensation in my nose and throat, and as he removed it I half choked.

"Spit it out, spit it out," he said. Too late!

"It's gone down," I gasped meekly.

"I can't do anything for you if you are going to act this way." Then writing something in the book, he told me to leave it where I got it, and so I left.

TRYING THE HOSPITAL

My mood was anything but cheerful the next day when I started out on my second visit. I had started it and I would persevere. I decided this time to complain of my ear. I had no idea as to the manner of treating such cases, but I felt confident that they could not attempt to amputate an ear. Anything but cutting for me. This visit was to the West Side German Dispensary, 411 West Thirty-eighth Street. It occupies the parlor floor in a small brick building with a high stoop. No one ever heeds the bell, so tiring out at last I open the door and walk into the uncarpeted hall, back to a half open glass door. In this room, waiting on the bare benches, are some half dozen men and women. One corner held a little drug store, and near it a conspicuous sign gave forth this warning:

"None but the poor treated here."

A man in a wet, worn suit sat shivering on a bench. I sat down between him and a woman who had herself and her baby wrapped in one shawl.

"Is the doctor engaged, do you know?" I asked the woman. She had one knee crossed over the other. When I addressed her she set the under boot into a soothing movement, for the benefit of her babe.

"Yah, him mit a sick voman."

"Has he been in there long?"

"Yah, mit some time already."

"Is your baby sick?"

"Yah, him vas sick mit him's ears."

"Oh, how sad!" I reply sympathetically. Then, with a harrowing remembrance of my throat experience, I ask cautiously, "How does the doctor treat your baby?"

"Dreat him? Vas es dot—doctor him? Yah, yah! Him dakes mine Yocob and runs him drough mit his nose to his ear. Mine Yocob schreams so loud as never vas, und den all der dimes mine doctor he runs it mit mine Yocob's ear again some more. Mine gracious! I shust tink der nefer vas notings so bad."

"Do you mean that he probes through the nose to the ear?" I asked in horrified accents.

"Yah, yah! Dot es it."

No. I did not stay to be probed. I got up and quietly made my way to the door. My breath came with more regularity when I was outside and my heart resumed a more dignified pace.

Over a half million people every year receive free treatment in the New York dispensaries and hospitals. It may be well to state here that dispensaries are maintained by charity. Many bequests are made by private people, and some of the dispensaries have been richly endowed. They are intended only for the use of the worthy poor, but many times are they imposed upon by people well able to pay. For this very reason some of the medical journals have protested against there being so many dispensaries. They claim that treating people who are able to pay robs young physicians. Then again, wrong can be done by a physician opening a dispensary and working it for an advertisement, at the same time charging a small fee "because he does not want to be blamed for taking patients away from his opponents." A ten-cent fee will make a dispensary pay very well. I don't think there is any law to prevent a doctor from opening a dispensary if he chooses, and the chances for abusing it are great.

I have understood that probably one or two dispensaries pay their physicians. The majority do not. Young physicians, while waiting their practice to grow to a supporting point, are glad of the chance to gain experience. Dispensaries are especially beneficial to young physicians who wish to make a specialty of any disease, so while benefiting the poor gratuitously they do the same for young physicians.

The Northwestern Dispensary, corner of Thirty-sixth Street and Ninth Avenue, was the next one I visited. Although the rain was coming down in torrents I found people going there as they go to church—in squads. I followed in their wake, up bare stairs, through empty, deserted looking halls, to a dark inside room. The only windows in it were shut off by the drug department.

IN THE CROWD OF CHARITY PATIENTS

This dark room was filled with benches. Each bench held from two to half a dozen specimens of humanity with all sorts of aches and ills. I quietly slipped into the last bench so as to command a view of the room. A pale, sad-faced woman with silver-gray hair sat beside me. On her knee she held a baby whose misproportioned head, half covered with a gray wool hood, reminded me of photographs I have seen of an 8-1/2 head on a six-month-old baby. The case of "big head" did not seem to interfere with the child. He beat a tattoo with his woolen heels on his mother's knee, meanwhile tugging away, with dirty fists and mouth, at something tied up in a linen cloth which had once been white.

On towards the front were women in shabby gowns, many nursing babies, others holding little tots by their sides. They were some few young girls who made an attempt at display in their apparel. Tottering, white-haired men, strong young workmen with bandaged arms or heads, sad little boys with large bottles were waiting. Everything was as quiet and orderly as in a church. Sometimes one woman would gossip in low tones with another. Then a mother would whisper, "Sh, sh," to her fretful babe. Then a new patient would quickly enter and take a place among us. A continual stream kept going with bottles and boxes in their hands to the drug window. An iron rail prevented crowding. They would hand in their prescriptions and bottle or box, as the case called for, and when it was returned moved more quietly out.

At last a man came into the room in a quiet, jerky way and took a stand near a hall door.

"Those to see the doctors come this way," he called, and an assistant helped get me in line.

"What is wrong with you?" he asked the first.

"An aching in my joints," replied the old man in a quavering voice.

"That room," pointing somewhere out in the hall. Then to the next, "What is wrong with you?" and so on down the line until it came my turn.

"What is wrong with you?" he inquired.

"My skin is rough," I replied.

"Breaking out?"

"Yes, a little," I answered, stretching the truth a trifle to fit the occasion.

"Room two. Next—What is wrong with you?"

I went into the room indicated. Two old men were waiting there. One sat in a corner in a drooping, despondent way; the other, in the opposite corner, leaned back with a rakish air as if the world pleased him well. He was old, but roguish. I was conscious that he was trying to catch my eye. At last when he did so, he gave a little smile. I was surprised at his audacity and looked again, thinking my sight deceived me. No, he smiled again, and I kept my eyes fixed on the blank wall thereafter.

A good deal after the right hour a young doctor came bustling in.

"First," he called, entering a small room at the end. One of the old men went in.

"Have you been here before?"

"Yes, sir," I heard the old man reply.

"Where's your card?"

"Sir?"

"Where is your card? You must bring your card if you want to be treated."

"I forgot it, sir. I will bring it the next time, sir. My leg, sir, is much worse."

"Have you received regular treatment?"

"No, sir; I 'aven't been 'ere more'n a month."

"You will never get well if you do not come regularly. Get this prescription filled and apply the salve every night. Good day. Next."

NEVER WASH YOUR FACE WITH SOAP

The third time he said "Next," I went in. I found the room as bare as the others. Two chairs, one table and a wooden box filled with sawdust, for the use of wood inebriates.

"Have you ever been here before?" the doctor asked, and

when I answered in the negative he asked my name, address and occupation, all of which he wrote in a large book on the table before him.

"What ails you?"

"My face gets rough when I wash," I replied.

"Do you use soap?"

"Yes."

"Well, no young lady can have a good complexion and use soap. It ruins the skin."

"But how will I keep clean?"

"Bathe your face in hot water and rub with a coarse towel. I keep clean and I have not used soap for eight years. Take this prescription," handing me one, "have it filled—you must bring your own box for it, you know—and every night, before retiring, bathe your face in hot water—as hot as you can stand, then rub this salve well into your skin. In a short time you will have a nice complexion. Come back next week, I may have to put you under other treatment. Always bring this card with you.

NORTHWESTERN DISPENSARY

ALWAYS BRING THIS WITH YOU.

Come at 2 o'clock

DISEASES OF THE SKIN.

MONDAY, WEDNESDAY AND FRIDAY

No. 76   Date, Nov. 26

DOCTOR S. J. O'NEIL, 421 E. 86

Keep this clean.   Do not roil or break it.

I went to the drug department and handing the man the prescription asked what it would cost.

"Ten cents," he replied. "Where's your box?"

"I have none today. I'll bring it back tomorrow. Do you ever charge any more for other prescriptions?"

"Certainly not. All prescriptions are 10 cents each."

HOW THE DRUGGISTS GET RICH

Hoping to gain some estimate of what druggists' profits are, I decided to have the prescription filled at an independent drug store. Dispensaries fill all prescriptions for 10 cents and yet they are said to clear all expenses by their drug department alone, and make a profit. What becomes of this profit? Whether it returns to the original charity fund I could not learn. This is the prescription I was given:

R.—
    Mag. Sulph……………………Z
    b. Appy
                              O'NEIL

A druggist near the union of Broadway and Sixth Avenue filled it.

"How much, please?" I asked as he handed me the small box.

"Fifty cents," he said, and I paid it. This makes the druggists' profit over and above the dispensary profit 40 cents, less the price of a small glass jar not costing more than two or three cents.

I did not wait to be treated at the Demilt Dispensary, corner Second avenue and Twenty-third street. It is one of the oldest in the city and is kept in splendid running order. In disguise I visited several more, among them Bellevue Hospital Dispensary, but found nothing of especial note differing from that which I have already described. In all I found the poor kindly treated, although in many instances the doctor's manners were quite brusque.

I have come to four conclusions—

First—That New York is the most charitable city in the world.

Second—That charity is daily outraged in numerous cases.

Third—That the poor have a much better chance to improve their conditions than those in moderate circumstances.

Fourth—That too much and ill-directed charity breeds pauperism.

The New York World
February 24, 1889

Nellie Bly a Prisoner

She Has Herself Arrested to Gain Entrance to a Station-House

Just What Happens to a Girl After The Police Seize Her

The Need of Many Improvements in Police Prisons Clearly Shows

Takes from a Hotel on the Charge of Larceny and Locked Up in Capt. Riley's Station House—Detective Hayes in the Double Role of Policeman and Feminine Charmer—Compelled to Disrobe in a Room While the Officers Peeked Through a Crack in the Wall—Scenes in the Cell Room During the Night—A Kind-Hearted Turnkey and Jolly Prisoners—Arraigned Before Judge Duffy at Jefferson Market and Discharged

The reasons for the undertaking which I describe below were:

First, THE WORLD wanted to know how women—particularly innocent women—who fall into the hands of the police are treated by them, and, second, what necessity, if any, there is for providing station-houses with matrons.

Undercover: Reporting for The New York World

About 10 o'clock Thursday a carriage drove up to the Gedney House, corner of Broadway and Forty-first Street, and two travel-stained women sprang out and entered the hotel. From their appearance even the most careful observer would have said that they could tell more about sowing hay-seed than about late suppers. They were so fortunate as to get the best room but one, and the hotel register soon bore these entries:

MISS JANE PETERS, Rochester, N.Y., room 130.
MISS F. KENT, Albany, N.Y. room 130.

Number 130 was a very comfortable corner room on the sixth floor, from the windows of which the two country women could see the crowds of muffled figures going into the Metropolitan Opera-House to the Arson Ball. But they had other things to think of, so they ordered a fire built in the stove, which filled a corner, and turned their thoughts to what they would have for supper. Apparently Miss Kent was the leader and from their conversation, which the waiters who fussed about could overhear, it seemed as if she had undertaken to make Miss Peters, whom she met for the first time on the train to New York, feel at home and enjoy herself. Miss Peters was very inexperienced and was charmed with the ease of her new found friend. Miss Peters was also very obliging and at Miss Kent's wily suggestion paid all the bills. Of course Miss Kent, in the sweetest way, assured her verdant acquaintance she would repay it all in the morning.

The waiters smiled and were more attentive to Miss Kent than to Miss Peters, strange as it may seem.

At 11.30 a dainty supper was served and the young women were very happy and amiable over it. Indeed they grew quite confiding, and Miss Kent charmed her friend with her tales of adventure and travel. No scene could have been lovelier, and the waiters smiled and pocketed their tips—from Miss Peters's purse, of course.

It was growing late and there were scarcely any carriages driving up to the Metropolitan Opera-House, save to the early-to-bed people. The hotel has become very quiet, and a waiter was removing the supper dishes when Miss Peters, who had gone to her satchel for some unknown reason, raised an outcry.

"My money is gone! Oh, Miss Kent, Miss Kent. I have lost my money!"

AROUSING THE HOTEL POOL

Miss Kent and the waiter hurried to the frightened woman and tried to quiet her, meanwhile aiding in a search for the missing money, It was not found and as Miss Peters insisted on raising an alarm Miss Kent became very indignant at the prospect of being connected with such a scrape. She put on her hat and remarked that she would leave, as she did not want to stay there and run the chance of having her name in the newspapers.

Instead of having a quieting effect Miss Peters immediately accused Miss Kent of knowing what had become of her money. For it was Miss Kent who advised her to divide her money and put half in her satchel, lest her purse be stolen and she lose it all. And after following this advice and putting two fifty-dollar bills in the satchel, had not Miss Kent been the only one to take charge of the satchel during Miss Peter's absences from the room and parlor car?

The bell boy went downstairs for the clerk and Miss Kent, now very indignant because of the charges made by Miss Peters, started to leave the hotel. Miss Peters excitedly promised an outcry if Miss Kent made the slightest move to go. With a cool little laugh and a sarcastic reply Miss Kent sat down to wait the pleasure of her frantic roommate. The clerk came and Miss Peters sobbingly related her story anew.

She was coming from Rochester to New York, and on the train she made the acquaintance of Miss Kent, who was so agreeable and nice that they became friends. Then Miss Kent suggested as they were both travelling alone that they stop in New York all night at the same hotel instead of Miss Peters going on to her destination—Orange. Miss Peters, being desirous of doing some shopping, and really pleased with her new friend and loath to part from her, acquiesced. Then Miss Kent had advised her not to carry all her money in her purse, for if she should have her pockets picked she would be penniless. Miss Peters, acting on this advice, had put two fifty-dollar bills in her satchel, which she had left in Miss Kent's care several times. And now the money was gone.

Leaving a man in charge of Miss Kent the clerk took Miss Peters down to the office. Careless and indifferent, Miss Kent stood by a window looking out, while the man in the room watched her steadily.

"Do you think she had the money?" he asked, at last.

ADVISED TO RUN AWAY

"Oh, yes, I saw it," said Miss Kent indifferently, shrugging her shoulders, but still looking out.

"Why didn't you get away?" he asked, going nearer.

"How?" asked Miss Kent shortly, turning to face him. He was of medium height, had a decided brogue and not an unkind face.

"Why, didn't you see me tip you the wink when she began to make a fuss?"

"I did not understand it," said Miss Kent.

"Well, I could've skipped you out then, an' I'll 'ave taken you to any hotel you wanted to go to. You could 'ave went across the street and they would never 'ave found you out."

"Oh!" Said Miss Kent, drily. "And why should I run away?"

"Haven't you enough to pay your bill?" he asked, apprehensively.

"I have," Miss Kent replied. "What is she doing now?" referring to Miss Peters.

"She's in the office trying to get an officer. I can get you out and over the stairway if you want to go."

Miss Kent was more careful of her money than of her liberty, for she refused to escape. As the man went out into the hall Miss Peters returned with Mr. Brugh, one of the hotel proprietors.

"Go out into the hall, Miss Peters, until I talk to Miss Kent," he said as he seated himself near to the accused girl. He was so kind and nice!

THE DETECTIVES CALLED IN

"Now, Miss Kent, I would advise you to give back the money while you have the chance."

"But how can I give back what I have not got?" she exclaimed.

"Oh, yes, I know, Miss Kent," he replied with a smile, "but now, look here, it can all be settled quietly now. If not, Miss Peters will insist on your arrest and you will be taken to the station-house, and tomorrow to the Police Court, and it will go very hard with you."

Miss Peters sat guard over her while Mr. Brugh went down for the officers. The case was hopeless, there was no escape for the accused girl; so with flaming cheeks and scornful eye she listened unmoved to the sobbing and pleading of her new acquaintance and now accuser.

No one ever waited so quietly to be arrested. Doubtless, Miss Kent's calmness and quiet was due to the hopelessness of escape. A man guarded the hall and elevator and Miss Peters guarded the room. So Miss Kent quietly awaited her fate. It came.

Mr. Brugh returned at last when Miss Kent had almost fallen asleep in a big arm-chair. He opened the door and invited the detectives in.

They looked very big and burly, and it's not surprising that even Miss Peters begged Miss Kent to restore the money instead of going to the station-house. They took everything off the bed and turned the mattresses. They pulled the wardrobe out from the wall and examined it carefully. The washstand, the bureau, the carpet, the stove and the chimney, but no money or remnants of money were found.

"You are wasting time and strength doing that," said Miss Kent, laughingly. "I did not take the money and it is not hidden in this room."

When everything was thoroughly gone over, the detectives took Miss Kent—and Miss Peters to tell her story—to the Thirtieth Street station-house.

IN THE STATION-HOUSE

The Nineteenth Precinct Station-House had the appearance, as usual to public places in early morn, of being half asleep. The gray-haired Sergeant rested his arm on his desk, while an expression of dreaminess stole over his chubby, flushed face. Two late reporters leaned against the railing which inclosed the Sergeant's desk, taking but little interest in the case. The fire in the stove, which marked the centre of the room, seemed to be tired of living, and the gaslight gave little spurts occasionally, as if to shake itself to wakefulness. Even the big old clock at the door, whose fingers pointed to 2 o'clock, moved as if it had began to tire of its long duty. The whole atmosphere of the place was filled with an air of languor.

The door was flung open and in from the darkness came four persons who ranged themselves in a line before that Bar of Complaint. Two women and two men. The Sergeant lifted his gray head, and his eyes flashed with positive pleasure. The reporters straightened up and smiled as they moved into the best positions to see and hear. A few dead ashes rattled through the grate of the stove and the fire grew brighter. Even the clock seemed to take up a more cheerful tick.

I—Nellie Bly—was Miss Kent, the girl who stood there accused of grand larceny.

Miss Peters, my accuser, stood beside a detective on my right; the other detective stood on my left. Miss Peters is not the verdant spinster she represented, but is a very bright and well-known newspaper woman. I concocted this plan for my arrest for the reasons given in the first of my article, and owing to Miss Peters' most able assistance I had now reached the threshold of my goal.

"Sergeant," said the detective on my left, as he flung my satchel on the desk before him. "I was called into the Gedney House to arrest this girl. She is charged with stealing two fifty-dollar bills from this woman." After repeating Miss Peters' story of our meeting he added: "We searched the room all over, but we did not find anything."

TAKING THE PEDIGREE

"What's your name?" asked the Sergeant in a gruff way.

"Must I tell," I asked faintly.

"Well, it'll go all the harder with you if I give you a name," he replied.

"What will I do?" I asked the detective. "I don't want to tell my name."

"Say Jane Smith, anything will do," he whispered.

"Well will I give you Jane Doe for a name?" asked the Sergeant.

"Jane Smith," I said by way of reply.

"Where do you come from, Jane?" he asked.

"Where?" I asked, turning to the detective in a pseudo-helpless way. It is always so much easier to allow someone else to do one's prevaricating, and there are always so many ready to do it.

"Gedney House," whispered the detective.

"Gedney House," I said to the Sergeant, and the reporters wrote it in their note-books.

"How old are you, Jane?" asked the Sergeant, lifting his eyes for a moment from the ledger in which he was writing all this new.

"Twenty years old."

"Married or single?"

"Single."

Then I kept quiet until the others helped "Miss Peters" to tell her tale of woe. They also helped her to a chair and I was allowed to stand. "Miss Peters" told her story with many a flourish, painting me blacker and blacker with every word until I began to half expect that I had stolen her money.

SEARCHED BY A LODGER

Some poor man, whom misfortune had overtaken, was brought in and stood beside me at the railing. He was given a chance to tell his story, but I don't see of what avail it is. The officer is always believed in preferences, and let the accused tell what he may, it never saves him from a night in the cells.

"Come with me, Jennie," said my detective on the left, and I followed him through the gate into a small room.

A poorly clad and unkempt woman was there. She was not strikingly clean and her face showed traces of a wearisome life. I felt sorry for her.

"This woman is a lodger here, Jennie, and is to search you," the detective informed me.

I had intended to buy her off—that is, if it had been a paid matron, but I had not the heart to tempt a poor creature who had to beg lodgings. I did not want to be the case of any misery to her, so I quietly submitted to being searched.

"You will have to undress, Jennie," said the detective, whose name I had learned was Hayes, and then he went out and left me in that little pigeon-hole alone with the woman.

As I began to undress I thought I detected an eye at a crevice, and, horrified, I got back as far out of the range of it as possible. I managed to keep the searcher between me and the crevice while I wondered what sort of a man a Sergeant must be who would permit such things. I gave the woman all the money I had, which she handed to the detectives. She was altogether an unfeeling creature, and no more fitted to search women than a vulture is fitted to nurse a sick lamb. She was utterly regardless whether I was seen dressed or undressed. Of course, the fifty-dollar bills were not found on me, and I was taken out through the station-house to a little low building.

LOCKED IN A CELL

A little old man with kind eyes and grayish whiskers and a cap and a great black pipe, from which came dense clouds of smoke, received me and I breathed a sigh of relief. I was locked in where the cells were and the detectives were locked out.

As far as I could see in the dim light the cells went to the top of the building, and as there was but one tier of cells the building must necessarily be low. All these cells had big iron doors. Snoring was about the only thing I heard as I followed my jailer around the stone corridors. Indeed, there was so much snoring, and it was so loud, that when he said:

"Do you want a cell close to the stove or a bit away?"

I had to yell back: "What's that you said?"

But one becomes accustomed even to the noise of a cannon. When the snoring began to resemble the sounds of a heavy sea tearing down things that were meant to stand I found I could talk.

"Don't put me too near the stove," I yelled above the chorus of snores. "It's very warm in here."

So he led the way past a cell where a young man stood looking through the bars, past where a woman leaned her pale face against the bars, away down to a place where half a dozen doors stood ajar.

"Is there no way to get a drink of water during the night?" I asked.

"Oh, yes, I will give you a tin cup which you can keep in your cell," he replied.

I went into my cell. It was not luxuriously furnished; indeed, some might call it bare. There was a bare cemented floor, brick walls painted brown half way up and then whitewashed; a brass faucet where I could get water. The bed was the very personification of simplicity. It was only a board fastened securely to the wall about two feet from the floor. There is no saying that there was no spread or pillow or any of those little things we think we can't do without at home, because there was only board and nothing but board. My jailer fastened the grated door. I was not very sleepy and felt inclined to talk. I peeped out between the bars, catching alternately a cloud of smoke and a glimpse of his kind old face.

CHATTING WITH THE TURNKEY

"Say, what are you called?" I asked by the way of an introduction.

"A Turnkey," he answered, peeping back at me.

"Well, now, if that stove would fall down out there how could we be saved?" I asked.

"I don't know, I'm sure," he said, with a smile.

"Would we all have to roast here in our cells?" I continued.

"Yes, I think that would be the end of you," he laughed; "but there's no fear of it; it can't catch fire here."

It was not very pleasant when I was alone with nothing to think about except the different varieties of snoring. I began to have a fervent wish that someone would waken and move. I felt cheated of the company I had expected to have in the yells and cries and songs of the different prisoners. As if in answer to my wish, I heard some door rattle, rattle, and then a voice—a woman's voice—cried:

"Say, Captain, Captain. Come here, won't you?" and rattle, rattle, rattle went the door.

"Ho, now. What do you want?" I heard my jailer ask.

"Say, open this door for me, won't you?"

"And what do you want the door opened for?" he inquired in a cheery voice.

"I just want it opened, that's all. Open it, won't you? Please, Captain."

"I'm afraid of you. You'll bite me if I open the door," he said, and she laughed at this quite heartily.

"No, I won't bite you. Open the door; do open the door."

"I can't, I'm afraid you'll bite," he still replied lightly; and pleased, the poor woman laughed again and then went to sleep.

SCENES IN THE CELL ROOM

I heard him open the grating of another cell and then heard him say: "Come, come, now! Don't double up that way. There, that's better," and the grating was locked again.

"Is anything wrong?" I asked, as he came down the corridor. I was still looking through the grating.

"No. There's a woman down there that I'm afraid may smother," he said, putting his face close to the bars.

"What is she in for?"

"Drunk," he replied shortly; "and I just now found this,"

holding a still burning cigarette between the bars, "beside her, and I'm afraid of her smothering."

"What brings the largest number of women here?"

"Drink. We have five drunks for any other one complaint," he said sadly. "We've got four in here now."

"What time is it, turnkey?" someone asked.

"Hello there, officer!" yelled another, "let me out! I can't stay in this cell."

Occasional spells of silence would come which were very tiresome to me. I began to feel weak from standing, so I decided to lie down and take to rest. I folded my jacket for a pillow, and wrapping myself in my silk circular tried to sleep. Just as I was dropping into a pleasant doze the turnkey returned.

"Here," he said, unbarring my door, "I found this comforter. It may be some good to you."

"You are very kind," I said earnestly, "and believe me, I am very much obliged to you. Tell me," to change the subject, "do you have much trouble with the women brought here?"

"I have to watch them, because they are ill and they will do anything, especially when drink is wearing off. Right in here—no, in the next cell—I had one of the finest girls in the world die on my hands. Oh, she was a beauty and such a fine girl—as fine a girl as you'd ever see. I left here after talking to her at the door. Ten minutes afterwards when I made my rounds she was lying there dead."

THE TURNKEY REMINISCES

"Did she kill herself?" I asked quickly.

"No; heart disease," he replied softly. "She went off in a minute, and a fine girl she was. I had another, in this very cell you're in, hang herself. Yes; I was away from her just a few minutes, and when I came back she was hanging to the cell door. I cut her down and I was sure that she was dead, but they brought her to." I sigh, relieved, and reserve my decision to ask to be removed. "I watch them carefully all the night and I always talk to them cheerfully to keep their spirits up, but they will sometimes give up all hopes."

"What do you do with their bodies?"

"Dump them in a box and haul them off," he replied quite cheerfully. We've had babies born in here, too, and we always bundle the women off to the hospital the first thing. But I must make my rounds. Try and rest a little, and if you want to pay for a cup of coffee I'll have one sent in to you in the morning."

"Thank you—good-night," I said, and he called back quietly as he went down the corridor. "Good-night."

I folded the comforter into a pillow and found it very easy. I don't know when or how I went to sleep or how long I had been asleep, but I was wakened by some man yelling.

"Say! *Say!* SAY!" he yelled, "What am I locked up here for? I haven't a cent. I don't know what you lock a man up for as hasn't a cent. Say ! *Say!* SAY! I want to get out. Unlock this door."

"Shut up." "You're drunk yet." "Go soak yer head." "Bag his mouth." "He's ---- crazy," were a few of the remarks the awakened lodgers hurled at him, and one began to sing. *"Where is my wandering boy tonight?"*

From this on there was no quiet in the station-house. It was not yet daylight, but I have no idea of the hour. It was very funny to hear the remarks of those who had been brought in dead drunk the night before. One man yelled, "Mary, ---- you, Mary; come open this door! What did yer shut it up for? Is breakfast ready?" which excited the merriment and remarks of his more sober companions. I felt a little relief that "Mary" was not present, and I drew a hasty mental picture of that brute at home.

"HELLO BIRDIE"

Some time early in the morning the watch was changed and my kind-hearted old jailer was replaced by a younger man. I moved slightly when he passed my cell and he yelled in:

"Hello, Birdie, are you awake? Say, Birdie, give me that tin cup you have." I got up and taking the tin off the faucet-handle handed it to him.

"Say, where did you come from?" he asked curiously as I

came near to the door and into the gaslight. "What are you in for?"

"That doesn't make any difference," I said crossly.

"Wait a minute, I'll be back," he said when he returned, and I repeated again the story of my arrest, making it as black as possible for myself.

"What are you going to do if you are discharged?" he asked afterwards.

"I don't know. Why?" I asked.

"Well, if you are going to stay in town I would like to see you again."

"Oh!" I said simply. I was surprised.

"Will you stay in town?"

"No, I will leave on the first train after I am released." And off he went to answer some call.

By this time they had begun to remove prisoners. One after another the doors were unbarred and some prisoner went forth to face a Judge. I could hear everything, but could see nothing. Most of the prisoners were talking among themselves in a friendly way. At last a woman evidently recognized a voice, for she called out to two young men who were the most vulgar and profane talkers I ever heard.

"Hello! Petie. Is that you?"

"Yes. Is that you, Mamie?" he responded.

"Judge Duffy's on today and he's all right. I'll put my bangs back and he'll say: 'Well, Mamie, they charged you with being drunk and disorderly again. What have you got to say?' I'll say, 'Go to ----,' and Duffy will say, 'Ten days or ten dollars.' I haven't a ---- cent."

Everybody laughed at this as if it were very funny, and someone called out:

PRISONERS EXCHANGING PLEASANTRIES

"Say, Mamie, give me your address and I'll call on you when I get out." The conversation became very foul, and addresses were exchanged and friends were made as well as promises to meet at Jefferson Market, and signals agreed upon so they would recognize each other. A station-house is a good place for bad people to become worse.

The new turnkey returned to me and offered me a towel, if I wished to wash my face, so I would look clean and bright in court. He was very nice and kind, and also ordered breakfast for me. I heard many of the prisoners speak of his kindness.

Many of the "drunks" had to be awakened. One man, with a deep bass voice, was called and commanded to wash the blood off his face. When the turnkey went out another prisoner advised the newly awakened man not to wash, but to go before the Judge in his bloody condition. It seems, from their conversation, that this man had been a bartender on Broadway for seven years. This was the first time in his life that he had ever been arrested. He was drunk and went to sleep in a doorway, I believe, and a policeman clubbed him into insensibility. However, he washed his face, as he had been ordered, and removed all traces of blood.

That bartender was very honest compared with the others in the place. His questions and his other greenness and simplicity about court proceedings amused me. The others understood that he was new, and Mamie immediately gave him her name and address and asked him to call. Then she asked him if he got out first to either pass her cell or meet her at Jefferson Market. At last she told him to listen carefully, and in a low voice asked him to lend her some money. He immediately consented. Then a man, who said he was a street-car driver, said that he had only six cents in his pockets and that if he did not get out by 10 o'clock, which was his hour to go to work, that he would lose his "job." Then he asked the bartender if he would pay his fine, which he thought would be $5. The bartender said he would.

"And if it is $10 will you pay it?" the driver asked, and the bartender responded that he would go $10 on him.

TAKEN TO COURT

My breakfast came—a steak, fried potatoes, a pot of coffee, several rolls, sugar and salt. The waiter told me that it was 45 cents and I gave him 50. He thanked me. The turnkey considerately turned up the gas so I could see and I was left alone to eat. It seemed an eternity before the hour came for me to be taken to court. Nearly every one had gone before me and I began to fear that I would be forgotten. At last Detective Hayes, looking very sleepy, made his appearance.

"Good morning," he said, and the door was opened for me and I left the cell where I had spent such a long night. We went out through the station-house and taking a Seventh Avenue car were soon at Jefferson Market court.

I was put into a large cell with some twenty women. I have nothing to tell about it that could be published. The men in charge seemed to take a delight in the horrible remarks which the women prisoners hurled at them, and the women seemed to be having a contest to see which could say the most horrible things. Those who had no breakfast were having coffee served to them. One woman spoke to me and told me that she had been found drunk on the streets the night before. She was a very plain, homelike-looking creature, so I asked her where she got her load, which I had learned was the expression used.

"By picking up strangers on the streets and getting them to treat me," she said. "I haven't a cent to pay my fine, and I guess I'll be sent up. I feel very shaky."

THE SHYSTER LAWYER ON HAND

I was the last one left in the cell. Detective Hayes came to me and said there was a lawyer outside who wanted to see me. I stopped at an interesting passage in the Prado story now running in THE WORLD. The gate was unlocked and I passed several officers who knew me well, but who failed now to recognize me, and into a quiet room where a thin-looking man was waiting for me.

"Miss Smith," he said to me. "I am a runner for Lawyer McClelland, and as your case is going dead against you I thought you would like to have some advice. If you retain me I will run over to McClelland's house, which is just across the way, and he will come over and fix things. He is a politician, and has a pull on all the officers and the Judges, and he can fix you. Will I go for him?"

"I don't think you will for me. I am innocent, and I am not afraid," I replied.

"They have got a dead case against you, and the woman whose money is gone is out there with two witnesses to appear against you. You give me $10 to retain me and McClelland will fix you all right."

"I'll think it over," I answered.

"It's too late to think. Take my advice. The money's nothing to me. I don't want your money. But if you don't do it, I'll stand out there beside you and"—I looked at him scornfully and he changed his taunt to—"see you put under $1,000 bail and then the Grand Jury will get you. You'll be sorry."

I went back to the cell, and presently Detective Hayes came for me and I was taken out before the little Judge, whose kind heart is ever with the unfortunate. The detective began his story about my doings. I corrected him in several misstatements. Then Judge Duffy told me to lift my veil.

"Why this lady hasn't the face of a thief," he said warmly. "I have seen lots of thieves and she hasn't the look of one."

I gave him a grateful glance and repressed an impulse to give him a wink to try his recollection of the time he sent me to Blackwell's Island as a crazy girl.

"Where's the woman who made the charge?" he asked.

"She promised to come here," said the detective, "but she hasn't arrived."

DISCHARGED BY JUDGE DUFFY

"I suppose she has found her money. This lady never stole it. I know. She is discharged."

I did not say "Thank you," although I was very grateful for the good opinion of one of the kindest-hearted men in New York. I followed the detective down to another place, where he told a man who had seen me quite often that Miss Smith, arrested for grand larceny, was discharged. Then we went out of the courtroom together, several men stopping the detective to inquire about the case.

"Where are you going now?" asked the detective as we reached the corner.

"I am going to the Gedney House to pay my bill," I replied. "I will send for my satchel."

"Am I not to see you again?" he asked.

"I hope not," I replied, purposely misunderstanding him. "I never want to be in such a scrape again."

HOW ABOUT THIS MR. HAYES?

"I don't want to see you that way, you know, but if you will let me know where you are going to stop"—

"I don't see what you want to see me again for. I hope never to see you."

"Tell me your name," he urged, "or where you live."

"Not for worlds."

"Well, what if I know it? Your name is Kent and you live in Albany."

"I think that you would want to stay in town and get rested," he said, after we were on the Seventh Avenue car. He had informed me that I could not get my satchel by sending for it; that I had to apply in person and sign a receipt for it. So we were on our way back to the station-house. "I can take you to a hotel to stop where no one will ever find you."

"I am going directly out of town," I insisted.

"What is to be my reward?" he asked.

"What do you mean?"

"Well, I have been good to you. Instead of you being dismissed I could have asked the Judge to remand you until we could get more evidence, but I let you go free. I am not glad you got into trouble, but I am glad of meeting you and I would like to see you again. I think I have been kind to you."

"Oh, yes, you have," I replied. "Everybody has been very kind. I expected to be clubbed to death."

"We are not such a bad lot, and we never club until the last moment."

"Jennie Smith, discharged, and wants her satchel," he

said to the pleasant man in the station-house behind the desk. "She thought she would get clubbed by the police."

"She is more likely to get embraced than clubbed," the man laughed.

"I believe that," I replied, and the detective held the door open for me.

"Won't you let me hear from you?" he said, as he took off his hat.

"I may," I laughed. "I know your name and you may hear from me."

REFORMS BADLY NEEDED

I walked up Seventh Avenue, rang a bell in a flat-house, went up several flights, inquired for a family that never existed, and came out at last satisfied that if any one was following me I had put him off the track.

I have come to several conclusions:

First—That a regular woman-searcher should be employed in station-houses.

Second—That the male officers should be given no opportunity of squinting through a peep-hole at women who are being searched.

Third—That innocent women who fall into the hands of the police are not necessarily badly treated.

Fourth—That the male and female prisoners should not be kept within earshot of each other.

Fifth—That if all the turnkeys are as kind as those I encountered no woman could ever fill their places, because women are never so kind to their unfortunate sisters as men are.

The New York World
April 28, 1889

Shadowed by a Detective

Nellie Bly Makes a Test of the Private Spy Nuisance

After Dogging Her Steps for Three Days the Hound Triumphantly Submits a Report to Her Supposed Husband—Keeping His Victim Always in Sight—How Evidence is Secured for Divorce Suits

Do the "shadows" employed by detective agencies to dog the footsteps and observe the behavior of suspected persons invariably make truthful reports? Can a "shadow," no matter how expert, honest or industrious, be depended upon to conceal his or her purpose, and continue on the trail without making a mistake or losing the scent?

THE WORLD answers both these questions today and tells a good deal about "shadow-tag" that is decidedly interesting. It gives the result of an actual experience, in which presumably clever detectives were fooled with the greatest ease and not only deceived for three days in succession, but actually "shadowed" themselves without any knowledge that every movement they made was watched. To follow, observe and report the actions of a suspected man or woman forms the bulk of the business done by every agency in the city of New York, with one exception. There are at least a score of these agencies, with reputations varying from "very bad" to "first class." Evidence on which to base a suit for divorce is probably the most sought after, and so long as a customer is willing to pay just so long will reports be furnished. With the purely disreputable concern there is no attempt to make a truthful return. Let the seeker after information display a keen anxiety for incriminating evidence, and it is furnished until the fires of jealousy and hate burn with a fierceness that does not abate until the empty purse shuts off further information. Then follows, perhaps, a tragedy, a scandal or the hiding of the manufactured skeleton in a closet.

There was just one way to know positively what these private detectives were capable of doing and that way I adopted. I was to live at a hotel for several days and a detective should be employed to shadow me. I was to be out as much as possible, so as to give the man a chance to earn his money. I was to keep a faithful account of everything I did during the time, so that our statements might be compared. I have done so and this is the result of my work.

WAITING FOR THE "SHADOW"

On April 22, at 5.50, I tucked myself and satchel into a hansom-cab and told the driver to take me to the Broadway entrance of the Morton Home. Fifth avenue was crowded, and the driver having a fancy for weaving in and about the other vehicles, after the fashion of a darning-needle in the hands of an old darner, consumed more than the ordinary time to reach my destination. My room at the hotel had been engaged in advance, so I merely handed a card—not my card—to the hall boy and asked him to get the key of my room. While he was gone I watched the driver, who was still at the entrance. I knew that a detective, furnished with a description of me, was already waiting for my first appearance. I was afraid that he would see me arrive and by questioning the driver learn that I cam from the New York Central Station instead of from Jersey City, as he had been led to suppose. I felt greatly relieved when I saw the hansom cab and the driver, who charged me double fare, disappear unmolested up Broadway.

As he became lost to view, a porter with the key took my baggage and went in advance to my room.

"What time is it?" I asked the porter as he set my satchel on the dressing-case, and as he looked out of the door he replied:

"About half-past 6. Is there anything you wish?"

I had but one wish, and that was to immediately join the gentleman who was to assist me in giving the detectives a chase. We had set the hour for 6.30, at which time a WORLD man, acting the part of employer to the detective, was to be waiting near the hotel, so as to point me out.

Giving my key to the hall boy, I was soon on Broadway.

Almost the first thing I noticed was the detective's employer trying to dodge around a pole which Mayor Grant's little hatchet had missed on the corner of Broadway and Fourteenth street. I had intended to walk east, but then I changed my mind and deliberately passed the pole, so as to give the detective a good chance to know me. I quickly crossed the square to the east side and walked rapidly along, looking straight ahead, and darted up the stairs to Ricadonna's restaurant.

I naturally concluded that everything had gone right and the detective was after me, but up to that moment I had not seen him. I walked along the hall and, entering the restaurant near the rear end, joined the gentleman according to previous arrangement. Suppose I call him Mr. X for brevity's sake? He was looking over the evening newspapers while he awaited my arrival. Of course, remembering the watchful eyes of the detective, I greeted him as if I had not seen him a few hours before.

While eating our dinner we watched every one and tried to single out the detective. In this we failed until a man with a dark mustache and a slight droop of the shoulders walked through, and then—as if unable to find an empty table—out again. He did not look clean nor happy, so we decided he was the man who intended to shadow our footsteps for that evening.

AN UNHAPPY DETECTIVE

My first sensation was one of enjoyment. I hardly knew whether to prolong my dinner and keep the man on the outside in the agony of waiting indefinitely or to rush my dinner so as to have more time to give him a merry chase. At last I decided to dine at leisure and allow the after events to take care of themselves. It takes the flavor out of life, just as it does out of cooking, to rush things, you know.

About 8.30 o'clock we left Ricadonna's and walked across Broadway. We did not look around and failed to discover anyone "shadowing" us. After peering in a window for a few moments we crossed Broadway and went along Twenty-second Street to Fifth Avenue. Still we didn't see anyone. Going up Fifth Avenue we stopped in a doorway to decide where to spend the evening. The detective had not yet been seen and I began to think that after all he hadn't the shrewdness that I had credited him with.

We made up our minds to go to the Eden House, and as we went down Twenty-third Street we saw a man who was walking in advance glancing over his shoulder. The action was so perfectly performed that it identified him as our "shadow." He went on past the Musee and we went in. Mr. X went to the office door and spoke to Mr. Gerkins, who came out and opened the door for us and followed us in.

We saw the shadow as he rushed hastily in after us, and then after seeing us standing so quietly, looking at "Lee's Surrender," he assumed an air of such indifference that we were highly amused.

Walking further on, we stood examining a group of figures near a stairway which led to the Chamber of Horrors. The detective slowly moved about, and, when we saw his back towards us, we merely stepped down the stairway and into the basement, which is filled with noiseless tortures and tragedies.

We waited at the foot of the stairs, and I know by the haste with which the shadow rushed down that he thought he had lost us. After he found we had not melted away he walked about looking at the different figures and pictures. I asked such questions concerning them as I thought likely a country woman was likely to ask. The detective was not going to lose sight of us again, so he kept very close to our heels. At one time Mr. X excused himself and walked away. He wanted to know whether the detective would speak to me if the chance came and offer to sell out the other side but he did not, he merely waited back of me and never moved until we started upstairs again.

We went up to the gallery, the detective behind us. We sat down; after the microscopic views had been shown we went into the Turkish smoking-room, and sat down on a corner divan. Evidently the detective expected to see us come out the other door, and when we did not he thought we had found some new stairway, for he came rushing in, and when he saw us sitting in the corner he turned and fled.

HANGING TO AN "L" TRAIN GATE

But he did not fly far. He waited close by outside, where he could command a view of both doors, and when we went out he was after us. After speaking to the man at the door, we went out into Twenty-third street. The detective, to give us the lead, went towards Sixth Avenue, carelessly lighting a cigar.

"Let us see if we can get away from him," I suggested, and accordingly we started in his direction and quickly ran up the stairs leading to the Sixth Avenue elevated. It was very amusing to see him try to look as if it were nothing extraordinary that he should rush after us.

A Harlem train came along. We made a move as if to get on it; so did the shadow. We stepped off again; so did he. Still he tried to look as if it were nothing unusual for everyday mortals to mimic each other's movements.

The next train was bound for Fifty-eighth Street. We waited until everybody was aboard and then got on. The detective got on, too, and we were no better off than before. We were on the second car and had the two seats directly by the rear door. The detective was on the front platform of the same car watching us through the window. We cold see him and the guard very plainly and he could see us just as well.

The first stop was Twenty-eighth street. Several passengers got on the train and came into our car. We sat very still until we heard the gate on the rear car close and the conductor near us get the signal. That instant we jumped up and stepped off. The guard slammed the gate after us, pulled the bell-rope, and the train started with our detective on board.

But he had seen us get off when too late to help himself, and frantic at being thus foiled, he sprang for the bell-rope. The bell rang and the train stopped. Everybody in the cars rushed forward to see what accident had happened. The guard grappled with the struggling shadow and the train started again, and as it moved off from the station the detective managed to swing himself half way over the gate. Thus he was hanging when that part of the train passed the platform. There was a terrible scream and the train stopped for a second time. I ran up to the end of the platform fearing the poor fellow had dropped to the street below, and was just in time to see him grabbed by several guards and given a terrible blow in the eye, which persuaded him to ride on to the next station.

All the people who were on the platform of the station were curious to know the cause of the trouble, but, as usual, the employees knew absolutely nothing. It is needless to add that we offered no explanation.

As the detective had been effectually given the slip for that evening anyway, there was nothing for me to do but go back to the Morton House and feel satisfied that so far I had decidedly the best of it.

After lying awake for four hours the next morning in fear the clerk would let me sleep too late, the porter called me at 9 o'clock. Half an hour later I had breakfast in the small restaurant which adjoins the reception room. When breakfast was over I walked across to the Third Avenue Elevated and rode down to City Hall station. Then I boarded another train and rode out to East Eighty-second Street. No detective was after me, so I decided to return to the Morton House and give them a chance to do something.

THE SECOND DAY'S WORK

I sat a while in the reception room reading. I had little desire to walk about in order to furnish employment for a stupid man, but I knew as long as I sat in the hotel he would not be earning his bread, so, about 2 o'clock, I started out.

I never could dawdle along and waste time. When I start out on the street I have always some objective point and generally get there in the shortest possible time.

Immediately I crossed the street a thin young man, about 5 feet 5 inches in height, with light hair and artificially blackened mustache, followed me. He was not the man who had done the shadowing the previous evening. I went into Brentano's and asked about the price of tickets for the Centennial parade. I walked down Fourteenth Street and stopped in a little store, but, making no purchase, I left again in a few moments. I then went into Macy's and directly up to the restaurant. It was well filled with women, so the detective stood outside the door by which I entered watching me.

I ate my cream and strawberries leisurely, and while doing so I decided to make the man who was doing such unskillful dogging meet me face to face. There are two glass doors which open into this restaurant. One leads to the china department, where there is a stairway. The other leads to the millinery department. As the detective was in the millinery part, I went out the opposite door and deliberately stepped aside and waited. He came rushing, he looked at me, then began to lazily study the different things about him. I moved around to several different quarters and then retraced my steps through the restaurant.

I rather liked to hurry the fellow so I skipped down the stairs, rushed into a young man who was going the wrong way. We both:

"I beg your pardon?"

"I beg your pardon?"

And I rushed on.

I stopped long enough downstairs to ask the soda-check girl if she sold bromo-caffeine, and as she did not I went out, rushing headlong into a woman who was trying to handle four swinging doors, a baby carriage with a crying baby in it and one of those old-fangled, newly revived parasols which look like a plate when a juggler balances it on a straw. If there is one event which prompts one to leave New York for a better sphere it is to encounter one of these women who takes her whole blessed family of ten, with nondescript dolls, a pug and a baby carriage thrown in, out shopping with her.

FOILED ONCE MORE

After I escaped the woman I stood for awhile on the corner of Sixth Avenue, then walked over and took a Broadway car. I saw the detective follow, and I decided to give him a cheap airing. I made no move to get off, and when the car was near its last stopping place, Fifty-ninth Street, the detective jumped off and walked as if going to the Park. I smiled and sat still,. The car started on its downtown journey, and the detective, seeing that I was coming back, came running after. He caught the car and he looked very warm and sheepish, but I did not even take the satisfaction of smiling.

At Thirty-third Street a large crowd had collected to see the last of a pole which the workmen had stripped of usefulness. I got off to watch it fall, and when it was down a balky horse decided to take a rest in the center of the street. This caused a blockade and the cars were unable to pass. I hired a hansom cab and started down Broadway. Just then the balky horse thought about his dinner and kindly made way so the horse-cars could move. The detective was in the first car, so I ordered the "cabby" to drive across town, so as to compel the detective to hire a cab also, but he didn't do it.

At 6.30 I gave the hall boy my key and started out. The shadow who had missed me for two hours was patiently waiting on the corner and was on the Broadway car almost as soon as I was. I rode up to Twenty-fifth Street, where I got off and went into the drug store on the corner. I asked the clerk for some bromo-caffeine, and, after drinking it, I sat down to wait the coming of Mr. X. I began to get very hungry, the result of my unusual exercise, and wished I had named an earlier hour for dinner.

When Mr. X came he wanted to know where I wished to dine. There was one thing to be avoided, and that was to go where it was at all possible that we would meet someone who knew us. We walked down Broadway as we tried to decide, and then along Twenty-third Street. By the time we reached Sixth Avenue we had decided on O'Neill's.

We went in the Twenty-second Street entrance and selected a table back in the hallway, or arm, which connects the two main restaurants.

While we were eating the headwaiter walked to and fro along this hall. As he passed us I heard him talking angrily to himself. I also noticed that the waiters glanced at him apprehensively every time he neared one of them.

"That man is either insane or has an attack of delirium tremens," I whispered to Mr. X, but he did not seem to think it worthy any attention.

Just as we had finished dinner there was a scream, followed by a great scuffling in that part of the restaurant facing on Twenty-second Street. Mr. X went front and returned to report that the head waiter had suddenly become frantic from the mental view of snakes he was having and that three waiters had put him out into the street so that he would have more room to tussle with his wriggling visions.

AND THE SHADOW WAS LEFT

The scuffle collected a large crowd around the entrance. I felt positive the waiting detective would be among them and would forget—if he had sense enough to know—that there were two more entrances to O'Neill's restaurant besides the one by which we had entered. We decided to go, as we had finished, and I relied on two things to help us to elude our persevering but indiscreet sleuth. He would doubtless be so interested in the fight among the waiters that he would forget his mission long enough for us to escape unnoticed, or he would watch the door we had gone in and never think to watch the others for us to come out.

So we came out of the entrance furthest from that by which we had entered. We walked across Sixth Avenue, and taking the downtown Elevated, rode to Eighteenth Street. Before we got on we noticed what people were on the platform, and when we got off at the next station we looked to see if any of the same people would get off. They did not, so we were sure that for the second time we had eluded our shadow.

We walked across town to Third Avenue, and down Third Avenue across Thirteenth Street to Broadway. In order to avoid being followed home Mr. X left me at the corner, he going back to Third Avenue, and from there over a circuitous route to his home, and I, mingling with the people just coming from the Star Theatre, was in a moment safe within the Morton House.

The next morning I took a walk about and at 1 o'clock, finding myself still free from a "shadower," I came home, and so ended my three day's experience in being watched and followed by men who are credited with being able to outwit ordinary people—and certainly to keep track of a woman.

NELLIE BLY

The Detectives' Side of the Story

There is a marked discrepancy between the real story of the three days' adventures and the story as told by the shadows themselves—sufficient perhaps to make valueless the result of the work, had an important issue thereon depended. How ingeniously does the shadow explain away his failures! How punctilious he is as to minutes, and how lacking when it comes to producing tangible proof that would stand a legal test!

On Tuesday afternoon last a reporter of THE WORLD went to the Morton House and made the following entry upon the register:

"Mrs. V. L. Cooppee, Philadelphia." The clerk was informed that Mrs. Cooppee would arrive before 6 o'clock and would remain as a guest for probably two or three days. The customer rate was paid and "Mrs. Cooppee" was assigned to room No. 135 on the second floor. Immediately after leaving the hotel the reporter, first announcing that he intended to return to Philadelphia, crossed the street and entered the office of Fuller's Detective Bureau, No. 841 Broadway, where he was received by a young gentleman with a worried expression of countenance.

"I want a woman watched," said the visitor. "I want to know every movement from the moment she leaves the hotel where she is now staying until she returns to it—every movement, remember, written out in full. What will that service cost?"

"Seven dollars and a half a day and expenses," was the reply. "Where is the lady and how can she be identified?"

There was no questioning either as to relationships, or as to what the visitor desired to establish. He was not even asked his name. Mr. Fuller's representative made out a receipt, and then touching an electric bell summoned a "shadow." This was a man about thirty years of age, of swarthy complexion, and with a pair of keen dark eyes, and a manner that bespoke the sleuth in every gesture, every look, "This man will meet you at Fourteenth street and Broadway at any hour you name, and you can then point out the lady to him," said the detective's secretary after having first obtained a description and written it on a piece of paper. The shadow was instructed to be at the rendezvous at 6 o'clock. He appeared according to promise, and strolled down Fourteenth street with the reporter. The pair returned to their post about 6.15 o'clock, and fifteen minutes later Mrs. Cooppee emerged from the hotel and started across Union Square. In an instant the "shadow" was in close pursuit, and so thoroughly intent on his purpose that his manner attracted attention from at least half a dozen persons. The reporter watched "Mrs. Cooppee" until she entered Riccadonna's restaurant, and then, knowing that she would remain there for at least an hour, went into Worth's Museum, looked at the freaks for a while and then spent a half hour in Theiss's listening to a mournful strain from the big organ.

The rest of the evening was spent in "shadowing" the shadow and in speculating as to how that enthusiastic but misguided specter would account for his time. At 11 o'clock the reportorial shadow took a trip downtown, and to avoid being watched or followed made several detours before reaching THE WORLD office at midnight.

THE FIRST REPORT

On Wednesday about noon a call was made to receive the detective's report and following is a copy of the "shadow's" description of his work, *verbatim et literatim*.

April 23, 1889

Mr. Coopee, City:
DEAR SIR; We respectfully submit the following as our report in your matter for the 23d inst.:

Operator went on post in the vicinity of Morton House at 6.15 P.M. and at 6.35 P.M. a lady left the hotel who answered the description given in every particular. Operator them motioned to Mr. C., requesting to know if that was the party, and Mr. C. signified yes by motion of his head.

Operator then followed the lady, who walked to Fourth Avenue and entered Riccadonna's restaurant, No. 42 Union Square. She remained there until 8.15 P.M., when she came out with a young gentleman of the following description: Age, about thirty years, 5 feet, 8 inches tall, slim build, sallow complexion, wore a high silk hat, light drab overcoat, dark pants and carried a cane.

After leaving the restaurant they walked to Broadway, up Broadway to Twenty-second Street, through Twenty-second Street to Fifth Avenue, stopped under the shadow of the Cumberland Building, corner of Twenty-second Street and Fifth Avenue. They remained there fifteen minutes, and then started up Fifth Avenue to Twenty-third Street, and through Twenty-third street to the Eden Musee. The gentleman left the lady standing on the stoop, and he entered the Musee. He came out in a few minutes with another gentleman, and then they all three entered the Musee.

Operator followed them in, and they entered the smoking room on the upper floor, over the music stand.

After they had entered the smoking room they both

sat on a sofa pretty close together. The gentleman ordered refreshments. They remained there until 11 P.M. then came out, the lady having the gentleman's arm. They walked to the L station at Twenty-third Street, and as they acted very suspiciously, operator did not follow them too close. They mounted the stairs leading to the uptown track and operator followed. When he reached the platform of the station they had just boarded a train. Operator endeavored to board the train but the gateman shut the gate and would not permit operator to enter, so he was compelled to discontinue. Yours very respectfully,

J.M. FULLER

C.F. COSTA, Superintendant.

As the putative husband finished reading this report the "shadow" came in. He was rather a disconsolate looking "shadow." His right eye was blackened and bruised, and the skin was broken. "I tried to get on an Elevated train at Twenty-third street," he explained, "but the guard shut the gate and punched me in the eye."

"We'll have to attend to that fellow's case," remarked Mr. Fuller, with some severity of manner.

"Well," said the reporter, "this is not at all satisfactory. Your man made a miss of it just at the wrong time."

"It's very unfortunate," replied Mr. Fuller, "but it couldn't be helped."

"Give me another man for today," demanded the visitor, assuming a tone of annoyance. "I must have this information."

"Very well," answered Mr. Fuller, and tapping his bell he called for "Fred."

"This," said Mr. Fuller, "is one of the best 'shadows' in New York. He has been in the business a number of years, and is really one of the cleverest men in the business."

"All right," was the reporter's reply. "Put him on the case and see what he can do. Now, understand, I want everything—everything!"

Then a further payment of $7.50 was made, together with 80 cents additional for the expenses of the 'shadow," who received the smash in the eye, and operator No. 2 started on his hunt a little after 2 o'clock. Again the reporter kept track of the "shadow," who went about his work without attracting the same attention as his predecessor; but it wasn't long before he discovered himself to "Mrs. Cooppee," and then his usefulness was ended.

WORK OF A GREAT "SHADOW"

Mr. Fuller was inclined to deprecate the efforts of his employees when called upon for a report on Thursday. "I don't think you will be satisfied with this," he said. "But my man did the best he could. Here is the report," and he handed the following statement as the work of "one of the best shadows in New York":

APRIL 24, 1889

Mr. Cooppee, City:

DEAR SIR: We respectfully submit the following as our report in your matter versus lady for the above date:

Operator was on post at the Morton House at 2.15 P.M., and almost immediately the lady left the hotel and went to Brentano's book store, on Union Square, came out in a few minutes and went to Allen's corset store, 2 West Fourteenth Street; remained ten minutes, came out and went to R.H. Macy's and entered the restaurant and had something to eat, remaining there twenty minutes; came out and left the building and walked through Fourteenth Street to Broadway, and boarded a Broadway car and rode to Fifty-ninth Street. At the end of the route she did not leave the car, but rode back to Thirty-second Street and there alighted and stood watching some men who were removing a telegraph pole.

She then entered a hansom cab and was driven to the Morton House, time, 4.15 P.M.

At 6.30 P.M. she again left the Morton House and, boarding a Broadway car, rode to Twenty-fifth street and entered Caswell's drug store on the northwest corner of Twenty-fifth

Street and Broadway, remained there fifteen minutes and came out with a gentleman of the following description.

Five feet eight inches tall, dark complexion, thirty or thirty-two years of age, of medium build, light brown mustache, and dressed in dark clothes and silk hat.

They walked down Broadway to Twenty-third Street, then to Sixth Avenue to then to Twenty-second Street and entered O'Neill's oyster house on the northeast corner of Twenty-second Street and Sixth Avenue, time, 7.05 P.M.

Operator covered the place until 1 A.M., when the oyster house was closed, but did not see the lady or gentleman leave. Operator is positive they did not leave the place by the main entrance.

There are four entrances to this restaurant, three on Sixth Avenue and one on Twenty-second Street, about fifty feet from the corner, and it is simply impossible for one man to cover all of those entrances. At 1 A.M. operator discontinued. Yours very respectfully,.

J.M. FULLER
Per. C. F. COSTA, Superintendent

"Now," said Mr. Fuller, when the reporter had expressed his utter and complete dissatisfaction. "I have a proposition to make to you. I will put two men on this case instead of one. Two men can certainly 'hold' her. If they do not I will not make any charge for the extra man. But if they get what you want then you pay $12.50 instead of $7.50. Yesterday's expenses amounted to $1.

The proposition was accepted and Mr. Fuller was impressed with the importance of keeping on "Mrs. Cooppee's" track and not losing sight of her for an instant. The result of this attempt was the most dismal failure of all. This is the report that Mr. Fuller made on Friday:

APRIL 25, 1889

Mr. Victor Cooppee:
DEAR SIR: We would submit the following as our report in your matter for the 25th inst.,

Operatives G. and L. went on post at the Morton House at 1 P.M. and remained until 6.10 P.M., up to which time the lady had not put in an appearances. Supt. Costa then called at the Morton House, wrote a name on a card and requested the clerk to forward it to room 135, Mrs. Cooppee. The clerk then informed Costa that Mrs. Cooppee had paid her bill and had left the hotel that morning.

Costa then returned to the agency and reported the above to J.M. Fuller, who thereupon instructed Costa to detain Operative Moore at Messrs. Caswell & Massay's drug store, corner of Twenty-fifth Street and Broadway, and to detail Operator Lopez at Riccadonna's restaurant, in Union Square, to see if the lady would put in an appearance at either of the above places.

Both of the operatives remained on post in their respective places until 9 P.M. and, not seeing the lady, discontinued. Yours respectfully,

J.M. FULLER, per F.M.

The alleged jealous husband thought he had enough. He said so, and asked Mr. Fuller if the bargain made the day before held good. "The understanding," said Mr. Fuller blandly, "was that we could 'hold' the lady, but as the operators did not see her, they could not 'hold' her. So…"

"Then I owe—"

"Five dollars," replied the detective, and for this amount he gave a receipt marked "in full to date." Half an hour afterwards, Mr. Victor Cooppee had resumed his own name and personality, and the quick-witted and swift-footed Mrs. Victor Cooppee became Nellie Bly.

The New York World
October 1, 1893

Nellie Bly as a Salvation Army Girl

Pathetic Scenes at the Food and Shelter Home in Front Street—Exorbitant Charges by the Booths for the Salvation Bonnets and Books—The Good They Do

I have been devoting myself to the Salvation Army for the last ten days.

I began with an idea that it was some sort of a nonsensical hulla-baloo, run by a lot of fanatics incidentally for the amusement of the curious, primarily for the financial benefit of a chosen few. And I end—how?

I don't know. I can only tell without frills, precisely what I saw.

I am without prejudice. Others may judge. I do not care to.

I was walking up Fourth Avenue, just opposite Cooper Union, when I met two girls.

Even the most ignorant would have drawn from a single glance that they were members of something besides the common mass one sees upon the streets. They were both clad in painfully plain dark blue gowns, and the smaller of the two wore a poke bonnet, with a plain twist of navy blue silk across the top and frilled in the spreading front, while two broad bands of ribbon tied it rather coquettishly under the left ear.

This girl carried under her arm a great lot of newspapers.

She was a pretty little thing. Her eyes were dark brown, and as clear and as bright as a babe's. Her pretty, smooth, clear olive skin was tinted a very fetching pink, just where the actress gives a touch of rouge to brighten her eyes.

In addition to this she had an extremely pretty nose and a mouth with beauty in every curve.

Her companion, a round-shouldered, great big, black-eyed, sallow-faced girl, wore a plain black sailor hat, and carried a small book that showed constant use.

I would hesitate to address almost any unknown woman upon the street. When occasion demands I always prefer to speak to a man. But I had no fear of these girls. There was a gentleness, a subtle something in their faces that drew me to them.

"I have wanted to see some of your people," I said, as I stopped, and they stopped with me. "I have a friend that I wish to get interested in your meetings. She is melancholy over the death of her sister, and I think if she could be induced to take an interest in something else, it would prove a blessing to her."

They listened to me in a very sympathetic and encouraging way.

"Bring her to one of our meetings," spoke up the one in the poke-bonnet. "We will talk to her and see if we can get her interested. I am sure we can do her some good, for we have had such people before."

"I also thought," I went on, "that if you would take her with you when you go out selling your papers that it might interest her in other things besides her grief."

VISITING THE POOR

"We would gladly do that. Or, we can take her with us when I go visiting," suggested the dark-eyed girl in the sailor hat.

"Whom do you visit?" I inquired curiously.

"The poor," she answered simply.

"What for?"

"To pray with them if they will let me. We think a visit encourages people and helps them."

"And is it your duty to sell newspapers?" I asked the other one.

She smiled gently.

"I visit, too, when I can," she answered. "When I have time I pay visits and sell War Cries, but I have to work and can't devote as much time as I would wish to the salvation work."

I began to be interested.

"Suppose you let me go with you today," I begged eagerly. "I would like it so much."

Both girls smiled.

"Certainly; if you wish you may come along. I will take you to headquarters if you like, and they can tell you all about the army," said the one in the bonnet.

"And I will take you visiting with me tomorrow if you will go," offered the other.

"I am delighted," I assured her. "What is your name and in what way are you addressed?"

Just then a voice at our side said cheerily:

"How do you do, sister? How do you do, sister?"

I had a glimpse of a smile on the face of a tall, plainly dressed girl, and a backward nod of good fellowship as she passed on with a poorly clad man.

"That is a missionary. She works among the slums," explained the little newspaper girl.

"A Salvationist?" I asked.

"No, she belongs to some church mission."

"Do they all call you 'sister'?"

"Some do, but the practice is generally confined to members of the army. My name is Ray Kemp."

She also gave me her companion's name, but for reasons which I shall explain later I shall call her Star.

By this time we had moved on down Fourth Avenue and stood by the door of the Hall, Nos. 14 and 16, where Salvationists congregate every night to give thanks and praise to the God they worship.

TROUBLE IN CAMP

Star said she had to go in for her bonnet, and begged us to wait for her, which we did.

In a few moments she reappeared, still in her sailor hat and with a look of unhappiness upon her face.

"I saw the Captain," she said to Miss Kemp, "and he

asked me why I advised a girl to disobey his orders. I told him I did not, and he says she said I did. What shall I do?"

"Did you do it?" Miss Kemp asked, gravely.

"No, I did not. You just said that I never talked or got into any trouble and now this has happened."

"What do they accuse you of doing?" I asked, with more curiosity than breeding.

"The Captain told a girl who had done wrong not to wear her badge, and she did, and then she told him I said to her not to mind him but to wear it anyway. I never did."

"What is the Captain going to do about it?" Miss Kemp asked, anxiously.

"He says he wants me to face her tonight. He said I was never disobedient or told him a story, but if she would tell such a thing on me, she would face it out. What would you do? Would you go out?"

"Yes, go up and get your bonnet and come on."

Star did as she was bid, and came down in a few minutes with her bonnet on and a lot of War Crys in her arm.

"Did he say anything more?" Miss Kemp asked.

"No; he just asked me if I was going out. Here he comes."

A rather boyish looking fellow, but having withal a serious and strong face, clad in the Salvation uniform of jacket and cap, went past us, raising his cap as he did so.

Then we girls started off together, walking three abreast, I being in the middle. "I feel awful about this talk," Star said, referring to her trouble. "I thought perhaps I had not right to come out, feeling that way."

"Did you kneel down and pray before you left?" Miss Kemp asked. "Always ask God to help you. He will comfort you."

"Tell me how you became a Salvationist," I said to Miss Kemp a little later. "I always thought the Salvation Army was a noisy thing that made money by calling people in to scoff at it. You seem to find real work in it."

"I used to think it was a good place to go for fun," she said laughing, "but I understand now that there is a motive in all the noise. We want to attract people, to arouse their interest, their curiosity, anything to get them in.

"As I say," she continued, "I went to laugh, became interested and then converted. I am a Hebrew, and my people said I was the first, as they called it, to disgrace my name. They banished me, but I have God and a place that I never knew before. I work in a dress-shield store on Broadway, and my employer is very kind to me, although he is very much against the Army. He is always saying that he can't see how such a nice girl," with a little smile, "can be a Salvationist. I asked him if I am very different from what I was before, and he says he doesn't notice any change except that I am quieter. Why, once I was so noisy and impatient and fond of running around, and cared so much for dress, and now all I care for is the Army, and my temper and impatience have vanished, and I wear nothing but this you see."

Here Star stopped at a door to sell a War Cry and we went on.

"Does Star work also?" I asked.

"She works at home," was the answer. "Her mother is dead and she does all the housework for her father and the family. She manages to have every afternoon and evening out, always going home at 5 to get the supper, and in this way she is able to do a great deal of work for the Army."

HOW SHE SPENT HER VACATION

"I wish I had more time," longingly. "This summer my employer gave me a two weeks' vacation, and told me to go off to the country and enjoy myself, but I spent every day visiting the poor and selling War Crys. I couldn't have had a happier vacation."

"Are you ever badly treated when you are selling newspapers?"

"Sometimes people are rude to me, but we do not mind that. The worst experience I ever had was with a man in a saloon. I asked him to buy a War Cry and he swore and told me that I should be ashamed of myself; that the Salvationists were a disgrace to the city. I asked him how he would feel if any one spoke to his sister as he had spoken to me, and he replied that if his sister was a Salvationist he hoped some one would kill her. 'Suppose she was a lost woman then, and we found her in just such a place as this, and we made her our friend and took her away with us and stood by her until she was good again?' 'Is that your work? Do you do that?' he asked me. 'Yes,' I said, 'that is our work.' 'Then I have wronged you. I shall think better of the Army,' he said, and I am sure he meant it.

"That was my worst case," she added, "but men, you know, try not to be funny at our expense, but we pass them by. When I asked a man one day if would buy a War Cry he said 'What for? Is there any tips in it on racing?' 'No,' I answered, 'but there are tips in it on salvation.' 'Give me two,' he said."

"Do you sell many newspapers to women?"

"Women are not as nice to us as the men. I asked a woman one day to buy a War Cry and she turned on me, saying:

'How dare you address me? I do not know you. I am a lady of position and means. How dare you speak to me?'

" 'Madam,' I answered, 'if you spent more upon your manners and less upon your clothes your money would be a blessing.' "

Star did not appear again, and Miss Kemp took me to the headquarters.

SALVATION ARMY HEADQUARTERS

High Prices Rule for the Bonnets, Caps &c.—Papers Published

The Salvation Army's headquarters is at No. 111 Reade Street, a street composed almost entirely of business houses, not one of which, I am sure, does a larger business than No. 111.

First, the posts all over the United States send their daily reports to headquarters. It is also the place of publication of their official periodicals The War Cry, The Conqueror and The Deliverer. The first is weekly, the others monthly. Commander Ballington Booth's name stands as proprietor of these publications.

A short visit at No. 111 will convince any one that a rushing business is done there, and that a handsome profit must be the result.

In addition to these papers, and it is claimed that 75,000 copies of the War Cry are sold every week at five cents a copy, they publish Salvation song-books, histories of the Salvation Army, of its charities, &c.

It is claimed that in England the Army has a manufactory of its own, where all their cloths and caps and badges are made. These are brought to this country, and the soldiers are made to dress the Salvation Army uniform. There is but one source of supply. That is headquarters. Soldiers either pay these prices or do without.

It has been asserted that the Booths make money out of the Salvation Army. If they do, it must be in this way.

An idea can be formed from the following prices:

PRICES OF SALVATION GOODS

Take a Salvation Army bonnet, for instance. There are two grades. A coarse straw, with the fold and frilling of navy-blue china silk, costs $2.50. The fine straw costs $5.

In the first place, I think that among people who claim to care so little for the pretty things of this world, it is rather pandering to woman's vanity to have a coarse and a fine bonnet. Why should they not all be coarse?

And then $2.50 for a coarse, ordinary bonnet. The frame at the very most is worth 25 cents. Two yards of good China silk, granting there are two yards upon a bonnet, can be had at many places for $1. A Sixth Avenue trimmer would charge 25 cents for making the bonnet. This at outside prices makes the bonnet come to $1.50. The Salvation Army, manufacturing this bonnet by free labor, should sell it for even less.

It is the same with other things. An athlete's "sweater" costs from $2.50 to $3. A Guernsey, about the same thing, costs at headquarters $3.75. A yachting cap sells in the Broadway stores for $2. An army cap, not quite so good, sells for $2.50. Trousers sell for $5; a summer coat is $5 and a winter coat is $10.

There must be a handsome profit in this for someone.
For whom is it? To what is it contributed?

Hall rents count up rapidly, and officers excepting those in the slums, who do, in my estimation, the real work, and as everybody knows the heavy work, are paid from $7 to $12 a week. They are also furnished with their board and lodging.

It is the rule of the Army that every post, every charity, shall be self supporting. While this is not always done, it is almost done.

There must be a surplus.

Look at it as one will, one feels that there is a profit, and a large one.

If so, who benefits by it?

THE BOOTHS LIVE PLAINLY

We can't believe that the Booths are misers, who get this profit only to hoard it. All evidence so far as I can find goes to prove that Ballington Booth and his wife, who live in Montclair, N.J., live as plainly and poorly as their humblest soldiers.

It is even said that Mrs. Booth went to the hospital that she might save expense when her child was born.

But this proves nothing. It may have been for effect or it may have been because she believed she would receive better care there.

Although I feel there must be a handsome profit in the headquarter business, still as it is said that the Booths live and dress like their poorest soldiers, I cannot see why they should get money to hide it away.

I do not claim to know anything about the financial side of the question. I only say they charge too much for the wares they make.

I also say they seem to be running things for their own advancement in some way.

Look at the advertisements in the War Cry.

" 'In Darkest England,' by Gen. Booth, Price $1.50. The first edition of this book was sold within three hours after its publication. The fifth edition is now ready, 200,000."

There is a small fortune in that book alone.

Here is another.

"Read this. The Life of Mrs. Gen. Booth, the Mother of the Salvation Army. A thrilling and profitable record of a remarkable woman. No officer or soldier should be without these memoirs and should at once procure a copy. Price, $3.50 net."

What does this mean? In the column I find:

"The Training of Children. How to Make Children Into Saints and Soldiers, by Gen. Booth," and above it:

"Watches. By this special arrangement we are enabled to offer a good watch at an exceptionally low price, and all watches offered are guaranteed to be the latest product, and all are stemwinders and setters."

It is followed by a long advertisement stating among other things that No. 1 is a gentleman's solid silver watch; price, $10. No. 2 is a "nickel composition, looking like silver, and wearing as well," price $7.

Any jeweler will sell them for $5, and be satisfied with a handsome profit.

No. 3 and No. 4 repeats the same thing to "ladies" at the same prices.

The advertisement ends in this way:

"Every opportunity is now offered for our officers and soldiers to procure a watch, as we place them within the reach of all. We are also in a position to supply superior watches at an equally low figure. Write for particulars. Order at once."

Has Gen. Booth deserted salvation for trade, or is he merely mixing one with the other?

Besides selling books and songs and watches and photographs, he sells motto fans and autoharps from $3 to $20.25.

Why should Gen. Booth, whose sole pretext is the salvation of souls, go into trade and inveigle his own followers into buying of him?

Judging from the list of advertisements the Booths are in the jewelry and publishing business. They publish nine newspapers, which would cost $16.10 a year. There is no end to their books and pamphlets, and no one but the Booths, apparently, are fit to write for the Salvation Army.

Looking down the list that might appall a wholesale bookstore, I see:

"By the General," "By Mrs. Gen. Booth," "By Mrs. Ballington Booth," "By the Commissioner," "By Mrs. Maud Booth," &c.

I care to say no more on this particular subject.

NELLIE BLY AN AUXILIARY

I decided while at Headquarters that I could in all honesty become an auxiliary member.

I stated my intentions to Lieut. Newcomb, who told me, without asking any questions, that the fee was $5.

I told her that I wished to know all about the Army, and desired to visit the different posts.

She was very kind, and said that as an auxiliary member I might do so.

My $5 got me a little red book inscribed "Auxiliary League Pass." Within it said:

"The bearer, _____ _____, is a member of the Salvation Army Subscribers and Auxiliary League. This pass is available until Sept. 21, 1894, when it should be returned, together with a renewal subscription, to

AUXILIARY DEPARTMENT.
No. 111 Reade Street.
No. 2,481.

Further on it said:

"The Auxiliary League is composed of those persons who, while not perhaps indorsing and approving every method used by the Army, are sufficiently in sympathy with the great work of reclaiming drunkards, rescuing the fallen and saving the lost as to give it their prayer, influence and money."

The badge I got consisted of a simple little letter S, which cost probably five cents a hundred. Accompanying it was this suggestive note:

"We have a more substantial pin than this, for which we charge 30 cents."

AT THE FOOD AND SHELTER

Seven Cents Will Pay for a Night's Lodging—The Food

Wednesday night was a cold night for a man to spend in the streets.

I noticed the men on Broadway, clad in warm clothing and possessing an after-dinner air of satisfaction, button their greatcoats a little closer and keep their gloved hands deep down in their pockets.

I thought how bright the lights looked in Delmonico's, the St. James and Hoffman's and with a little pang of envy at man's privileges, I noticed the cafes were unusually crowded. The men seemed to be lingering happily over their dinners, as if they did not care to leave the warmth and comfort to face the chilly blasts outside.

As I walked along, thinking of the joy of being a man, I caught passing remarks of "beastly cold," "frost, sure," "darned chilly." But it did not interest me. I knew they were well-clad and well-fed, and I said to myself, what a great country this is, and what blessed people we are, and then I got into a cab and drive down to Front Street.

If you have never been there you may judge from the name that it is near the river, and being near the river must necessarily be devoted to warehouses and such business places.

It is crooked and narrow, and at night very quiet and dimly lighted.

All the buildings are dark and tightly closed, and if you see any one upon the street, it is a slouching figure with bent head, and hands thrust deep into bottomless pockets.

I said all the buildings are dark. There was one, a dismal three-story warehouse with a fire escape on the front, and grated windows on the ground floor, where by looking sharply I saw, through an open door, the flicker of a weak light.

I left the cab a few doors beyond, and going back climbed upon a platform built for the accommodation of truck loading and not for pedestrians.

Entering this barn-like door I saw a long, low room lighted by two gas jets. The brick walls were white washed and the unplastered ceiling was held up by a number of posts. The floor was divided by a continuous line of plain board tables set at right angles.

In the front by the window was a high counter enclosed by wire netting, and in the rear was an ice-box, a cupboard containing dishware, a flight of stairs leading to the floor above, and back of all, crossing the extreme end of the room, was a small partition that hid a range.

The head of one man was visible above the partition wall. I knew him to be the cook. Another, a short, boyish fellow with half-parted lips and guileless expression, the one I had first seen at the Slum Nursery, stood near the end of the table line. Seated upon chairs that stood against the wall were four miserable men in that peculiar curled-up attitude that always makes me think they would like to crawl within themselves and go to sleep and forget.

"I have come down to see the Food and Shelter," I said to the boy. "Is supper over?"

"Supper was over at 7 tonight," he said. "Come and sit down and I'll call the man in charge."

He disappeared up the new flight of stairs and reappeared very shortly with a beaming smile and a coatless man.

"I am an auxiliary member of the army," I said to him, rising from my chair, "and I have come down to see the Food and Shelter because I am more interested in the slum work than any other."

"I am glad to show you all there is to see," he said, very cordially. "Supper is over now, and at 8 we close and go to the meeting in New Chambers Street. I always get back here by a quarter past 9, for we admit the men from 9.30 until 10.30."

"Then I shall also go to the meeting and return here when you do," I answered. "But first tell me something about the Food and Shelter. Is there any other place like it in New York?"

SEVEN CENTS FOR A BED

"It's the only one in New York, but the Army has another in Boston. There are lots of cheap lodging-houses in the city, but the Food and Shelter is the cheapest. We charge seven cents for a night's lodging and a bowl of soup or a cup of coffee and two slices of bread."

The menu card that does service for all is a blackboard 2x3, which leans against the wall facing the table. Upon it in very legible writing was:

> Bowl of coffee..3c
> Corn beef and cabbage.......................................5c
> Bowl of Soup...2c
> Beef Stew...5c
> Stewed apples..3c
> Regulation dinner..10c

"Regulation dinner means the entire bill of fare."

"I suppose you have hours for meals," I said.

"We have breakfast from 6 to 7.30; dinner, 12 to 1.30; and supper from 5 to 7.30."

As no one is allowed upstairs from 7.30 A.M. until 9.30 P.M., I went up to see how men slept for seven cents, including a bowl of soup or coffee and two slices of bread!

I found the rooms nothing but lofts, but they were clean lofts. Along the whitewashed walls was an iron structure, forming an upper and lower berth. On these berths, without pillow for a head, that did not rest comfortably low, or a coverlet for one inclined to be chilly, were leather-covered straw mattresses. That and nothing more.

They looked hard to me. Doubtless they would have looked unendurable to those men I saw in Delmonico's and the St. James and the Hoffman, but they are a luxury compared with a bench in City Hall Park, a corner on a pier, a doorstep or an empty wagon.

They were clean, the floor was clean and if the lodgers were inclined that way, there were iron sinks at the end of the room where they could wash their faces.

"Do you give them towels?" I asked the man in charge.

"Yes, although many men carry their own towels or a bag of cloth to dry upon. I do the best I can for them, but as there are only four of us at this post, the work is very heavy. I give two towels to a floor and I change them once a week. I would change them twice if I had time enough to wash them."

"I suppose you get paid for this work," I ventured.

WAGES 50 CENTS A WEEK

"Oh, yes, I get 50 cents a week and my board and lodging, which is exactly the same as is given to these men who pay their seven cents. We eat the same food and sleep in the same beds."

"What do you do with your 50 cents?" I inquired curiously.

"Well, we are supposed to use it for writing paper and stamps, but you see, sometimes on the day I get paid some poor fellow comes and begs for a bed. I can't give it to him. It is against the rules, so I buy him one with my own money, and more come along and I do the same until I've got but a few pennies."

"And then?"

"Then," with a little smile, "some one comes in for something to eat and I scrape up my pennies and put them with a few pennies this boy (indicating the first one I spoke of) has left out of his 50 cents, and together we can buy the man something."

"That must be a very discouraging financial condition for you," I suggested.

"But if you could only see these poor, miserable men,"

he cried, warmly, as if to justify himself, "created in my maker's image, and brought to this terrible condition. You can't picture it. Why, some nights I look around at them when they are lying over the floor, the beds all filled, and I can only kneel down and bless God that he has let me, so poor and helpless and unlearned, be of some service to my fellow man. It is very little, but I thankfully give up my whole life just to be able to do that little."

"Why don't you wear the Salvation Army uniform?"

He looked at me for a moment, and then said, frankly:

"I can't afford to buy one."

"Do they cost much?"

"Well, too much for me. I have no money."

At this time I asked his name, which I learned was Charles Ingraham, and boy said his name was Luvery.

"What is your first name?" I asked.

"Willie," he answered with a smile; and I smiled, too.

As I stood near the door, talking to them, I saw a bent, grizzled, ragged old fellow walking up and down the platform in front. Every few moments he stopped in his walk to gaze longingly into the room where we were.

"Who is that old man? Does he stay here?" I asked.

"He has stayed here," Charles Ingraham answered, "but he is penniless now and can't even afford our poor lodgings."

"Where will he stay, then?"

"Upon the streets when he has no place else."

"It is rather a cold night for an old man to be out," I said. "Does he drink?"

"Never since he has been here, two weeks now."

So I went out and spoke to the old man.

He was badly in need of a shave and his clothes were ragged and his calico shirt all frayed and buttonless.

"Where are you going to stay tonight?" I asked him.

He took off his battered hat and looked at me as if frightened.

"I don't know, Miss," he said, slowly, "I have been staying here, bit I haven't got enough to pay for a bed, and so I suppose I'll have to stay in the street."

Not enough? Think of it! Only seven cents!

And he looked longingly, wistfully into the barren hole.

"It's rather a cold night for an old man like you to stay in the streets," I ventured. "Tell me how did you get in this penniless condition?"

"Bad luck, always bad luck," he said slowly. "I was a farmer once and had a wife and one child, a daughter. She was a nice child, smarter than her old dad, but one day her mother put her out of doors and told her she was a disgrace, and she went away and I never saw her again. Then her mother died, and I couldn't stand the farm, so I left and went off to work on boats, and now I'm out of a job. I'm looking for work every day, but times do seem hard."

I looked at the poor, distressed old creature and with a strangeness of heart I thought it would be better for him if he remained out all night and froze to death.

"What if you don't get work, and midwinter comes on?" I asked.

He turned his hat awkwardly in his hands.

"I don't know what I'll do," he answered slowly, "if worse comes to worst."

"I think worse has already come to worst."

He gave a little gasp that might have been a laugh if he had not forgotten how.

ONLY AN ODD JOB

"Maybe it has, and maybe you're right. But if I could only find some odd job to do I'd be a happy man."

Some odd job! Cursed are they by fate and fortune whose living depends upon some odd job.

"How much will it cost for this man's lodging for a week?" I asked Charles Ingraham.

The old man looked at me wonderingly.

"It will cost 49 cents," was the reply.

The old man's face changed from half hope to utter despair.

"And that will give him bread, soup, coffee and bed every night for a week?"

"Yes."

"Then let him stay here; I shall pay for it. I hope," turning to the old man, "that in the mean time you will find work."

He looked at me with blank amazement upon his dirty old, wrinkled face. He gasped, tried to speak, his voice broke and, rushing blindly down that platform, he leaned his face in the corner of the window against the iron grating, and I heard husky, hoarse sobs breaking jerkingly from his throat.

I don't make any professions of any kind. I have been deceived so often that my heart is very hard to touch, but the memory of this scene lived with me, and the following morning when I sat down to breakfast and accidentally noticed that the liver and bacon I had ordered cost 40 cents, I thought of the 49 cents, and the old man, and I was ashamed to eat.

We walked away and left the old man alone, and, as it was almost 8 o'clock, I said I would drive up to the meeting in New Chambers Street.

My departure aroused the old man, who, thinking I was leaving not to return, rushed after me saying in a voice he was plainly ashamed of, but could not keep steady:

"I don't think I'll live long."

"Why?" I demanded, in surprise.

"Because you've made me so happy. I feel so unlike myself, I'm sure I'm going to die."

I couldn't help it. I laughed at him.

"If you think you are going to die," I said to him, "you would better come up to 91 New Chambers Street to the Salvation meeting."

"Are you going there?" he asked, quickly.

"Yes," I said.

"Then I shall go," he answered promptly, and he hobbled off.

THE MEETING

The room was well filled when I reached there, and although I drove I was scarcely seated until my old man came in and, with a friendly nod, seated himself a little way off, pretending to listen to the services, but really slyly watching me.

Charles Ingraham and Willie Luvery came in shortly, and then a slum sister rose, one that I call my angel, to state that the Captain had been called away to do some other service for the Lord, and that the meeting would have to be conducted without her.

My slum angel's cold was somewhat better, but she was very pale, and I noticed that when speaking she frequently pressed her hand to her chest, as if it hurt her.

I looked around that strange assemblage. I looked at those men and women upon the platform who have given their lives to a Christ they believe in and others who have left home, family, comfort, to live among and labor with life's lowest and most depraved creatures, and I asked myself, Were those low ones worth it?

Then I saw some seated well up in front who had accepted the same spiritual belief, and I noticed that while their clothes were poor and ragged, their faces were clean and their manners gentle. The scoffers were dirty and rude, yelling at the top of their voices senseless remarks they considered wit, but ever gentle, ever mild, those Salvationists answered every scoff, every rude remark with "God bless you."

My friend, Charles Ingraham, beat upon the bass drum, and had I not known how sincere and honest was his heart, it would have been ludicrous to me to see him lay down his stick to tell of his conversion.

A RUFFIAN INTERRUPTS

But the spell of their enthusiasm was upon me, so much so that when a soldier in a red waist and broken English spoke of his conversion and was called a fool by a dirty hoodlum in the rear, I wanted to give the ruffian an emphatic hint as to an epithet fit only for him.

My anger was cooled by the soldier's calmness.

"You call me a fool," he said with a look of happiness; "I may be one. What do I care since God has heard my prayers and put a sweet happiness in my heart as I can't explain to you? I may be a fool; but why need I care since God has taken away from me every wicked thought and filled my heart with only the desire to be good and to serve him?"

The hour passed all too rapidly when Charles Ingraham and Willie Luvery left, and I knew it was time to go to the Food and Shelter.

When I walked out my old man followed, and my opinion of his spiritual devotion went down several notches.

Quite a little crowd of men hung shivering around the door when we reached the Food and Shelter. Charles pulled off his coat and in his shirt sleeves took his place behind the wire-enclosed desk. Like a flash Willie removed his coat, pulled on a linen jacket and, dumping some coffee into an enormous tin pot, poured water upon it, set a match to an oil-stove and placed the coffee-pot upon that.

The bread he had cut before he went to meeting, and it lay ready in huge piles upon a little table.

At the same time the cook's white-capped head appeared above the partition, and from the inner depths came the odor of soup.

It was good soup, too, I know. It had the smell that bespeaks good, fresh and wholesome ingredients. It made me hungry, I know, and being quite well fed, living as I do in the hotels, I am slow to hunger, and very particular about what I eat.

So my hunger spoke well for the soup.

I remember a few weeks ago when I went to the penitentiary to see Claus Timmerman. I had an honest hunger from missing my luncheon. As I turned up from the river road to walk up the drive to the penitentiary the smell of the kitchen reached me, and as a smell it was enough to make the mummies in the Metropolitan Museum bilious. It was fish, and fish I have foresworn forevermore. Hunger vanished for that day.

Naturally, I thought of this when I smelled the soup.

As the coffee was boiling the men formed in line before the desk.

FEEDING THE HUNGRY

One by one they gave their names, which are put upon the hotel register; then they put down their seven cents and received in return a brass check for their bed and a paper one for their supper.

From the desk they go immediately to the table, where Willie, as spry as a squirrel, called out, "Soup or coffee?" and quickly served them.

There was no waiting for the order there, and Willie was just as particular about wiping the bare table after every man as would be the best of waiters.

That long line of men! With what interest I scanned them!

Some were old, and some were young; most of them were ragged, and most of them dirty.

I must say that, with two exceptions, the men seemed to be sober.

One was Martin, who was rich. He had ten cents, and must have had more, judging from his gait and breath.

"Give me ould noomber," he said to Charles Ingraham, who carefully looked over his brass checks to accommodate him.

"Here you are Martin, and I owe you three cents."

Martin staggered off to the table.

"Ye shouldn't kape us out so long to fraze," grumbled one tall, shaggy fellow. "The doors should be opened arilier."

Every crowd must have one growler, and this was the only growler I saw that evening. The others seemed to feel that they were thankful to get even what they did.

WELL-DRESSED YOUNG MEN

Along down the line I saw two young men that were very well clad. They were to all appearances German students of refinement and learning. Their looks and clothes and manners showed they were strangers to such places and scenes.

Very carefully they counted and divided the painfully few pennies they had.

One of the young men saw me and his handsome face flushed scarlet, and, although I would have liked to have spoken to him, I felt too sorry for him to do it.

When the poor fellow came up and laid down his few pennies, his white hand trembled and his eyes were fastened upon the floor.

I still watched him when he went to the table, and I noticed how hungrily he drank his soup and how slyly he slipped his slice of bread into his pocket, as if it were gold he was stealing.

There was only one colored man in the lot.

"Gib me de same bed up near de windy," he said, with a soft chuckle as if this world had used him as well as he could wish.

"You always want the same bed, don't you, Ben?" said Charles Ingraham.

"Allus like to sleep in me own bed, sah," laughed Ben, and he hobbled off.

The table was crowded. Willie was flying to and fro, the line of wretched humanity was getting smaller.

"I'm going to share my bed with this man," said one wretched fellow, pushing in seven pennies.

Whether they were all his, or he and his friend had raised seven cents between them, I do not know, but I do know that sardines in oil do not lie straighter than these men would need to to share that bunk.

"May I keep this check for something in the morning?" a pale-faced man asked wistfully. "I'd rather have something before I go out."

"No, that check is only good for tonight," Charles said, and the man sighed heavily.

He ate, though, as if he needed it then as much as he ever could.

NO TRUST

"Will you let me sleep here for five cents? It's all I've got," said a plaintive voice, and a good-natured, bloated face appeared at the grating.

"You know I cannot do that; it is against the rules," was the decided answer.

"Won't you trust me for two cents?" coaxingly.

"We never trust here."

"I've only five cents," in a pleading tone.

"You should not have spent the rest for drink."

"I drink?" innocently.

"Yes, Brown, you've been drinking. Now, either give seven cents or go away."

"I've only five"—he began again, when he espied me.

"Will you kindly lend me two cents, miss?" he asked, very wistfully.

"No," I answered; "I will not give or lend money to a man that drinks."

"It was only one glass of beer," he said, pleadingly. "A friend treated me; just one glass."

"Why didn't you tell the friend you needed that money for a bed? You preferred to spend it for beer. Why don't you go back to the saloon-keeper and ask him to give you a bed? Or, having made your choice, why don't you make that glass of beer take the place of a bed? You knew your condition, you knew you needed a bed tonight, and if you wasted what little you had, I have no money or sympathy for you."

"You are right," he said. "I know you are right. You see what I am (he straightened himself up)—I am Henry Brown, mechanic. Who has spent sixty dollars a day once, and didn't mind it. Now you see what I am—almost a tramp."

I looked him over. His face was bloated and dirty, his eyes were bloodshot, his shirt was collarless, and a short coat was pulled on over a long one. I wondered why he did not wear the short one underneath, but I did not question him.

"You see what I am," he repeated. "Almost a tramp."

"Almost?" I echoed. "Quite."

"You're right, lady, I'm afraid you're right," he said, and I saw his eyes grow dim.

"Were you born in America?" I asked him.

"Yes, lady," was the humble answer.

"You should be ashamed of yourself then. In this great

country, where you have a chance to be what you will, to come to this. I am ashamed of you."

"So is all my family," he muttered, hopelessly. "I am the black sheep. It was drink, drink!"

"And you drank today, and you'll drink tomorrow," I added, sharply.

"If I get a bed I won't have any money; if I sleep in the streets I'll have five cents."

He turned away. I hate a man who drinks, and yet I could not let him sleep in the streets, undeserving as he undoubtedly was, for two cents.

"Come back, Henry Brown," I called. "If I give you two cents will you promise me not to drink for two days?"

HIS PLEDGE

"I will not drink for a year," he answered.

"You know you won't keep that promise, and I would rather have you tell me the truth—even to say you will drink. Can't you promise me to stay sober for two days?"

"Two days, Miss, and a year. You can take my word. This man (Charles Ingraham) knows me, and can tell you if I break my word. Will you shake hands with me? You've spoken to me in the right way. You're a lady, every inch of you, and I'll keep my word to you."

It sounds well, but I have heard such promises before. However, he gave his ticket, and give me a beaming smile of gratitude, took off his battered hat, made a profound bow and went to bed.

A HAPPY OLD MAN

Then came my old man, as happy as a schoolboy, his wrinkled face all lighted up with a smile that was simply glorious. He got his ticket, tried to thank me, broke down and rushed off to gulp down his sobs with hot soup, casting adoring glances at me between swallows.

Ah, unhappy power of money! My intentions might have

been just as kind or kinder, and if I had not possessed the great sum of 49 cents for a week's lodging he would not have adored me.

It was getting late. The table was almost deserted, and the men were disappearing up the stairway, beside which on a long red banner were these words:

"Remember your mother's prayers."

I could scarcely reconcile myself to the thought that those miserable creatures were ever laughing babes with fond mothers to play over them. I am sure it was not so in the majority of cases. They must have been brought up with blows and cross words instead of love and prayers.

There was no longer any line, and Willie announced that the soup was gone.

"I wish I could gather up all homeless people and bring them in tonight," I said.

"Many a night I've slept on the streets," Willie ejaculated suddenly, "cold nights, too. But that was before I was saved."

"Saved?" I repeated, questioningly.

"Yes, saved. I was saved just before Easter. My father and mother died, and I was all alone. I couldn't do anything but odd jobs, and I couldn't find any of them to do. Then I went to the Salvation Army, and was saved, and they let me work here."

Work there! Bless his simple heart! He works like a hero.

Up at 6 in the morning, he and Charles Ingraham. Floors to scrub, food to buy, cooking to look after, accounts to keep, meetings to attend, and not to bed until after 11 o'clock every night.

For pay? They tell me with tears in their eyes and exultation in their faces that God pays them by putting a joy in their hearts that makes all life glorious.

You may scoff at their religion, at their enthusiasm. I only tell you what they say, and I do add with all my heart, whatever it is that, as Charles Ingraham expressed it, makes temptation unknown to them and leaves only in their minds the desire to be good and do good—whatever it is, I say, it is a beautiful thing.

I was about to go when two men came in with a letter from a missionary, asking that they might be kept over night at his expense. They had no place but the streets when he found them.

Shortly after them came three men also hearing a letter from a missionary, who said the men seemed honest, but he was unable to provide for them. Would the Food and Shelter do it?

No; it was against their rules, so I talked with the men.

HUNGRY AND PENNILESS

They were Swedes, and sailors. Their boats were laid up, and for weeks they had been out of work. For two weeks they had been penniless, sleeping in the streets at night, living in the day—heaven only knows how.

"Did you have anything to eat today?" I asked the leader.

"I had something yesterday morning," he said, slowly.

"What did you have?"

"A piece of bread."

He looked ashamed to tell, and with flushed cheeks said, hurriedly:

"I had no money. I begged it from a baker."

"When did you," I said to the second men, "have something to eat?"

Pointing his finger at the first, he said simply and with a pathos that brought tears to my eyes:

"He shared his bread with me."

Not friends, only brought together through the same fate of being hungry and sleeping in the streets, but he had shared his bread with him.

"You must be hungry," I said, softly.

"Not so hungry as I have been," answered the first.

I told Willie to get them something to eat. Soup was done, but he found three plates of hash left over from dinner and that with coffee and bread they ate ravenously.

They thanked me awkwardly when they finished and went the way I pointed out to them, up the stairs, past the mother's prayer banner.

"Does the Food and Shelter pay its expenses?"

"Almost. That is, we don't pay any rent, but we run about even on the food. It costs about $2 a day for food."

"How many men came in tonight?"

"Just sixty-seven. We usually have more."

I remembered the poor fellow who wanted to save his food ticket for morning. I thought it must be hard to stay out in the morning with a craving stomach to look for work. Hunger robs a man of courage.

"How much will it cost to give to your lodges coffee and bread in the morning?" I asked.

He counted it up very carefully and told me that 42 cents would give sixty-seven men a bowl of coffee and a slice of bread each.

"Then give it to them," I said, "at my expense."

That is the Food and Shelter. Don't let my story move your heart to send it a lot of money. A few pennies rightly given does more good than dollars donated foolishly.

I don't want you to send money to the Salvation Army Headquarters. Put on your old clothes, and when a cold night comes, go down to Front Street and watch these unhappy wretches come in. If they have not seven cents, give it for them. Don't give more. If you have work for them, blessed things, clothes, good; but money given only pauperizes.

The New York World
February 18, 1894

The Siren of the Coleman House

A Nest of Eager Gamblers; a Big Broadway Hotel as a Screen and a Clever Woman as the "Capper."

The Wiles and Tricks of a Skilful Adventuress and Schemes to Victimize Women Who Have Money

The Hushed Mystery of the "Boston Club," and Its Select Membership of Notable Children of Fortune

Pat Sheedy, Gambler, Appears

His Quick Eye Recognizes Nellie Bly, He Gives the Alarm and Her Dear Friends Suddenly Disappear

And a Word About This Coleman House and Its Distinguished Coterie of Guests and Mysteries

There is a "club" in the Coleman House—mysterious rooms, with drawn curtains and a colored man inside the door who answers the raps. I came very near getting into the rooms the other night.

There is a woman in the Coleman House whose business it is to catch victims for gambling games, as well as for several other little games on her own book.

I came near being her victim last week. Only an accident saved me.

It happened this way:

I was told to meet a young man whom I shall designate as Mr. Knight and plan with him some way to make the acquaintance of this clever woman of the Coleman House. This hotel, I suppose everybody knows, is on Broadway, from Twenty-seventh to Twenty-eighth street, in the heart of the "Tenderloin" district. You can always find a crowd of gamblers, bookmakers, and sporting men there.

Now, Mr. Knight, being a young man about town, had, in some of his various and vast experiences, met this woman, so it was not difficult to plan a meeting for my benefit.

MEETING THE SIREN

It came in this way, a natural way one must confess, and one not liable to arouse suspicion. Mr. Knight called upon the clever woman of the Coleman House and, saying he had had no luncheon, invited her down into the restaurant with him. I came into the restaurant a few moments later and walked past their table to one at the other end of the room.

I had not been seated long when Mr. Knight crossed to my table and in a sweet, affable way asked apologetically:

"Am I mistaken, or are you Mrs. Clark?"

"So you've forgotten me!" I exclaimed in a reproachful manner.

"Not now, oh, no, not now," he assured me sweetly. "How are you, and when did you come to town?"

"I'm well, as usual," I reply, "and I've been in town just long enough to be bored. What's going on? I'm dying to have some fun."

"If you are along," he says, "come over to my table. I'm with a very jolly friend whom I want you to know. You'll like her, I am sure."

This was all said and done of course for the benefit of the clever woman, and I, feeling the way was sufficiently paved, got up and followed him.

EXAMINING HER PROSPECTIVE VICTIM

"Mrs. Clark," he began solemnly. "I want you to know my friend, Mrs. Clemishere."

Mrs. Clemishere and I shook hands across the table. Then I sat down and devoted my attention to Mr. Knight, while Mrs. Clemishere's sharp eyes estimated the cost, to a penny, I'll wager, of my attire. She may have, and results proved so, thought she estimated the character of the girl, but for once, and for the first time, her sharp eyes and clever wits were led astray.

I had a rapid tongue and I devoted all my conversation to Mr. Knight, as was seemly in such old friends after so long a separation. Occasionally I appealed to Mrs. Clemishere, as a woman will to another when they are "simpatico." And, of course, we were "simpatico," for my aim was to make Mrs. Clemishere believe that I had taken one of a sudden and unaccountable likings for her that sometimes do occur between strangers.

"Are you still as crazy on gambling as ever?" Mr. Knight asked in a tone that conveyed utter disapproval of my horrid and shocking dissipated accomplishments.

"Of course!" I rattled on. "What else is there for a poor girl to do? We women must have some kind of excitement. Don't you think so, Mrs. Clemishere?"

Mrs. Clemishere gives me a sweet and approving smile such as a fond mother bestows upon her dear, darling Tootsie-Wootsie, aged five, when it sings "McGinty" in the key of X for the company.

GETTING POINTS

"I play Wall Street sometimes," she says indifferently. "What do you play?"

"Oh, anything," I exclaim with an airiness that I regret later on.

"Poker?" she asks mildly.

"Poker and faro and roulette when I get a chance and races in the summer and, in fact, anything that offers any fun and excitement."

Mrs. Clemishere beams on me with delight. I am a very willing victim and she does not find her work hard.

She takes a paper and scribbles all over it in a dreamy and aimless manner. After a while she asks my address and I name the first street number that comes into my head, which Mr. Knight writes down on a slip of paper for her. Then she tells him to write her address for me, which he does.

I take the paper and on it is written:

Mrs. Allie Clemishere
Room 312, Coleman House

Some more aimless scribbling is done by her and then she gives Mr. Knight a tip, which he instantly takes. It is to go away and leave clever Mrs. Clemishere alone with her pliable victim.

Of course I pretend to see and know nothing. Mr. Knight makes his excuses and I am left alone with Mrs. Clemishere.

She leans on the table and looks at me very pleasantly and I seize the opportunity to study her appearance.

THE SIREN

Mrs. Allie Clemishere is a woman of marked personality. I have met but very few persons that do not in some way, feature, expression or mannerism resemble someone else. Mrs. Lizzie Halliday is one of the few. So is Mrs. Allie Clemishere. She does not look in the faintest like any other woman.

First, she is about five feet six, as closely as I can judge, and generously developed. That is where Mrs. Clemishere's resemblance to other women ceases.

Her face is a striking one, long and thin, the thinness not meaning leanness. Her mouth is small, her lips thin and not noticeable in color. Her teeth are like her lace, long and thin. Cruel-looking teeth they are, as a rat's teeth look cruel. Mrs. Clemishere's teeth are not strong, as every one in view bears gold filling.

The nose is long, straight and sharp. The eyes may be the worst or best feature, as different persons may view them. They are a sharp gray with a touch of blue and are large and bright. It is in expression they are faulty. So keen are they, so swiftly do they rise or fall, so shrewdly do they glance around or over one, that they invite suspicion and dislike.

These remarkable blue-gray eyes wear dark rings naturally, but a pencil is always used to darken both lashes and brows. A cautious and knowing use of paint and powder makes a very presentable appearance of what would naturally be a sallow complexion.

IN MOURNING

This face, so peculiar in its way as to impress one with its power and strength, is set off by an abundance of black and gray hair—hair not black and gray mixed as one always sees it in people, but black on the top of her head to the width of her forehead, with the sides snowy white. It is combed straight back from a very good brow and is gathered in a high knot directly on the top of her head.

Mrs. Clemishere dresses in deep mourning. So much for her appearance.

As she leaned over the table, smiling and confidential, I waited for her to speak.

"Do you really mean what you say about gambling?" she asked hurriedly and with a manner that seemed to suggest that she was going to do one a good turn by telling one something great.

"What? That I like to gamble?" I inquire.

"Yes. Listen!" She glances around and turns back to me. "I do a little of it myself, and when I get a good thing I'll let you in on it."

"How?" I ask densely. "When you find a good place to gamble?"

"No, child," with a smile that said 'What a great, sweet, charming baby you are!' "I mean in stocks. I do lots of it and I make lots of money. Why, I've made $1,200 in the last month. The next good tip I have I'll let you in on it. You give me $100 and I treble it for you."

TOO EASY A GAME

I did not wish to bid a fond and final farewell to $100 quite so easily. So I began to shy.

"Wall Street is so stupid," I cry wearily. "You put up your money and presto! It's gone and no excitement for the price. It's like betting on a horse, you know, and having to get the excitement of the race through a sporting extra."

"But I don't lose my money, my dear," she says, winningly: "I make money."

"What's the use of even that unless you have the excitement of the game?" I ask, with the air of one surfeited with enough greenbacks to carpet the Brooklyn Bridge an inch thick.

"Well, I like to make money," she said pleasantly, "but if you like to play poker I know where you can go."

"Like it? I adore it!" I gasp, with clasped hands.

"I can take you to a place, a regular gambling resort, where you can play all the poker you wish," she ensured me.

I say carelessly, "Big game? Poker is so stupid unless it's for something big."

"I guess you can lose from five hundred to twenty-five in an hour. Most people consider that quite significantly large," she answered, with a slightly sarcastic laugh.

"That's promising," I say, "When will you take me there and where is it?"

She glances around and turning to me says swiftly and distinctly: "It's right above your head. It's known as the Boston Club."

I do not speak for a moment.

"Meet me here tomorrow," she goes on rapidly, "and I'll take you in. Come at 1.30. I'll be waiting in the parlor for you. Hush, not a word to Mr. Knight."

"I'll be here," I promise her as Mr. Knight reappears and

carries me away, and Mrs. Clemishere parts with me with every evidence of cordiality.

THE SECOND VISIT

I make my appearance at the Coleman House at 2 o'clock the following day. I am purposely a half hour late, for I thought it was more politic to make her anxious than to show anxiety on my own part.

Mrs. Clemishere is waiting for me in the parlor. She rises at my approach and slipping her arm around my shoulder kisses me on the cheek. I do not turn the other.

"How late you are, you bad girl," she says with tender chiding, and I laugh and tell her that I was out lunching.

In truth, I had been spending several hours learning the beautiful game of poker that I had declared was my chief delight. I did not know a blessed thing about poker and I was determined not to display my ignorance as soon as I was taken into the gambling room.

I had worked hard at the game, I confess, and had learned all about three of kind beating two pair, and a "royal flush," and a "bobtail flush" and a "full house." As for "bluffing!" Well, I showed my teacher a trick or two and beat him at the game he was teaching me. He simply said "You'll do" in a dry sort of a way, and on that recommendation I went down to the Boston Club in the Coleman House.

But Mrs. Clemishere was not ready for me to leave her clutches just yet. She wanted to see if a disappointment in the game of poker would not send me back to her own game, Wall Street, mysterious stocks, &c. Why give me into the hands of card sharps so long as there was a hope of getting everything out of me on her own account?

"I'm so sorry," she said, "but I did not get to see the man that was to take you into the Boston Club. He is one of the proprietors and they've had some big games on and he hasn't been able to come out to talk to me."

"That is too provoking," I answer with a little shrug.

Mrs. Clemishere slips her arm around me again.

"I haven't had my breakfast yet," she says. "Come down and let's eat. I've been waiting for you until this hour."

My old friend Mr. Knight arrives at this moment, and together we all go to the dining room. Mrs. Clemishere orders luncheon for herself. Mr. Knight takes a drink. I refuse to have anything. I am afraid to trust anybody. I had been told that a "knockout" drug put in food or drink was one of the weapons employed by such people on the victims, and I had no intention of being caught in such a trap.

WALL STREET AGAIN

"Go away and leave us alone," Mrs. Clemishere says to Mr. Knight. "I want to say something to my little friend."

Mr. Knight is very affable and obeys.

"I've just heard from my cousin," she begins at once. "He is the one who conducts all my Wall Street business. He tells me that he knows of a good thing, and for me to be ready to send him several hundred dollars at three hours' notice. Now, if you want to play, I'll let you put up a hundred dollars."

"What's he going to buy?" I ask innocently.

For a moment she is cornered, but only for a moment. She rallies so quickly and with such an unmoved countenance that I begin to admire her cleverness.

"I never ask what he buys," she says, with charming indifference. "I give him the money and he always sends back a big return for it, and that's all I care."

"What is your cousin's name?" I ask.

"Hartshorn. He is very rich and only goes into Wall Street for amusement," she assures me.

"I'm not fond of Wall Street," I say again, and this time very decidedly. "I like to play any gambling game where I can get some excitement out of it. Wall Street is no fun. Now, I thought I was going to have a good time today playing poker or roulette."

"Well, if I'd got to see that man that has the game upstairs, I'd have got you in. I'll see him tonight for sure, though, and if you come in tomorrow at 2 I'll introduce him to you."

Now while we sat there I saw Mrs. Clemishere glancing very frequently towards the hall and I noticed, though I pretended not to, that several men had been passing in through the Twenty-seventh Street entrance out to the office, out the Broadway door and in around the same way again.

They were looking me over and I knew it.

Of course Mrs. Clemishere did not speak to or recognize them in any way except in one instance. That time she merely raised her eyebrows to one man and he passed on without a word.

Knowing that I would not get into any gambling den that day I made excuses and went away, promising to return the next day.

CLOSETED WITH A VICTIM

I did so.

At 2:30 the next afternoon I walked into the Coleman House parlor and found Mrs. Clemishere sitting with a young girl near the Broadway window. They had their backs to me, so I sat down and waited. Mrs. Clemishere was talking to the girl in a tender, confiding, sympathetic way—a way in which she is beyond competition.

She asked her where she lived, if she was married, how liberal her husband was with her, if she ever went out on any little secret jaunts, if she liked a jolly time, and all that. She did it beautifully, I confess, in a way that the girl could never suspect she was being cross-questioned.

I interrupted them at last, and Mrs. Clemishere rushed to me with a sweet smile on her lips, clasped me in her arms and kissed me as she had done the day before. Never once did she express the slightest annoyance at my tardiness. Not she! There was nothing but sweet smiles and tender words.

"We don't want to sit in the parlor," she said at once. "Come with me."

She led me down the hall and seated herself beside me on the sill of a window facing Twenty-seventh Street.

"Are you going to take me in to gamble today," I asked eagerly.

"The man that I was to see told me everything is closed up at present. He says there is no place to gamble, and he is an all-round sport and knows," she said decidedly.

I am provoked and bored, and I show it. I am at a loss to understand why she is putting me off until I decide that she and her friends are not quite sure of me. They are taking no risks these days.

AFRAID OF SUPT. BYRNES

It is not easy to escape the eye of Supt. Byrnes and the gamblers know it.

"I'll fix it all right for you tomorrow, though," Mrs. Clemishere says. "The truth is that I've had a little trouble with the men in there (pointing to the mysterious rooms) and I'm going easy."

"How," I ask, and am surprised when she tells me.

"It was a misunderstanding," she said, "and since then I hate that man."

"That man" had just come down the hall, passed the parlor and with a latch-key was letting himself into a door that was half glass and covered with a dotted mull. The mull was rather short and had a red mustache.

"Who is he?" I asked.

"His name is Heineman, and he is one of the members of the Boston Club," was the reply. "I knew a man, a real brainy chap—and I do love brains—who knew about the Boston Club. He threatened to have it pulled, so I told them and they think I was in the scheme."

"What scheme?

"Blackmail," she answered. "He did it to get money out of them and they blamed me with being in with him. But I was not. I told him I would warn them, and I did. The whole thing was settled, but it cost a lot of money and they are sore on me ever since. That's why I intend to introduce you to the head man and let him steer you in to the game. He's coming here tomorrow at 3. I made an appointment for him to meet you. I'll introduce you and leave you to fix it with him to take you into the rooms."

"Who is the man?" I asked.

"A professional gambler—Pat Sheedy!"

I sit in perfect silence while I try to regain my nerve.

"Did you ever hear of Pat Sheedy?" she goes on. "He is a famous gambler."

Do I know Pat Sheedy? Of him, and by sight, most emphatically I do; but I do not tell Mrs. Clemishere this.

"Why, poker is not unlawful," I say guilelessly, "A club may play poker and no one has power to stop it."

"But this is different," she explains. "They have a 'kitty' and they have cappers."

"What are 'cappers'?"

"Men whose business it is to draw other men into the game, to go out and meet fellows and induce them to come here and play," she says.

THE BOSTON CLUB

The situation of the rooms could not have been better for a "club." They form a little apartment all to themselves, surrounded on three sides by halls and the fourth side facing Twenty-seventh Street. There are eight doors to the rooms—three in the hall where I sat, facing the parlor, one in the back hall and four in the hall above the "Ladies' Entrance."

While I sat there I saw from a dozen to fifteen men go into the rooms, some with larch-keys, and others had to knock for admittance. Those carrying keys, although Mrs. Clemishere said she knew them all, never gave her the faintest sign of recognition, but they all watched me closely, and I supposed their frequent trips to and fro were all done to place my appearance in their minds and to judge if I were a safe victim.

Meanwhile Mrs. Clemishere was not losing time. She was "pumping" me, gently, cautiously and cunningly. Unknown to her I was doing the same thing—"pumping"—and she was being "pumped." It may not have been to any very great extent but at least I gained facts that have been verified, and she got in return an exquisitely beautiful ghost story.

"I imagine you have had trouble with your husband, my dear," she said sweetly. "Am I not right? What was it? Did he object to your having a good time?"

"That he did most emphatically," I answer, with a laugh. "You know how selfish men are? They want all the fun on their own side. I objected."

"Is he rich?" softly, the steely eyes studying my face.

"What do you suppose I married for?" I ask, laughing again. "What do women marry for these days? Didn't you marry for money?"

"My husband and I both had money," was the evasive reply.

"And you loved him?" I say.

This time she laughs. It is rather a high key and is not unmusical.

"When he died I went to my mother and I said 'Thank God Jack's dead. I'll know where he is now.'

"Why, we parted twice before he died. We lived in San Francisco. It was there he got in an accident and I went back to him then and nursed him for a year until he died. He's been dead six years now, thank God!"

"And you still wear deep mourning for a man you never loved?"

"You can bet all your worth I don't. I'm in mourning now for my father. I've been in mourning for eleven years steady. It suits my business, but I'm going out of it. I'm having a gay dress made now."

A SURPRISE

Mrs. Clemishere had slipped her arm around my waist, and now I felt her hand go creeping towards the pocket in my sealskin jacket, like a live animal with cat's eyes.

I am just thanking my lucky stars that my purse is in my muff when I feel her hand come in contact with something, and she stiffens all over as if she had received a deadly electric shock.

Then I remember! I had a revolver in my pocket! For an instant I am seized with varied emotions. I don't know whether to yield to the laughter that is even then making me shake like a monkey with the ague or to throw up my hands and confess that I was afraid to enter that gambling den unarmed.

Like a woman, I do neither, but turn the subject to my mythical husband.

"You should be quite free now that you have no fear from your husband," I say feelingly. "I wish I was. I would wear mourning, con mucho gusto."

"Don't you know where your husband is?" (Her voice is strained, and at the sound of it the old desire to laugh almost upsets me.)

"No," pushing up my lips scornfully. "He may be in New York for all I know. The last I was told of him he was in Scotland. But I expect to run across him any day, and when I do you'll hear of my having my head shot off. That is, if he's quicker than I."

"Why, what do you mean?" she asks.

"He's threatened if he ever sees me with anyone else to shoot on sight," I add. "I've made up my mind to die hard. When I see him, if I'm not alone, I'll shoot first. Wouldn't you?"

"Indeed I would. So you go armed? That is right, I don't blame you. I'd do the same thing." She assures me and I wink the other eye in self-congratulation. I flatter myself I have explained that revolver in my pocket very satisfactorily.

"Do you know any men?" she asks me. "I mean men with money, with more money than brains, though I do love brains. I'm just dying to meet some man with lots of money."

"They generally know how to hold to it when they have it," I say.

ALWAYS SUCCESSFUL

"I'd like to see the man I couldn't work for his money," she laughs. "I've never failed yet and I've had men of all kinds, young and old. Why, I have one now—he's in California at present—who is dying to marry me. He has a wife, but he says he'll leave her and get a divorce if I'll marry him. I don't know whether I want to marry or not. Sometimes I think I will marry this one. I told him last week that he could settle $200 a month on his wife and that would take care of her. Then, I said I'd take a flat and he could room and board with me. For I don't care what the world says. The world has never paid me a salary. He wrote back that the thought was heaven and he had decided he couldn't live the old life any longer. So I expect him very soon. If I take a flat within the next ten days, will you come to live with me? You may do just as you wish, paint the place as red as you please, so long as you don't have me put out."

I was beginning to be bored. It was tiresome to sit all the afternoon in that window merely to have the men going in and out of those mysterious rooms to inspect me.

"How do you live?" I asked at last. "Did your husband leave you money?"

"No, he left me poor, but I worked several things until I had $10,000. My brother-in-law's mother-in-law, Mrs. Crawford, had $10,000 and she went in with he to buy a coffee plantation in Guatemala. We had a $15,000 mortgage on it, which we paid off last year. Now it will pay us $50,000 a year apiece. Mrs. Crawford is now in Chicago. She has some business to do there and I had business here."

"What business have you now?"

"Lots of things for my cousin, who is a very rich man. He's dead in love with me, although he has a wife, and she's awfully jealous of me. I tell you I can work money out of him. He's very liberal. All the men seem to take to me. I'd like to see the one I couldn't get money out of. Pat Sheedy, that you're to meet tomorrow, likes me pretty well, too."

She laughed as if well satisfied with herself and everybody.

EAGER FOR VICTIMS

"Have you no rich friend you can bring around to me?" she asked, anxiously. "Some one with lots of money."

"I know one," I replied. "Son of a millionaire publisher. I might be able to bring him around."

"And he's got lots of money?"

"Oh, galores of it!"

"Then I'll tell you what to do." (See her clever plan.) "You tell him to call here to see you tomorrow. Tell him to send his card up to my room, 312, and I'll go down to see him. Of course you won't be here. You come at 3, and I'll introduce you to Pat Sheedy, and you two can go off somewhere and leave me to work Mr. Man. I'll come down and say you went out with a friend, and that you said for him to wait until you came back. Of course you won't come back."

"That's lovely," I acknowledge. "I'll fix it for you."

"You are sure he has money?" she asks again.

"Proof positive," I vow gravely.

The afternoon has passed away and I am cold and stiff from sitting in the window. I complain of a heavy feeling in order to get away, and that makes Mrs. Clemishere beg me to go to her room.

"You are looking ill and tired out," she tells me, sorrowful. "Do come to my room and rest. You can lie down and I'll rub your head. Do come."

I am afraid to go, so I am proof against all persuasions. I am afraid of those "knockout" drugs. She says she wants a Manhattan cocktail, and as she never has her purse with her, of which fact she carefully informs me, I tell her to come down to the dining room and drink at my expense. This she does. I will not take anything.

The next day I met her again at 3, and Mrs. Allie Clemishere is waiting for me in the parlor. She has her bonnet and coat on and does not move to take them off.

"Pat Sheedy could not come this afternoon," she said. "He has a big game on, and he didn't want to leave. But he is going to meet you tonight, and take you where you can play. It's better at night, anyway. Did you make arrangements for your friend to come to see me?"

"Yes, he'll be here at 5," I answer, and she is satisfied.

MR. SHEEDY INTRODUCED

Once again I buy her a drink and go away.

I go back that night. I am to be there at 9. It is five

minutes to 9 when I go upstairs. In a little alcove next to the parlor, barely containing a sofa and two chairs and darkened by heavy portieres, sits Mrs. Clemishere.

A man is with her.

She sees me and rises to her feet. This time she proposed in the afternoon I should be Mrs. Roberts, of Boston, because she doesn't think it necessary that Pat Sheedy should know I am Mrs. Clark, wife of a rich Pittsburger.

I know that is merely told me, but that in reality she tells Pat Sheedy or whoever she introduces to me all she thinks she knows about me. As she kisses me she leads me forward and the man rises awkwardly to his feet.

As I live, it is Pat Sheedy!

"Mr. Sheedy," she says, holding me by the hand, "this is Mrs. Roberts, a friend of mine from Boston."

Pat Sheedy held out his hand and I gave him mine.

"Glad to meet you, Mrs. Roberts," he says, and I reply with a slight inclination of the head and a smile.

We all sit down. Pat Sheedy proposes that we have a bottle of wine, but I am so afraid that I blurt out I really couldn't drink because I haven't had any dinner, and thereby get myself into more trouble. Mrs. Clemishere instantly proposes that we go down together to dinner. I ask Pat Sheedy to go with us.

"Not for $300!" he says emphatically.

"He never goes downstairs," Mrs. Clemishere explains. "He is always in the house, you know, but he daren't show himself around the dining room. He spends all his time in the game. Don't you, Mr. Sheedy?"

THE GAMBLER'S CONFIDENCES

"Some little of it," he confesses cheerfully.

"Who is in there? What sort of people?" I ask curiously.

"Bookmakers, some gamblers, two or three thieves and some youngsters from Boston. They're having a big game in there tonight."

"What are they doing?" I inquire.

"Everybody! That's what I'm doing," he says cordially.

Once again he begins to insist upon having some wine brought, and I am so much in terror of this that I instantly swear I am dying of hunger and head out.

"Go down then. I'll wait here till you come back. Then we'll have that wine. You'll see my father in the restaurant," he says to me, and then to Mrs. Clemishere: "He went down to eat."

"Am I going to play roulette tonight?" I ask, and Mrs, Clemishere cries quickly:

"We'll see all about that when we come back," and drags me away.

At a table near the window sat a man with a bald head and red-gray mustache. He was inclined to flirt with me, but did not recognize Mrs. Clemishere in any way, although she had been talking with him upstairs a few moments before.

"That is the man Sheedy called his father," she says to me. "Go on and make a mash. He is the only member of the club upstairs that has any money, and they say he's got loads of it. He is a bookmaker. His name is Joe Cotton."

"Why don't you speak to him?" I ask.

"I never speak to any of them," she says. "They all know me and I know them all, but we never recognize each other anywhere. I never even speak to Mr. Sheedy before people. Don't you think he's nice?"

"Very," I answer cordially, and begin my dinner.

We had not proceeded far when Pat Sheedy came in and went over to Joe Cotton's table. Sheedy did not even look at us, although there was no one but the waiters and the cashier in the room. He stood there talking earnestly to Cotton, while Cotton looked at me. I made up my mind I'd make Sheedy speak, so I called to him:

"Who gave you more than $300?" I inquire, laughingly.

"What do you mean?" he asked with a smile.

"You said you wouldn't come down here for $300, and here you are," I explain.

Sheedy laughs, and so does Cotton.

"I was sent for," Sheedy explains. "A newspaper editor wanted to see me on a little business."

He mentioned the name of an editor that sent my heart away up in my throat. The editor is, as I know, devoted to roulette, and doubtless dropped in to see Sheedy in connection with it, but if he knew how near he was to seeing me there, I fancy there would have been some surprise all the way round.

MR. SHEEDY REAPPEARS

We followed Sheedy upstairs very shortly. He had gone into the "club" house, but Mrs. Clemishere explained how she could get him.

"I do not need even to speak to his valet, Warfield, who is always on duty at the door," she said. "All I have to do when I want Mr. Sheedy is to merely raise my eyebrows. Warfield understands and goes for Mr. Sheedy, who'll quit the biggest game any time to come to me."

She spoke the truth in one respect. Warfield made his appearance at the door to admit a visitor and Mrs. Clemishere never spoke, but almost instantly on Warfield's disappearance Sheedy came walking out.

"We must have that bottle at once," he said, and I said, "None for me."

My determination not to drink put a damper on the crowd. No one felt especially jolly over it.

Mr. Sheedy looked perplexed and thoughtful.

At last, at Sheedy's request, we left our old station in the window in the hall and returned to the alcove.

Hardly had we been seated when we were joined by a tall, thin man with gray hair and close gray whiskers.

He was introduced as Dr. George Dalton.

"I am a horse doctor, ladies; that's the only kind of doctor I am," he said.

"What is he, really?" I ask, turning to Sheedy.

"Anything," he assures me. "George scuttled two ships and was caught scuttling a third, and he did time for it; didn't you, George?"

George laughs, without seeming to appreciate this frank confidence.

"George is mad tonight. He's one of the partners in there (pointing to the 'club' rooms), and he ordered a lot of baked beans for the boys tonight and Pearson, the hotel proprietor, played a joke on him."

"Is there a big game on tonight?" Mrs. Clemishere asked.

"Yes," says Pat Sheedy; "a pretty big one."

"Am I not to go in?" I plead.

"Not tonight," Mrs. Clemishere answers hastily.

"Why not?" demands George Dalton.

"Because Mr. Sheedy says at present there is no game for women in New York," Mrs. Sheedy says, warningly.

Pat Sheedy says "No, there isn't," in a way that is not convincing.

"Well, can't I even peep in to see what they are doing?" I coax, and again George Dalton says "Why not?"

But the other two are not quite ready. They want me to drink first, and even to get in the rooms. I could not take the risk of drinking drugged wine.

"How old are you?" Mrs. Clemishere asked to make conversation when we all grew silent.

"How old do you think?" he demanded.

"Thirty-five or forty," she says.

"If you'd been hangin' since I'm forty-four you'd be pretty stiff," he said with a laugh. "I'm forty-five. I've been around the world four times. I stubbed my toe first in Boston twenty-seven years ago. Before then I'd walked the streets all night to keep from sleepin' and I'd walk 'em all day to keep from eatin'. Yes, I'm an old man now. I've got two boys and a girl older than this girl (pointing to me). My girl is in a convent. She is goin' to be a nun."

"Have you any business besides this?" I asked.

"I had a gambling house at No. 45 West Twenty-eighth street, but it's been closed since last July. I'm paying rent right along, and all the fixtures and everything's there just ready, but I daren't play."

"Why? Are you being squeezed for more money?"

"That's it," he says. "Will you come around to see my place?"

The conversation was drifting easily and I felt everything

coming my way. Everybody had thawed out and talked unreservedly to me.

RECOGNIZED AS NELLIE BLY

Suddenly Pat Sheedy cried out in a frightened voice and with a warning glance at the others:

"My God! You're smart enough to be Nellie Bly!"

That was more than enough. Instantly and at the same moment Mrs. Clemishere and George Dalton sprang to their feet, pale and trembling. George Dalton ran as fast as he could to the gambling rooms and Mrs. Clemishere ran down the hall. Pat Sheedy did not run, but he went hastily after George Dalton and disappeared into the "club" rooms.

"Well," I gasped to myself. "And who is Nellie Bly, that her very name should strike terror to the hearts of such fearless people?"

I looked at my watch. It was 11.30.

"Well, my chance for seeing that game is done forever." I sighed.

But, I mused as I left the hotel, what happens to other less fortunate women who are caught in the snares of these people?

The New York World
March 18, 1894

A New Trick in "Bargains"

Nellie Bly Discovers an Enterprising Woman Who Makes You Think You Are Getting Things Very Cheap

Pianos, Furniture, Pictures

A Bogus Bill of Sale Which Misleads Customers as to the Real Cost and Value of the Wonderful Bargains

An Interesting Household

A Striking Illustration of How Clever People in the Big Town Manage to Live on the Credulity of the Unsuspicious

Of all bargain frauds, I believe, the bargain furniture fraud comes very near being the worst.

Look in almost any newspaper and there will be found these alluring advertisements:

ALL THE *magnificent furniture pertaining to a first-class private residence must be sold immediately, consisting of superb Turkish parlor suit, also silk tapestry suit, $40; paintings, magnificent grand upright piano, $140; silk couches, screens, portieres, magnificent hand-carved oak buffet, table, leather* *chairs for bedroom suits, fine velvet carpets, $14 and $18 each; all like new, used four months; sell separately, 127 W. 47th St.*

Alluring? Yes; and to the very people who can't afford to be swindled.

Advertisements, changed slightly in form, but always retaining some special features, such as "silk tapestry suit, $40; magnificent grand upright piano, $140," have appeared daily for some months from No. 127 West Forty-Seventh Street.

I began to wonder why it took so long to sell that furniture, and at last I decided to see it.

The house is a four-story high-stoop situated between Sixth Avenue and Broadway. It is the most pretentious house on the block, and has an impressive hall door, adorned with heavy hinges and stained glass, that makes the old houses across the street shrink back fifty feet in very shame.

I went up the stoop rather timidly for a "bargain-chaser" and touched the electric bell that sent a jingle through the house. A man answered my ring, a well-spoken fellow, who admitted me to the hall and then paused inquiringly to hear my business.

"I have seen your advertisement," I began in the same old way, and the man inclined his head with a pleasant smile. I needed to say no more.

"Will you wait one moment, please, until I call the lady of the house," he said, and off he went through the hall to the rear parlor.

This gave me a chance to look about, and the hall bade fair to maintain the pretentiousness of the front door. There was a large fireplace in it filled with gas jets and above the mantel were a cabinet and two gas jets.

The front and rear drawing-rooms were hidden from me by cheap chenille portieres.

What amused me most at the moment was that someone began to play the piano the moment the man went into the rear room.

"That is the $140 piano, and they intend to draw my attention to it," I thought.

Just then the front portieres were drawn aside and a little stubby woman, rather too stout for her height, invited me to enter.

"I want to buy some furniture," I said to her, as her sharp, dark eyes scanned me closely.

The woman is far from prepossessing. Her eyes are dark and have a bad expression—keen, cruel and unscrupulous. Her hair is very dark and very banged and curly about the face. Her nose is "pug." She began in a very business-like way.

"What kind of furniture do you want?" she asked promptly.

"Oh, every kind," I answered, airily. "I am furnishing a house."

"We are selling off everything, if you will state what you wish to see," she replied, a trifle testily.

The piano kept going in the back room and I said that I would like to see a bedroom suit.

GAUDY AND BRAND NEW

The woman evidently did not expect to sell bedroom furniture, so, for an instant, she was rather disconcerted.

"I have some beds to sell," she said at last, "but I have some friends visiting me and I cannot show them today."

So I turned to look at the things that were before me.

The floor was bare of carpet, but filled with furniture of every kind. Chairs, sofas, tables, lamps, bisque statuettes, cabinets, and all of the gaudy style that catches the general bargain hunter.

The tables and cabinets were gold, and the chairs and sofas were upholstered in light-colored cotton brocades with trimmings of velvet; such furniture as one sees in the windows of every cheap furniture store.

It was very evident that not a single article had ever been in use.

"How much do you ask for this little gold table," I inquired.

"I will sell that for $25. It cost double only three months ago," she answered.

The table could, I should judge, be bought in any store for $10 at the very most.

I saw that the walls were covered with cheap oil paintings, regular sawed-out things of impossible colors, so I inspected them.

"Have you any by noted artists?" I asked.

"There is one by Murand," she answered, pointing to a ghastly thing, "and there is one by Watson."

"Who is Watson?" I ask, meekly.

"Don't you know Watson, the celebrated artist?" she ejaculated, with cutting scorn, which I bore with Christian fortitude, for I did know Watson, better than she could ever suspect, but more of that later.

"Have you any etchings? I don't care much for oil," I say, to turn the subject.

She has no etchings. The class of people that search for bargains are usually fond of gaudy oils in deep frames.

"Are these the only chairs you have?" I asked, nodding towards the pink and blue brocades before me.

"I have some back here," she said, leading the way to the rear room. "I have elegant dining-room furniture, if you want any."

The back room was more furnished than the front. There was a carpet upon the floor, a business table in the center, the $140 piano against the wall and a number of chairs standing around. The dining room, with a high window of cut glass that succeeded in making the place frightfully gloomy, was yet further in the rear. An ordinary oak table was there, with six oak chairs. And there were several upholstered chairs, a roll of lace curtaining and a roll of carpet—that she said was sold.

COST $600, WOULD SELL FOR $140

While we were looking at these things the man that admitted us was thumping with great energy upon the piano, and naturally I spoke of it.

"I believe you mention a piano for sale," I suggested. "Is it a good piano?"

"Try it yourself," the woman said quickly, as the man rose up to make way for me. "There is no better make, and I have a five years' guarantee."

I looked at the manufacturer's name, Sears R. Kelso. It was unfamiliar to me and I said so.

"Oh, well, that may be," she replied, in a tone that suggested I didn't know much, "but the firm is well known just the same."

"You can see this, that will tell you all about it," spoke up the young fellow at the table, as he handed me a circular that stated that the piano cost $600. It was a black ebony case, and I considered the one before me a very plain affair for the price.

"I will sell it for $140," the woman added, "and I've only had it since last August."

"That is quite a bargain," I say, pleasantly, and then I turn to other subjects.

"I should think you would be sorry to sell your furniture and leave such a pleasant home," I observe, amiably, but she doesn't grow very confidential.

"We must do according to our circumstances," she answers, carefully.

"Is this house for rent?" I go on.

"No; it's been rented," she answers, quickly, "but it's for sale. We have power to sell it for the owner."

Promising to return the next day, I depart. Then I set about to look up this woman's record. I find a history that, though short, is interesting, presenting another phase of New York life. Between thirty-six and forty years ago Fanny Ford was born somewhere in West Virginia. Her parents were poor people. Her father, now a man of perhaps seventy years, was for forty years a pilot on the Ohio River.

SHE WAS FANNY FORD

The family moved to Gallipolis, O., and something like ten years ago Fanny Ford married a man named Walsh, who tried to practice medicine in Cincinnati.

It is said that Walsh made a failure of medicine, and that

then Fanny went into the furniture business, just as she is in it today, buying cheap furniture, at wholesale prices, and selling it by alluring misrepresentations to would-be bargain-finders.

Less than three years ago Walsh died and left his wife with three children whom she idolizes. There is Lucy, nine years old, who has a governess, for her fond mother will not permit her to attend public school. Next comes Tiny, a little five-year-old girl, and last is Elmer, three years old, the baby and only boy.

After Walsh died Mrs. Walsh had about $10,000 that she had scraped together, and with that amount and her three children she removed from Cincinnati to broader fields.

In other words, she came to New York and rented No. 17 West Twenty-fourth street, where she opened a boarding-house.

Her first boarder was Victor Cadieux, a Canadian youth, less than twenty-one years old, who attended to the stereoscopes in the Eden Musee.

No one knows whether it was the widow Walsh who made the first advances, or the boy Cadieux, but be that as it may, they say that in less than eight months after her husband's death, and with courageous, if not admirable disregard of the almost double difference in age, the two were wed, and Victor gave up the Eden Musee, with its motionless inmates, for the boarding-house and its spry mistress.

The boarding-house proved a failure. I don't know why, for though Fanny didn't sell furniture during that time she sold carpets.

Having lost considerable on the boarders, she removed to No. 138 West Forty-sixth Street, where she went into the business in which she is at present engaged.

But trouble will come to those who deal unfairly, and at last too many had lost money through her to make home very comfortable, so she gave it up and went to No. 48 West Twenty-seventh Street.

She only remained there about six months when she sold her lease, at $100 increase, to a Mrs. Gibbs, together with $800 worth of furniture.

It was only six months from the time she lived in West Twenty-seventh Street until she sold and moved to No. 127 West Forty-seventh Street, Feb. 1.

She buys her furniture at wholesale prices from Pierce & Co., West Nineteenth Street, near Sixth Avenue, and this furniture she represents as having cost enormous amounts, and succeeds at swindling her customers into buying at prices that exceed the real value, giving Mrs. Cadieux a most handsome profit.

Her pianos are bought from Sears R. Kelso, One Hundred and Thirty-third Street and Lincoln Avenue, and by examining the following receipts, it will be seen how buyers are easily misled and swindled.

The first receipt, dated March 5, 1894, giving the number of the piano and price, $100, is the real receipt. That was meant only for the Cadieux family. The second receipt, dated Aug. 26, 1893, and giving the number of the piano and the price as $600, is the "fake" receipt, given by the firm of the Cadieuxes to help them swindle the public into believing the piano cost a great deal and that at $140 ($40 increase in real price) they would be getting it at a great bargain.

The carpets are furnished by Dobson & Co. Most of them are made in the house, and when they are shown it is always done in the hall, so that a buyer cannot judge how small the carpet is.

I was shown one that was actually not more than ten feet long and four breadths wide, and was earnestly assured that it covered the floor of a very large room.

They have more trouble over their carpets than with any other article. They tell most dreadful lies about the size, and their victims are helpless when they discover the truth.

A queer lot compose the household at No. 127. On the top floor are two women, Mrs. Tona Banie and Mrs. Richardson. They live well, dress gaily and enjoy life generally.

ARTIST WATSON ET ALS

Then there is a Mr. Wilson, or Nelson, who once did a Japanese act at the Eden Musee with Olive Nelson, who is his wife, and lives there with him.

Besides these are a trio of queer fellows who came from Cuba and have joined their fortunes with Fanny Cadieux and her boy-husband.

There is James Brown, a Scotchman, who helps to move around, and in and out, the furniture. He also attends to the door.

He might properly, being the most useful, be called No. 1 of the tribe.

Tom Watson is No. 2. He is an Englishman and tries to paint. It is his name that honors some of the elaborate "oils" in the drawing-room. One, a Venetian scene, is considered especially fine. Tom is very handy at copying pictures and painting over lithographs.

No. 3 may not be useful, but he is ornamental. He says he is the Marquis Daniel de Cardamus. The Marquis, in his ornamental weariness, sits around in the easiest chairs admiring Jim Brown's muscle, Tom Watson's paintings, and Mrs. Cadieux's clever sales.

Besides all these Mrs. Cadieux has her father and mother with her. They confine themselves to the rooms on the floor above the drawing room, where they help the nurse to attend to the three children. There are three servants in the house.

While I have described how business is done at No. 127 West Forty-seventh Street, it is folly to imagine that it is the only place of its kind in the city. But it is the largest and most successful.

Only remember in the future that everything worth having is either unattainable, or expensive, and—beware of bargains!

The New York World
March 25, 1894

Worked by the Hindoo Idol

Nellie Bly Sees Through the Pretended Supernatural Wonders of the Nimble-Fingered Jugglers

The Basket Trick Explained

A Private Séance with the Oriental Magicians Who Mystified Visitors to the Midway Plaisance

Their Very Clever Legerdemain

But the Wily Hindoos Insist that Their Tricks Are the Miracles of the Sun God "Ramswamy"

There were Seyid Jamal, Sheik Jamel, Sheik Lail, Sultan Meah and Mohamed Khan, not to speak of the tum-tum, the stuffed god and the bagpipe. And I went to see what these Hindoo magicians could do with the aid of their god Ramswamy last summer, and now they are in town giving private exhibitions.

They are from Rudyard Kipling's land—India, and they are all jugglers, even the tum-tum, the stuffed god and the bagpipe.

I confess with grief that my faith in all things is weak and my curiosity of an investigating turn, but having been told to sit still and look on, I tried to curb my natural impulses and to believe that the Sun God of India would work wonders to behold through these pajamaed jugglers.

It is the fashion to call anything partly or unusually clad "picturesque," so I suppose the jugglers in their white muslin pajamas and enormous turbans and their copper-colored, bare feet were picturesque.

The half-dozen that composed the audience sat down and gazed on the jugglers, every face wearing a ludicrous look of responsibility. All except my own. I was not permitted to investigate, but I could be amused.

Sultan Meah and Sheik Lail perched themselves upon the edge of a table and played an overture on the "hooduk" and "dhole," that if I had not been informed was music, I should have believed the most ear-splitting noise I had ever heard. Sultan and Sheik looked notable and the audience important, so I made up my mind to stay as long as the others would.

Mohamed Khan is the dude of the jugglers. He is the smallest man of the troupe, and wears a salmon-pink turban and an enormous hoop earring set with semi-precious stones. He has a sweet smile, and besides doing a lot of drinking, does odd jobs for the stars.

He brought forth a carpetbag, a stuffed rag baby, an antique bagpipe and two strings of sleigh bells and laid them upon the floor before us.

While Mohamed was thus engaged, Sheik Jamal proceeded to dress himself for his part. Around his thin brown legs were folded his white muslin pajamas, and he fastened them with a string of sleigh bells. Then he was ready for business.

Taking up the "tumdl," he joined in, regardless of time or place, with the other musicians; but failing to outdo them in noise, dropped to his knees on the floor, searching the carpetbag and uttering a continuous string of something that sounded like "Yuh-yoh-yoh-yoh."

"Ramswamy!" he said, picking up the rag doll and handing it to me. "Sun god of India. Much good help."

Gently and gingerly I took Ramswamy into my hands. He was a marvel to behold. It may be that the son of India had shone too generously upon his ungodlike form, and he had suffered from a fever that had played roguish pranks with his make-up.

However that may be, I must truthfully state that Ramswamy, the Sun God of India, has baby-blue zephyr-yarn hair that stands upright in a way that suggests the tail of a cat at an accidental and unexpected meeting with a strange dog.

Ramswamy is more than twenty. He has whiskers. They grow all around his neck and are strangely like a bit of rabbit's skin, but I suppose, being a Hindoo God, Ramswamy is allowed to be original in the way of whiskers. Ramswamy's arms are of stuffed green silk, and, like Pacquetette's, reach all the way around his body, which is also a stuffed bit of cloth, probably a good yard long and two inches through, narrowing down to a point at the feet.

The jugglers claim that it is by Ramswamy's aid alone they are enabled to perform their feats of "marvel," the manager explained, as the Sun God was handed back.

The music grew quieter as Sheik produced a bit of stone that transformed within his hands into two silver dollars. These are thrown upon the floor to prove that they were genuine.

He picked up the money, asked "How many? How many?" and closed his hands upon them. Immediately he reopened the tawny hands, and, of course, the money was not there. Then he closed his hands separately and asked in which the money would be found. It was not found in either. Then he suddenly cried out with a pain in his nose, pretended to blow it, and the silver dollars fell to the floor.

"Much big nose!" Sheik said in tones of satisfaction.

Of course, if Ramswamy and his standing baby-blue hair had not been lying right before Sheik I should have sworn that it was simply a sleight-of-hand trick that any one with nimble fingers could perform. But then it would be so impolite to doubt the power of a stuffed Sun God, especially one with standing baby-blue hair. Ramswamy, through Sheik, could do more with money, so we found. One of the men in the small audience was asked to hold two silver dollars very tightly within his closed hands. Ramswamy was placed on his head, and then the young man blew very hard on his hands, while Sheik played madly upon the "tumdl," and Lail and Meah on the "hooduk" and "dhole."

Suddenly the music ceased. "Do you feel the money?" cried Sheik. "Have you my $2 fast tight?"

"Yes!" answered the subject in a "you-can't-fool-me-I'll-hold-on-to-this-money-and-see-your-trick" tone that made my courage almost bubble over.

Sheik took Ramswamy from his perch upon the young man's head, uttering "Goo! goo! goo! goo!" as rapidly as he could, and making all sorts of pauses and signs with the bilious sun god. Suddenly the god was cast upon the floor, the closed hands were knocked asunder, and out fell two copper cents, the size of the silver dollars.

Everybody said "Ah!" with a great deal of feeling, and Sheik raised a howl.

"My moneys! My two dollar" he cried, in distress. "Give my money."

"I haven't got it," the young man said very earnestly and gravely. "You see I haven't got it."

"You take my money. I get policeman," Sheik threatened, adding angrily:

"You no got my money? See!" He pulled the young man's nose and the money went dashing to the floor. Of course, Ramswamy did it all, but it wasn't a pretty trick to play upon a stranger, especially when he's bashful.

The little stone that turned into money made its appearance a second time. Sheik brought it from the bag and, after showing it to us, pretended to swallow it. He grunted and groaned when it went down, just as any of us would do if the victim of a similar mishap. Then he invoked the aid of Ramswamy, and soon he groaned again.

This time he promised to do with the stone as the whale did with Jonah, and we watched in apprehensive silence for what we were about to gaze upon. I didn't think it was a nice thing to do in company and felt like suggesting that Sheik might retire to an adjoining room, but I recalled that I had been told to remain silent, so I waited shudderingly for the final moment when I would gaze upon what Sheik had seen at luncheon.

Catching himself by the waist and apparently in greatest agony, Sheik's mouth was seen to fill until he could keep it closed no longer, and opening it, he began to unload that which was therein.

He grabbed something. It proved to be a piece of yarn. He began to pull and pull. We gazed, thunderstruck, upon the many colored yarn as it came from within his mouth, yard after yard, until a goodly pile of it lay upon the floor before him.

"Goo! Goo! Goo!" he shouted, and the tumtum thumped in devilish glee.

Sheik picked up the bunch of yarn to show us; it was too big to go into his mouth again, when horrors upon horrors, he gave another groan, and it was seen that something more was there.

His brown cheeks bulged and his black eyes distended until his mouth opened slowly, to show a handful of nails about an inch and a half in length. Nails followed nails, until it seemed as if Ramswamy had started a nail factory in Sheik's internal arrangement.

There was a breath of relief when the last nail came, and Sheik picked up a flannel cloth to wipe his tongue, when a volume of smoke shot from his mouth. Ramswamy seemed to be raising Cain in Sheik's insides.

"Much smoke! Much smoke!" Sheik cried, gleefully, and he blew hard, but no result followed. He had to take the flannel cloth and wipe his mouth a second time before he could make the sparks fly.

But they did fly at last, and everybody was lost in amazement.

Of course if it hadn't been for Ramswamy and his standing baby-blue hair, I should have declared that sheik put a small ball of yarn in his mouth instead of the stone, and that when the yarn was unwound it naturally looked but was not in reality too large to go back again.

And when he pretended to show us that it would go back, he slipped the nails into his mouth, putting some in every time he took some out, and when he wiped his mouth with the flannel rag it contained something that could be blown into smoke and sparks.

Of course Ramswamy with his standing baby-blue hair precluded any suggestion of how the thing was done. One must be polite in the presence of a Sun God even if his whiskers are not up to date.

The Sheik, having done all these things, made his little bow and changed stage dress with Seyid Jamal—that is, he took off his sleigh bells and Seyid tied them around his own ankles. Besides his pajamas, Seyid wore a big canary yellow turban and black whiskers.

Seyid, besides being the largest man among the jugglers, is the only one, excepting Ramswamy, who boasts of whiskers. Seyid seems very sure of himself. There was a look in his eye when he put on the sleigh bells that seemed to say: "Well, you have seen the other, but just wait till you see me."

So Sheik Lail and Sultan Meah played upon the "dhole" and "hooduk," and Seyid Jamal took up the "turndl," the mother of bag-pipes—a gourd with two reeds in it—and began to play and dance. As he danced he turned his toes up—or maybe Ramswamy did it for him—but it was very funny.

When the music was over, Seyid showed up a small ear of corn.

He shelled some of the corn and handed it around so that we might see it was genuine. The remainder he shelled and threw into a breadth of calico from two to three yards in length, which was held by two men. Seyid showed the corn in the calico, He then passed the marvelous Ramswamy over it, blew upon the bag-pipe and, taking up a basket-like arrangement, rattled with great rapidity the corn in the calico.

Lo and before our eyes appeared popcorn!

With a smile of triumph Seyid passed some popcorn around so that the audience might taste of it, and thereby be convinced.

I would swear, if it were not impolite, that Ramswamy was not guilty of that trick, or if he was, it was a shabby one to play upon his own follower.

The popped corn was concealed in the basket lid, but not so well that I did not see it before it was shaken out. Of course, the first corn did not pop at all, but it was hidden by the popped corn, not so well though that I did not see it when the trick was done.

One can't blame Seyid. He believes in Ramswamy, and if Ramswamy gets tired and plays prankish tricks upon his faithful worshipper, hiding popped corn in the basket lid because he was too lazy to pop it at the right time, why one can only say it's shabby in Ramswamy and extend one's condolence to Seyid.

Ramswamy did better with the turban trick. It is a pretty thing, and must have cost that brain beneath the Sun God's standing baby-blue hair some tall thinking before he accomplished it.

Seyid produced a strip of red cloth probably fifteen feet long. It was a turban as it appears before it is twisted around the head.

He asked a man in the audience to cut it, and thirteen pieces were taken off the end and thrown down upon the floor.

The cloth was then folded, and holding it in his hands Seyid requested the man to cut again. He did so.

"How many pieces now?" asked Seyid.

"Fifteen!" was the reply.

Once again the cloth was folded and once again cut.

"How many pieces?" Seyid asked again, and the reply was "Seventeen."

This long piece that had apparently been cut was not released from Seyid's hands. We only thought it was cut because of the way he folded it.

After all this was done, and it was said that the long cloth had been cut into thirteen small and four large pieces, Seyid gathered them all into a lump, the cut ends protruding from his hands, and had the man strike a match and set fire to the cloth. It burned slowly, but it did burn real fire, and was at last crushed out and rolled up quickly in a little wad and placed in the young man's hands.

"Hold tight! Hold tight!" Seyid commanded, and the young man obeyed.

Seyid did a little humorous decorating then. He placed Ramswamy on the young man's head, and on his lightly clasped hands a little red-wooded object without legs, which he said was...

"India Billy-goat, not 'Merican Billy-goat!"

This being done, Seyid played upon the lamdl and

invoked the aid of the blue-haired Ramswamy to make the cut and burnt turban whole again.

Ramswamy was good. Seyid jerked the cloth from the young man's hands, and lo and behold, it was neither burnt nor cut!

Of course, if we hadn't been told that Ramswamy, he of the standing blue hair, had power to do all this, I would have called their attention to a little worldly matter-of-fact thing—that the red cloth was at least two feet shorter!

But then, maybe Ramswamy is not exact as to measurement. One can't expect a Sun God to attend to all such little details. I confess, as I have before, my great failing of disbelief. Still, Ramswamy, with his standing blue hair, can afford to scorn doubting scoffers.

That Sun God was yet to show greater power than we had yet witnessed.

Seyid Jamal said he would put Sultan Meah into a basket and that Ramswamy would take away the material and leave only the astral body.

The basket, a large willow affair, with sloping sides, was submitted to an examination. Everybody pronounced it whole, with no openings except the usual one at the top.

Then a net bag was passed around, and we all examined it. Sultan was then put into the net, and the rope that drew it together at the top was tied into many knots, first by some of the audience and then by Seyid himself.

Seyid lifted the net-imprisoned Sultan into the basket and, with seeming effort, crushed him partly down, put on the lid and covered the entire thing with a sheet.

Then they played music and made a great deal of noise, and Ramswamy was invoked to take Sultan's physical body away.

They said he did. At least, the net in which Sultan was confined, holding nothing but the gay, yellow turban, came flying out and fell on my knee.

"There he goes! There he goes!" the jugglers all shouted, pointing beyond us.

"Why didn't you hold him?" they asked me, but I had

nothing to say. That uncontrollable disbelief of mine would not admit that Sultan was out of the basket.

I wanted to get up and stand on the other side of the basket, but these honest followers of Ramswamy declared I would interfere with the workings of the Sun God, so I was forced to retain my place. To convince us that the basket was empty Seyid took a stick and jabbed into it, but when I offered to do a little jabbing with that stick they refused to permit it.

Those jugglers are so particular when it comes to jabbing an astral spirit in a covered basket.

Once again the basket was covered up and the music set going, while Ramswamy was invoked to unite the physical body to its astral in the basket.

Ramswamy did it—that we know. If we didn't we would say that Sultan untied the net bag, tied the knots in the rope again, and then curled himself down around the edge of the basket. The jabbing was done above him.

By putting one of our own men upon the floor in the position sultan must have assumed, we found the basket covered him, and he had on his boots and hat, while Sultan had only his pajamas between him and Comstock.

It's an unpleasant thing to doubt, but if it hadn't been for Ramswamy and his standing baby-blue hair, I declare I would have thought the hindoo jugglers nothing but tricksters, and very poor ones at that.

All hail, Ramswamy!

The New York World
August 5, 1894

In the Biggest New York Tenement

Nellie Bly Spends the Two Hottest Days of the Year in the Largest "Double-Decker" in Town

3,532 People in the Block

One Family Occupying Only Three Rooms Has Eight Boarders and Lodgers

Sleeping on the Fire-Escapes

No Scenes of Disturbance or Disorder Among the Throngs of Over-Crowded Tenants

Strange Phases of Life in a Big City

An Interesting Chat with the Janitress of the Big Double-Decker Tenement-House

The most thickly populated spot on earth?
That is where I've spent the two hottest days we've had this summer—last Saturday and Sunday.
Three thousand five hundred and thirty-two people in one block! Actually in one block, Second Street on the south, Third street on the north, Avenue B on the west and Avenue C on the east.

No other block upon this earth, or same space of ground, is so densely populated. At least so it is claimed and, so far as statistics go, proved.

Thirty-five hundred and thirty-two people would make a good-sized town, and towns of smaller population have a mayor, a postmaster, constables, churches and bankers all of their own.

In one of the big tenements on this block, No. 228 Second Street, an apartment was hired for me, and on Saturday afternoon, when everybody else was taking a half-holiday and thanking heaven they were able to be out of the hot city over Sunday, I moved into my new abode.

My first intention was to dress very poorly, so as to look as much as possible like those with whom I was to live, but on second consideration, I decided that I had never found any excuse for the dirty poor, and that if I was to be poor it was not necessary to be also ragged and dirty. So I wore a plain gray skirt, a shirt-waist and a sailor hat, and in a small hand-satchel carried all the toilet articles I needed.

Although I was partly prepared for the crowded appearance of the block, still at the first sight of it I thought something must have occurred to cause such numbers of people to congregate in one spot.

The sidewalks were well-nigh impassable, but making my way along slowly, I soon found my number and, climbing over the people upon the dirty stoop, stood upon the threshold of a new and strange existence.

INTO THE TENEMENT

The hall was dirty and dark and forbidding. It seemed well-filled with children. I addressed a half-grown girl and asked for the housekeeper.

The girl shook her uncombed head; she could not speak English. I spoke to another, a smaller girl with thin, stringy hair and one solitary sleeveless slip between her and nudeness. I inquired for the janitress.

"The housekeeper's in there, if that's what you want," she answered, pointing to the first door in the hall.

The door was open. It opened into a very small kitchen. The kitchen opened into another room, a parlor, they call it, which was in front and was the only room that had direct light, it having a window facing the street. The kitchen also opened into a back room, a small, dark bedroom. There was a big stove in the middle of the kitchen and in the stove was a roaring fire, although the day was the hottest New York has been afflicted with in years.

I could not help glancing at the hot stove and from it to the small rooms on either side, and I wondered if some way could not be found to compel the builders of tenements to use some thought for the comfort of the unfortunate poor who must help to pay the 14 percent interest on the money invested. The kitchen built between the two living rooms may save money for the builders, but it means frightful discomfort for those who do not know what "a few weeks in the country" means.

'ARE YOU MRS. BROWN?'

They must eat, and naturally to eat must cook, and a fire in the stove makes the other rooms, especially the rear bedroom, insufferably hot. Seeing me standing there, the housekeeper left something she was looking after on the stove to come to me.

"An apartment was rented in this house for me, I believe," I said to her. And she looked at me with a smile. "I will take you up," she said, and she hurried into the rear room for the keys.

She led the way up the narrow, dirty stairs. I knew they were dirty, although I could see no more than I can at midnight when it is moonless and stormy; the vile stench made seeing superfluous.

With the instinct so exquisitely developed in dogs, I followed the housekeeper up the dark stairs, around a dark landing pregnant with the smothering smell of cabbage, and up a second flight. There she stopped and unlocked a door opening into a front apartment. They key was bent, and it took some time to accomplish this task; which being done, I walked into my new home.

Oh, the smell of it! It seemed to me that more than a million kinds of smell rushed out to embrace me in strong, if unseen, arms.

"Your furniture came, and I had 'em bring it here," she explained, pointing to a pile of stuff upon the floor. There it was, sure enough—furniture that had been bought for my use in the tenement.

IN NELLIE BLY'S ROOM

I glanced at the floor; it was black with filth left by the last tenant, and a sickening smell seemed to run from it.

The housekeeper next moved to the windows. "It ain't safe to leave 'em open when you go out," she explained. "There hasn't been anything taken yet, but it's better to be safe."

She opened the dust-covered windows as she spoke, and then she brought me one of my two new chairs.

"Will you scrub for me?" I asked, "and put things to place?"

She promised readily enough.

"I need odd jobs," she said.

Her arm was strong and willing, and in a short time the floor was as clean as it would come, and so hot was it that the wet boards dried almost as they were scrubbed. In fact, when she reached the doorside the entire floor was dry.

Then she set up the cot bed for me, put a chair at each of the front windows and a small table between them. My apartment consisted of three rooms, just like the housekeeper's; the front room, then the kitchen, in which there was running water, and the dark rear bedroom.

The rent was $10.50 a month and 75 cents deposit for the keys.

The rent is lower and the rooms are better than in the town of Pullman.

There was no way to have any cooking done in my apartment, so I went uptown for my dinner, returning to my new rooms about 9.30.

EVERYBODY ON THE STREET

Making my way through a task that looked impossible, I went to my room and, opening my window, leaned out on the fire-escape to watch the strange scene below.

The pavement on both sides of the street was filled with a mass of human beings. A woman sitting on the curb pushed a carriage containing two babies arm's length and back. Another woman held a fretful child in her arms and kept balancing from one foot to the other to keep it quiet. Four men clad in undershirts and trousers sat in chairs placed in a row on the curb. A woman was huddled down in a doorway, a shawl over her head and her face hidden between her knees. A group on a neighboring stoop were drinking turn about from a tin pail. An old man with an enormous beard and a long Dutch pipe stood smoking thoughtfully at the entrance to a dark hallway. A line of baby carriages, twelve in number, stood one after the other along the edge of the pavement, each carriage held one or two babies, and no one was in attendance.

Across the street, between the baker's and barber's front windows, was a soda fountain with three bottles of syrup, four long glasses and a mite of a showcase, a foot square, containing tobacco.

A bald-headed man sat hatless and coatless on a high stool behind the counter. Occasionally he sold a glass of soda to a woman or a child, or a package of cigarettes, with a picture and box of matches thrown in for a boy.

The strangest thing of all to me was the constant sound of voices which rose in one unbroken buzz from the street. Its like I never heard before, and so strange was it that I can find no words to describe it. It was one loud, continuous sound, much, I fancy, as would come from a mob advancing upon something. It was a distinct but distant sound, a constant buzz, with no distinguishable words. Within the tenement where I lived everything was comparatively still. It seemed to me that everybody must be out in the street.

After a while the housekeeper came to see me. She brought me a glass and pitcher and said she could buy the ice across the street.

SHE WAS A "WIDOW," TOO

She returned with the ice. She put it in a pitcher and ran water over it. The water was thick with a black sediment, which finally settled in the bottom of the pitcher. She placed the pitcher and a glass upon the mantel for my service. I noticed that she looked lonely, so I asked her to sit down.

"Are you all alone?" she asked me bluntly.

I had to account for the "Mrs.," which the man upon whom had fallen the duty of renting the room had credited to me, so I told her I was a widow.

"I'd never thought you were married, you look that young," she said, and then she signed.

"Are you a widow also?" I asked, for it seemed she wanted me to ask.

"Yes," she replied. "But my husband ain't dead yet," she added with an afterthought.

I looked at her curiously. "He can't live with me," she explained. "He's on Ward's Island; gone in his head, you know."

"Ah! That is sad," I say, sympathetically, and I see her dark eyes fill with tears.

Her eyes have the sad, appealing look of a dog, and I remember that is her hair is tossed and untidy, her little rooms are spotlessly clean, and I like her.

"He was a good man," she says, encouraged by my sympathy, "but he couldn't sleep nights. That's what was wrong with him. He never slept nights and his head ached so all the time. But he was such a good man."

"Could nothing be done to make him sleep?" I asked.

HUSBAND ON WARD'S ISLAND

"No; he was always taking everything, everything he read about or people told him about, but it didn't help, so the doctors said I'd better send him to Ward's Island. They said he'd get worse all the time, and when he couldn't work I couldn't keep him because they said it wasn't safe to leave him alone, so he had to go to the Island."

"Do you ever see him?"

"I go to see him every two weeks. I was there today, but he seemed bright today. 'Why do you keep me here?' he said to me, an' he cried. 'Wasn't I always a good man to you? Won't you take me home?'

"That's what makes it hard," she said with quivering lips. "He was a good man to me always and to the children. So kind and quiet! He never said a cross word, even when his poor head ached so."

"Is there no hope for his recovery?" I asked.

"No; the doctors say he has—I don't know what you call it; his brain is all soft. He'll get worse all the time, but they say he can live to be an old man; outlive me, for he won't be working and I will. I never had to work hard when he was with me. He was such a good man! That's what makes it hard."

She told me she had five children, the youngest about two and the eldest about ten.

"I worked hard, took in washing and went out cleaning and everything, but I couldn't get enough to keep them, so I had to give the three oldest ones to the home. They'll be kept there till they're sixteen an' I can see them once a month."

MAKING BOTH ENDS MEET

"It's better for them," she added, as if to assure me of her rightful intentions. "It keeps them off the street, an' my man wouldn't have liked them to grow up in the streets, an' they'll get a schooling."

"Yes; I should think they are much better off. How do you keep yourself now, and your two little ones?"

"I get my rent free for taking care of this house," she replied. "That's a good saving. Then I do washings or any work I can get. Work has been scarce for a year now, but I've had two boarders; two young ladies. They work in a cloak factory and they make $5 a week. I charge them $2.50 each for their board and wash. But they are going to leave Monday. The one is getting married and the other is going with her. I don't know what I'll do then."

A child came running upstairs for the housekeeper.

"The new people are down there," the child said, and the housekeeper said she must go.

"It's a newly married couple that's movin' in tonight," she explained.

"Rather a large move, isn't it?" I asked.

"Yes; but he wanted to help with it after his work," she said. "I left the lights burning in the hall because they were coming. I always put them out at 10."

Midnight, and I sat at my window watching the crowd below.

MIDNIGHT NOISES AND SIGHTS

The boys on the trucks made attempts to sing; children still darted hither and thither; men and women clustered on the sidewalks; that strange buzz of life was just as loud as ever.

Will they never go to bed? I wondered.

The noise, that unearthly buzz, exhausted me. I felt that I needed sleep and that I would be unable to get any. The bad odors from the street and house made my head ache.

Then lights came in a few of the windows opposite and men and women and children, each in a single undergarment, moved around as if making ready for bed. There was no attempt to close the shutters or leave down the blinds.

I lay down upon my cot and tried to sleep. People came up and went downstairs, stumbling in the dark or striking matches against the wall to give them light. The newly wedded couple below me were hammering their furniture together. The baby in the apartment overhead was crying lustily.

I may have slept five minutes; it couldn't have been longer. The baby overhead screamed so lustily and angrily that I felt half inclined to go up to see what was wrong with it. Somewhere else in the house I could hear a baby-carriage being wheeled back and forth on the bare floor to keep some child quiet.

I got a book and read.

THE FIRE-ESCAPE FOR BEDS

At 2 o'clock I went to my window. The bald-headed, hatless and coatless man at the soda-fountain was just selling a strawberry soda to a little girl who had to get on her tiptoes to reach the top of the counter. The men and boys were no longer attempting to sing, but were lying in a dark mass in the bottom of the wagons. The line of baby carriages had disappeared. One woman on the pavement beneath my window sat upright on a chair and kept a baby-carriage in constant motion with her foot.

I noticed a little dark heap of something on the fire-escape near my window. I could have put out my hand and touched it, but I didn't.

I merely watched it. Presently above the bundle of rags I saw a little curly head toss restlessly. A little girl was sleeping there.

I leaned out of the window and looked about. Beneath my fire-escape lay a man in his underclothes; a little beyond him slept a woman and child.

Because of the intervening bedclothing I could not see those upon the fire-escapes above, but I could get a view of the other side of the block and every fire-escape was transformed into a bed. The buzzing in the street never ceased; fewer people were moving about, though just as many as ever were sitting around as if they meant to spend the night where they were.

It was now nearly 3 o'clock in the morning. I went back to my cot so sleepy that I felt I should no longer mind the frightful heat, the smell and noise. Notwithstanding my weariness I laughed to find that the reporter who had been sent to buy my necessary household articles had only bought me one bedcover. It was a heavy woolen blanket!

And it was the hottest night in six years! And what was infinitely worse, to protect myself from mosquitoes I had to cover up!

I was so miserable and uncomfortable that I went to

sleep, and when I woke again two babies, in place of one, were scratching matches against my door.

I went to the window and found little change in the street below. The woman still sat stiffly upright in a chair, rolling her baby carriage with her foot, and the bald man at the soda fountain was sitting upon his high stool with folded arms and motionless.

Then a milk wagon rattled up to a shop opposite, and the driver deftly tossed five filled cans on the pavement and five empty cans into his wagon. Then he yelled to the storekeeper and rattled the garden door; the other wasn't closed.

This Mr. Sneider was holding the screen door open as the milkman whirled the cans inside. The quickness with which Sneider made his appearance proved that he had not undressed to go to bed. Nor did he return for a second snooze. He opened up shop at once, and as customers had not appeared, came out and sat before his open door.

I went to my cot again. When I woke the babies were still crying upstairs and the mosquitoes had disappeared, but their places were taken by busy, buzzing flies. I looked out upon the street. The soda-fountain man was still motionless on his high stool and the woman still sat by her baby carriage. A new woman had appeared. She was pacing up and down the pavement for the matter of ten feet, with a child in her arms. The child's face in the early daylight wore the color of death.

The people still slept on the fire-escapes, but the men had disappeared from the wagons, curbs and door-stoops.

The heat and the constant noise had worn me out. The air in my room was stifling and had a heavy, vile smell. Still, I went to sleep and slept on until 8 o'clock.

ONLY ONE SUNDAY PAPER

I went out for breakfast and came back to my post of duty a few hours later.

I found the strange block once again jammed with people. All the little shops, the butcher, the baker, the coal dealer and ice-man, the candy shops and the soda fountain, were wide open, doing business just as if it were a weekday.

I noticed that in the entire block only one man had a Sunday newspaper. No one else read. I also noticed that families had no particular hour for meals and that there was no ceremony about eating together. I also noticed that they mostly ate something with a spoon out of a bowl.

Just opposite three children were sleeping on a fire-escape, and above them two men in their under-clothing and bare feet took turns at drinking out of a broken pitcher, and on the fire-escape, still above them, a little boy of bilious yellow, clad only in a short shirt, kept crying to some boys in the street below, and never getting a reply: "Do you want a pussy-cat? Do you want a pussy-cat?"

As the day advanced the line of baby-carriages made its appearance upon the pavement, increasing steadily with the shade. The soda-water man did a pretty good business and the ice-man had constant customers. In fact, all the shopkeepers, including the barber, who, like the other men, wore only his undershirt and trousers, did a good, steady business.

I saw no fights and no disorder all the time I was there and I saw a policeman upon the block only once. The nearest approach to trouble was with an amateur baseball team who were howling themselves hoarse and bumping into everything in their limited field in the street.

At last the ball hit a small occupant of a carriage in the baby-carriage line, and a big, fat, dirty man with a pipe in his mouth yelled lustily for the baker's wife, and the baby squalled like a young Indian. The baker's wife ran out, wrapping up some cakes as she ran, and the baker, with his hands and arms covered with flour, came up out of the basement. Everybody clustered around the baby and the barker barber walked off in triumph with the ball, shaking his fist at the boys when they yelled "Hi, there!" to throw it back.

A LITTLE BOY VISITOR

A timid knock came upon my door, and I opened it to find there a pretty little boy in a white waist, and with his hair just as nicely brushed as it could be. He had big, trusting blue eyes, and he looked up at me and smiled, saying, pityingly, "Ain't you lonesome?"

I told him I was, a little bit, because I didn't want him to think I didn't want to see him, and I asked him in and gave him a chair at the window.

His mother, who proved to be my neighbor in the rear, followed him in to explain that the child knew I was alone and thought he would come in to cheer me up.

Then I talked with the mother. She told me the house was the kind known as a "double-decker tenement," and that there were four apartments to a floor, two front and two rear, of three rooms each.

She also told me that the largest family in the house numbered eleven, all of whom lived in three small rooms. She said that nearly all the people in the house kept boarders, and that there were three empty apartments at present and fewer people in the house than usual.

117 PERSONS UNDER ONE ROOF

We counted the number of persons under the one roof.

There were, by actual count, one hundred and seventeen people!

The largest family numbered eleven. The smallest was my own.

The family that lived above me have twins. It was the twins that cried all night—sometimes solos, sometimes duets. The woman who sat on the pavement all night did so because her child is very ill and the night air is better for it than that of the hot, stifling rooms.

Her son and my little visitor had been at death's door with diphtheria four weeks ago. For eight days and nights she sat without sleep or rest by his bedside, and then the doctor who told her to prepare for the worst at 10.30 one night shook hands with her at 6 and told her the little chap had "pulled through."

She hadn't cried before, but she cried then and cried herself to sleep. Her husband couldn't sit up at night, because he had to work to provide food for them. The husband is a clerk in a hat store and gets $10 a week. He works from 7.30 until 10.30 every day, Sundays as well as week days.

Since her boy got well, four weeks ago, two other children had died in the house, and a man, the father of the eleven children. He died very suddenly of inflammation of the brain. Thirteen of them lived in the three small rooms.

When he was dying, she told me, the eleven children and the wife gathered around the bed and cried so loud and went on so that he couldn't die; they wouldn't let him. He was dead, she declared, but their wild lamentations made him come back to life.

Then a friend came in and said: "You must go away; he can't die if you don't." And though it was because he was dying they cried so, yet they went out and gave him the chance. I thought if I had been one of the eleven and crying would have kept my father alive, nothing would have induced me to stop, but I didn't tell her my thoughts.

They weren't gone five minutes, she added, until the poor man closed his eyes, sighed gently and was dead. He could die when they didn't cry.

The New York World
December 17, 1894

In Trinity's Tenements

Nellie Bly Visits Many Miserable Homes Owned by That Corporation

Wretchedness and Squalor

Outrageous Rents for Filthy Dens in Foul, Rickety, Leaky, Unsanitary Hovels

Death, Too, Lurks in Many of Them

You Will Learn Here Something About the Real Life of Dismal New York

  Trinity! Meaning the Father, the Son and the Holy Ghost. Embracing everything that means love, mercy, justice, charity.
  The Trinity Corporation is rich beyond the dreams of avarice. It was within its power to solve the tenement-house question, to use its vast wealth to benefit the poor, but what has it done?
  I will tell you.
  They have been spending thousands of dollars to celebrate Christmas, ordering masses of green foliage and holly and mistletoe to delight the eye, and a special musical programme to charm the ear, while I have been visiting their poor tenants in their miserable tenements.
  I happened by chance to go first to No. 4 Grand Street. I did not know the part of the city in which the Trinity property is

mainly located, and when the Grand Street car suddenly swung around a corner and the conductor pointed down a street that stopped abruptly and went nowhere, as the end, or rather the beginning, of Grand Street, I was somewhat surprised.

I alighted and walked down the block, looking closely at the houses. They were small red brick houses, presenting rather a respectable appearance for a poor locality. Near the end of the street I saw a small, dilapidated, two-story frame and attic.

THE FIRST GLIMPSE OF SQUALOR

An empty wagon stood in the street and an ash can, overflowing and vile-smelling, was on the shaky frame stoop. There was no number upon the house, and though some inner instinct told me it was the one for which I searched, still I could scarcely believe it. But on looking closer I saw a badly made figure 4 in chalk upon the dirty door.

There was no knob with which to fasten the door, so I entered and found myself in a dark, dirty and ill-smelling hall. The floor was not carpeted, but it certainly was not bare. A layer of filth, the accumulation doubtless of months, covered it.

A knock upon the two doors leading to the rooms on the first floor was not answered, so I went up a flight of rickety stairs, four one way, then a sharp turn and three the other, and I was on a landing from which opened two doors.

I knocked upon the one nearest. It was opened by a little, clean-faced old woman, bent in form and sad of countenance. I told her briefly that I was looking at the Trinity tenements, and with her permission, would like to see her rooms.

The door was opened wide and I was invited to enter. I am used to tenements and sights of poverty, but the picture of misery that confronted me stirred me deeply.

The room was small, about one and a half times the width of a single bed, and one and a quarter times the length. A single bed that crossed two windows just managed to leave space enough for the door to open. At the end of the room and the foot of the bed was a small cook stove. Two wooden chairs, one with the bottom split and the other without a back, and a rickety table completed the furniture. A few ragged clothes hung upon the door, a wooden bucket containing water sat on the floor, and one cup, one plate, a dish and two knives were on the table.

That was all the room contained except three unhappy people—the little old woman, her daughter and her son-in-law, who lay upon the dirty bed propped up against the headboard, for pillow he had none. His face was thin and pale, and his breathing was loud and laborious.

"Are you ill?" I asked rather foolishly, for my eyes had answered my question.

"Yes," he replied slowly, and in a husky voice, "I had two hemorrhages Monday, and I'm feeling pretty bad."

I asked him questions, and he told me his story modestly and without complaint. He is a glass packer, but has been out of work for many months, except such odd jobs as he could obtain. Once he carried sample cases for a Maiden Lane jewelry drummer. It was during the very cold and wet weather we had a few weeks since. The cases weighed 106 pounds and he carried them, drenched to the skin and shivering with the cold, to Harlem.

ONE TENANT'S MISERY

That brought on his first sickness. Two weeks ago he got work at No. 72 Murray Street at his trade. On Monday, as he left work he had the hemorrhages, and doubtless by the time he is able to go back to work the work will be over for the season, as it is ended when Trinity rings in the New Year.

Still, the man must have shelter while he lives. And although the rain comes in the windows, which are pasted over with paper to do the service of glass, his room is infinitely better than the streets. Cook, eat and sleep in it, for the outrageous price of $2 a week.

There are eight apartments (so called) in the building. One in the basement, consisting of two rooms, for which the charge is $5 a week. The basement is dark, filthy and damp. On the first floor the price for the front room is $2.50 a week and $3 for the rear room. The prices are the same on the second floor, and the hall room is $1.25. In the attic are two pens called rooms for which the tenants pay $6 a month. The only water is in the yard, a small space, filthy, ill-smelling and filled with pools of stagnant water. The toilet, one for the entire house, has no roof and its floor is unsafe. It stands within a foot of the hydrant.

The tenants of the first floor and the basement were out, but on the floor where I found the sick man I saw in the front room an old woman partially paralyzed.

The plaster in the corner of her room was wet where the rain comes through the side of the house. In some places the plastering had fallen down and in all places it was filthy dirty. The floor was warped and uneven.

This old woman is supported by her daughter, a ragpicker who works from 7 A.M. until 6 P.M. for $4 a week, and then, owing to the dull times, is laid off more than half the week.

The hall-room tenant was out, so I felt my way up a twisting and dark stair, so narrow that two persons could not pass on it, and so twisted that I felt every moment as if I would tumble down.

First at the head of five or more steps was a door, a few boards roughly pounded together and put on hinges. It had no knob. No door in the house had. The sick man's had a nail fastened to a string. Stumbling on a few steps with my head bumping against the rafters, I hit against another door which flies open at my touch and shows me a low and narrow passage with a window at the end, from which a woman is hanging clothes on a line.

She was a nice little French woman, very tidy. Her room, if I can call it such, was merely a little space under the roof.

At one side, where the roof ran up to the rafter, the height was probably five feet. At the other side, where it sloped down, one couldn't have found space between the roof and the floor to tack carpets. It was practically a case of making two ends meet—the roof and the floor of a house.

A QUAINT ATTIC PICTURE

There was one window in the place. It was the kind that is cut in the roof and built to stand out. To reach it one would have had to crawl across the single bed, which took all the space, except what was occupied by the wee cook-stove.

It was the smallest place I ever saw for two human beings to live in. But the little French woman had it as clean as a combination of soap, water and hard work can make it, and it wasn't her fault that the sickly geranium on the window-sill found it always too warm or too cold for health.

As I did not believe in judging the Trinity Corporation by their houses in one street, I decided to make a jump and see if I could not find better ones.

I went to Clarke Street and I saw some good buildings that I thought were Trinity property, but when I inquired, I found that Trinity owned the ground, but lease-holders owned the buildings. I was told if I would go further up the street I would find four houses rented by Trinity. They were Nos. 9, 21-1/2, 26 and 28, the oldest, most dilapidated and disgraceful looking houses in the street.

No. 9 is a frame tenement of three stories. It is ready to fall down. The first floor is occupied by a toy and candy shop and is only one room deep. The proprietor lives on the floor above his shop and rents out the top floor for $6 a month. The water is in the back yard, a wet, dirty place, into which the sun never comes. There used to be a frame tenement in the rear, but the Health Board made the Trinity Corporation pull it down.

The floor in the house is anything but on the dead level, and even a short person could without the slightest difficulty touch the ceiling. For this the toy man pays $25 a month, and he thinks it's not very high, although he has to keep eight black and white cats and one Skye terrier to keep the rats from carrying away his stock.

I went next to No. 28 Clarke Street. It is an old frame that bears its misery on its face.

In the basement, where the floor looks like the deck of

a ship in a heavy sea, I found a nice old Italian cobbler, with his wife and two children. The old couple could not speak English, but their little boy, with the ideal face of a poet, answered all my questions promptly, intelligently and politely.

THEY HELP SWELL THE FUND

His father sometimes didn't earn a dollar in a whole month, he said, but he had two other brothers, one a little bigger than him, who "made ties" in South Fifth Avenue. The biggest brother had had no work for a long time, but the other brother got $2 a week for stamping the name on "the ties." His sister worked on "coats," for which she got $3 a week.

The combined income, $5, had to keep them and pay their rent, $10 a month. Their rooms are three-quarters under the ground and flat upon it.

There is the front and back room, and between is a dark space divided by the passage which connects the two rooms. This dark space holds on either side two beds, which touch the wall at the head and at the foot.

The floor is warped and the walls are damp, but still Trinity charges $10 a month for the place.

On the first floor of the house is the same arrangement of rooms, except that the width of the dirty hall is taken from them.

For this front and back room, with the dark space between that will hold two beds, the family pays $14 a month. The floor in these rooms is worn out, has been many years, but Trinity will not repair it and the family have been compelled to do so themselves.

"The Trinity carpenter said that the Trinity Corporation was like a woman," observed the girl I found in these rooms. "If she found a small hole she would patch it, but when it gets to be a big one she thinks it's useless to do anything and so she lets it go."

Of course there are many places uptown where for $14 a month this family could hire a four- or six- room flat, where they would have a bath, range and running water. But they cannot live uptown. Their work is downtown, and they must be near it. The two sons drive trucks when they have work, and the daughter works at feathers, and they together keep the father and mother.

By going up dirty and uncertain stairs, stairs that aren't mates, or even any relation to each other, I found on the second floor an Italian family that had lived there for twenty-six years. Their rooms corresponded with those below which I have already described. There are no accommodations whatever, unless running water in the hall is considered by Trinity a modern improvement. For these four rooms the family pays $12.50, and the rent has never been reduced in the twenty-six years, although the house has been growing older and poorer all the while.

And never until this month has the family been compelled to ask the wealthy Trinity Corporation to wait for its rent, the woman told me proudly, and she added that they had been very nice about it.

Considering that they have paid in rent the entire price of the house, lacking only $6.50, one would suppose the agent might be "nice" about waiting a day or two.

And that is the only thing I found in all my investigation that was "nice" about the Trinity Corporation.

A CRIB UNDER THE EAVES

On the top floor, if you could ever summon up enough courage to feel your way through blinding darkness to it, you will find a landing with four doors facing each other in space literally not large enough to turn around in.

The one door is from the stairs; the others open into "apartments." Had I not been told that people lived there I should certainly never have suspected it and never have found them.

As it was I pounded upon the wood I felt in the darkness and a man opened a door and reluctantly admitted me to his home

I have heard of birds that build their nests under the eaves of houses, but I never knew human beings to have homes there until I visited Trinity's tenements.

This man's room was like the one I saw at No. 4 Grand Street, only worse. It was smaller and poorer.

A bed stood under the slanting roof at one side; a crib shared the other side with a small stove. Between them was the space of about two feet. It was occupied by a cradle, rather cleverly made of a soap-box, pivoted at either end to two upright pieces of wood. It was certainly not a swinging brass bed, as one sees in the shop windows, but it was built in that style.

The man and I stood at the door. Of course, it was practically impossible to enter the room, or whatever one may call it. We could stand where we were because that happened to be the highest place in the roof, but even a wee baby mouse couldn't crawl where the roof met the floor.

Still that man, his wife and three children eat, sleep and live in that place. He has not been able to work for many months because he has heart disease, but he can mind the children while his wife goes out to get what work she can—washing, scrubbing, anything—to help make up $4,50 a month so the wealthy and charitable Trinity Corporation will permit them to go on living under the eaves.

Trinity has three other "apartments" on this "floor." They are all like the one I saw, so the man said. One is occupied by an old man and woman, who go out to work every day, and the other is occupied by an old man, who works all day, but, so far as is known, is absolutely alone in the world.

They pay $4.50 for each apartment, which means $13.50 for the floor; $12.50 for the floor below, $14 for the first floor and $10 for the basement, makes in all $50 a month for the miserable old tenement, which is estimated by Trinity as being worth $4,500.

Pretty comfortable interest on their money.

After that I visited a number of Trinity houses. At first I went to some that looked respectable and comfortable, thinking to be able to write that all was not black, but that the wealthy corporation had good as well as miserable buildings for their tenants.

But I was sadly disappointed. Although I spent three days looking after their dwellings in a totally unbiased and conscientious manner, I must state with regret that I soon learned one unmistakable fact:

If a house was painted and had a comfortable look from the outside, it was a Trinity leasehold, and its appearance was totally due to the owner.

On the other hand, if the house was the most dilapidated and disreputable-looking in the entire block, it was owned and rented solely by the Trinity corporation.

Nor did I visit houses in one street alone and base my judgment on them, but made my tour as varied as possible among the houses owned by Trinity in Greenwich Village.

At No. 82 Vandam Street I found a miserable two-story and attic frame building, with a collection of poor but interesting tenants.

Going down several steps into a basement that is almost entirely below the street, I found a neat housewife, as I judged by the tidy curtains at the windows.

She had only two rooms, the front one being a kitchen, dining-room and bedroom, and a rear cellar room, the air of which gave me a chill, serving as second bedroom and containing two beds, which left a space scarcely a foot in width between them.

The poor rooms were as neat as hard work could make them, and the woman was herself as clean as a new pin.

She was such a nice, motherly old lady; the kind that wins one's heart by a simple glance at her sweet face and white hair, and mild eyes that look straight at one and whose frankness shows that in their whole life they had never one wicked thought or deed to conceal.

I found her in the back yard, vainly trying to pile some good earth around the roots of a tree that had managed to live a starved existence in that poor locality. I love trees as much as I love all dumb animals, and so I naturally felt my heart go out to the dear old English woman.

"Certainly, miss, you may see my rooms," she said in reply to my inquiry, never asking my object.

And when I had seen them, and she told me the rent--$5.50 a month—and I had involuntarily said something about the outrageous price, she said quietly:

ENGLISH RENTS CHEAPER

"Do you think that much, miss? I have been told that was low rent for America. We have lived here three years, ever since we came over, and I had no way to know what rent was just."

"How does your rent compare with your rent in England," I asked anxiously.

"Well, miss," she answered, with a smile, "it is vastly different. I only know about Liverpool, where we always lived. We had a nice house there with six rooms; a better house in all, miss, than this, and with it we had a nice garden. For it we paid six six a week, for, you know, miss, we pay our rent by the week there instead of by the month as we do here."

I asked her how much "six six" was in our money, and she said she thought it was about $1.00.

In this family are the husband and wife, one boy, who "follows the sea," it being also the father's trade; two girls and an orphaned niece about fourteen years old. The husband has been unable to work for fifteen weeks owing to a sore leg. One girl lives out, but has no place at present, and the other earns $3.50 a week in a biscuit factory.

There is one other member of the family, a very dear one. It is a green parrot with a black bill and yellow spot at the back of his neck. He calls the nice old lady "Mamma!", whistles beautifully and sings with a decided Cockney accent "After the Ball is Over."

The floor above this interesting family is divided into two apartments, consisting of two small rooms each. The front rents for $8 a month and the back for $5.50. I did not see either, as the families were out.

From the yard one can walk up a flight of some ten or fifteen stairs to the second floor. It is also divided into two apartments. The front rooms are occupied by a woman whose husband goes to sea. She never speaks to any of the neighbors and has never been known to open her door in reply to any knock. However, all the neighbors know that she pays $7 a month for her rooms.

A little woman with a small baby in her arms admitted me to the rear rooms. The first room is small, and plumes on the hat of a medium-sized woman would touch the ceiling.

The room was comfortably furnished, for the family once lived amid better surroundings. The husband was a longshoreman, or, rather, the employer of longshoremen, a sober, industrious and saving workman. His wife was a neat and saving housekeeper, but exposure to all kinds of weather did its work, and five years ago the husband began to lose his strength.

He held out as long as he could, but the sickness was stronger than he, and now for ten months he has been unable to move from his bed, a victim of consumption.

DYING IN MISERY

There he lay, a mass of bones covered with a yellow skin. His soul seemed already to have gone beyond, for his eyes were dull and unseeing, giving me the same look of utter unconsciousness that he cast upon his wife and child.

"I have five children," the woman told me. "The eldest, a girl not yet sixteen, works in a laundry, for which she gets $4 a week. The boy next to her in age is an errand boy and is paid $3 a week. The boy next is at school and the one still younger you see out there in the yard cutting wood for me. The baby (the one in her arms) is not yet ten months old."

The family lives upon the $7 weekly income and pays $7 a month for their miserable rooms.

I was awfully glad there were three boys. They have to sleep in that bed on the boarded balcony. It must be dreadfully cold, and if it wasn't that there are three boys and that they have to sleep in a single bed, they would never be able to keep warm. And I am positive Trinity would not give them burial room if they froze to death.

They have to crawl over the foot of the bed to get in. I wonder if they ever laugh, and if they rush to see who'll get in first, and if they ever tumble each other over the footboard! Or I wonder if the poor little errand boy is too tired to laugh and play, and if the mother makes the other boys keep still so he can rest, that he may be able to work like a grown man and bring home his poor little $3 every Saturday to help pay the rent to Trinity!

I went up the stairs to the attic. There I found a young widow with two small children. She proved to be one of my human birds, whose nest is under the eaves.

LEAKS! ALWAYS LEAKS!

The roof is high at one side and meets the floor at the other. It has never been boarded over, and the rafters are all black and the light of day shows through the crevices. A stove is fastened to a chimney that goes zig-zag, so that, while it starts near the side of the house, it comes out of the roof at the middle.

When it rains the water comes through on the floor, but the widow smiles as she says it can't hurt her carpet. She has some bits of worn oil-cloth, but water doesn't hurt them. Sometimes the rain drowns out her kitchen fire and that makes her sorry, and when I showed her how wet and damp her walls were she said I must remember that the house must be very old!

She has to go to the yard for the water, as must every other tenant in the house. At night the halls are dark, but in the daytime anyone would note how wonderfully clean and tidy the tenants keep them.

For this attic the widow pays Trinity $5.50. She does not complain, nor do any of the others.

I do say, in all my experience among tenements, I never found poorer tenements or better tenants. They are all extremely poor, but they are respectable, clean, and not of the whining, begging class.

An inexperienced person is apt to visit tenements and consider people poor according to their filth. Where they find clean rooms and people they are most likely to fail to note the poverty.

Among the poor in New York I never found as clean and respectable a class as I did in Greenwich Village, though Trinity deserves no credit for that.

I next went to No. 88 Charlton Street, and I never found a New York tenement so poor. It is a miserable old frame that has stood so many years that it's too tired to hold up much longer.

On the ground floor is a tailor shop, where a lot of men and women, who pretended not to understand English, sat sewing.

Through the low hall, from which the damp and dirty plastering is hanging, I went up the creaky and unsafe stairs to the landing on the second floor, where I knocked in the darkness until a ragged woman opened a door and let me enter.

She was a poor, miserable, unhappy-looking creature, and was vainly endeavoring to clean a place that can never be made clean.

I never saw walls and ceilings in such a state of filth and dilapidation.

She had this room and one inside that was perfectly dark and had the damp smell of a cellar. The woman made a light and showed me the floor and walls, but the smell was so intense that I asked her a few hurried questions and went away.

A MISERABLE PEN, THIS

Her husband is at sea, and she has been compelled to put her two boys in a Catholic home. Her girl, not yet sixteen years old, earns $4 a week in the Empire laundry, and on that they live, unless she happens to get a day's scrubbing.

She pointed to a hole in the ceiling where the plastering had fallen down, and she told me that she paid $8 a month for the miserable pen.

"I think it's a little too much rent," she said, timidly, "I don't think it's worth more than seven. The halls are dark and filthy, and you should see the yard! We have to carry our water up from it, and it's awful. I do think the rent's too much. It's all poor people can do to pay it."

I asked her what she knew about the Trinity Corporation—what it meant.

"They're landlords, that's all I know," she answered, which amused me very much.

Next door I found a man and two small and very dirty children in two rooms that beggar description. The filthy and falling walls, the uneven and broken floor, and glassless windows, I leave to the merciful imagination of my readers, who, if curiosity is strong enough, can visit the place.

When I spoke to the tall, dirty man he set the baby he held in his arms down on the floor, and pointing to his mouth, made signs that he was dumb. I wrote on a bit of paper that I was looking at Trinity's tenements, and asked him how much rent he paid. He wrote in reply: "Eight dollars a month."

I shrugged my shoulders in disgust, and he held up his hands pitifully and helplessly.

I then wrote the following questions, to which he wrote the replies.

"How many children have you?"
"Three."
"Can you work at anything?"
"I am a longshoreman. No work."
"Does your wife work?"
"She is out peddling lace."

RICKETY AND FOUL-SMELLING

Just then a pretty little girl not more than five years old came in with a loaf of bread under her arms. She said the man was her father, that her mother talked to him with her fingers, but she couldn't say much to him. She tried, moving her lips and her little thin arms, but he failed to understand her.

At No. 35 Watts Street I found the front house is rented by a respectable widow, who pays Trinity $40 for it and sublets to tenants.

I also learned by this time that many of the Trinity houses are like the corporation—they present a good front.

Many of their old houses have a brick front, which, being painted, is apt to make a casual observer consider the houses very comfortable at a glance at the miserable frame rears dispelled this delusion.

The rear of No. 35 Watts Street is worse even than the yard house back of it, though that is bad enough, It is the only yard house the Fire Commissioners left standing. A short time ago every one of Trinity's houses had houses in the rear.

In this rear house are two apartments on one side, consisting of two wee cubby-holes, for which the family on the first floor pay $6 a month and the one on the second floor pay $9. On the next side the apartment on the first floor consists of one room, for which $5 is paid, and on the second and top floor is a room the shape of a flatiron, and scarcely larger, with a small adjoining closet that Trinity calls "room," for which $5 is paid also.

MISERY PAYS THE TOLL

The walls and plastering are in a frightful condition. The water is in the yard.

The front and rear houses are estimated at $6,000. The rent collected by Trinity for the same is $85 per month.

No. 259 Houston Street is estimated at $5,000 value. It is one of a long row of Trinity houses, but all the others are leased to tenants who sublet. No. 259 has always been leased, too, but the policeman who had it last said he could not make it pay and gave it up.

Two nice old women with snow-white hair live in the basement. They have been tenants of Trinity for the last thirty years. They keep their two basement rooms spotlessly clean and tidy, and it is entirely due to them that the paper on the wall is new and clean and that the ceiling, just an inch or so above our heads, is whitewashed.

But they cannot prevent the floor from being on the slide, nor can they stop the green mould from coming on the damp walls in the hall, or the green moss from covering the stones in the areaway.

When it rains the water forms in deep pools in the areaway and they have to dip it out, but still Trinity charges them $5 a month for living there.

The first floor has a front and a back room, with two dark rooms between, for which Trinity receives $15 a month. Eighteen dollars a month they get for the second, and the top is divided into two apartments, consisting of two rooms each, for which Trinity receives $9 from each family.

The widow in the rear top rooms is to be dispossessed. She has a boy who used to earn something by "putting in" coal, but he's been in the hospital for weeks now with spinal trouble. She has two girls. One scarcely twelve was a nurse in some family, but she is homesick. The other girl, a tall, thin, underfed soul, who was frying some foul-smelling fish, said she worked in a candy factory for four years. She used to earn as much as $4.50 a week, but work got slack and slacker, and now she has none at all.

That makes $60 a month Trinity receives on a $5,000 house. The majority of the other homes in the block are leased yearly for $66 a month.

I called at scores of other houses, but as the story of them is the same as that already told of others, I shall not enter into a description of each one. In the rear of No. 12 Clarkson Street I found some interesting people. I first looked at the dirty yard and cellar, there being pools of water standing in each.

Then I went in to see the tenement. It and the adjoining one, No. 10, have four floors, with two families to a floor. The halls are narrow, dirty and dark, and the apartments consist of one front room and one small pen dignified by the name of bedroom. Both houses are as filthy and damp as can be imagined, and there is much sickness among the tenants.

The same scale of outrageous prices are charged. For the ground floor $10, $5 for each apartment; $11, or $5.50 each for the second and third floors, and $9, or $4.50 each, for the top floor.

THE CEILING IS FALLING

On the second floor I found a woman who has lived there for seventeen years next June. Eight years ago her husband died and left her four children to provide for.

She succeeded beautifully. There is no water in the house, but every day of her life this energetic woman carried enough water up from the yard to do a washing. The clothes she had to dry in the one room in which they lived, as the bed fills the other.

Now she does not labor so hard, for one girl lives out, another is a "saleslady" (the mother tells me with pride) and the boy is in a grocery, leaving the little girl at home with her good mother.

In all these seventeen years Trinity has never done any repairing for their worthy widow tenant. Once she papered the rooms herself, but they are in very bad order now, and the ceiling is coming down. The first year after she moved in Trinity reduced the rent to $5, but the next year it was raised again to $5.50, and has remained at that ever since.

In one apartment on the top floor I found a tall, sickly looking man frying fish. A shapeless woman with an appealing look upon her face sat watching him.

He showed me the rooms, keeping a careful eye on the fish meanwhile, so that it might not burn. The walls in the bedroom were wet and the roof leaked in the other room.

The man told me that he used to be a boilermaker in the navy-yard, but his health failed and he was unable to work at his trade and was forced to do odd jobs when his health permitted. He has just returned from ten weeks spent in St. Vincent's Hospital.

I asked him what was wrong, and the shapeless woman in the chair answered for him.

"He's got the dropsy, poor dear," she said, the tears rolling over her cheeks, "an' they took twenty-six quarts of water from him in the hospital. I'm dying with the same thing. Look at my hands and legs! See, they ain't any shape to them. I sit here all the time waiting to die. I can't lie down in bed, 'cause I choke. An' I haven't a friend in the world. I'm no kin of his, but him an' his wife took me in. They're good, and they deserve better luck than sickness."

I asked the man how they managed to exist, and he said his wife worked in Gordon & Dilworth's factory for seven cents an hour. She works ten hours a day, which means 70 cents, and would gladly work longer if her strength permitted.

The man told me also that when he moved in the rooms were so filthy that he had almost concluded not to take them, but the Trinity agents said if he would clean them himself they would allow him for it. But they have never done so, though he papered and whitewashed. They have even refused to pay for the lime.

On the same floor with him is a widow whose sole support is a boy who earns $5 a week in a cracker factory. The woman has "rheumatics so bad she can't touch the floor."

Her daughter, about fourteen years old, does the housework. The widow says she has lived there for fifteen years and has never owed Trinity until this month. She is back one dollar, and she sent her daughter out to pawn some clothes so she can pay that.

And this is only part of my experiences among the Trinity tenements.

Sources

Nellie Bly Online
http://www.nellieblyonline.com/herwriting

Undercover Reporting: Deception for Journalism's Sake: A Database
http://dlib.nyu.edu/undercover/nellie-bly-new-york-world-0

The Library of Congress: Nellie Bly: Online Resources
http://www.loc.gov/rr/program/bib/bly/

Further Reading

Beasly, Maurine H. and Sheila J. Gibbons. *Taking Their Place: A Documentary History of Women and Journalism.* Strata Publishing, 2002.

Bly, Nellie; Jean Marie Lutes (ed.) and Maureen Corrigan. *Around the World in Seventy-Two Days and Other Writings.* Penguin Classics, 2014.

Brian, Denis. *Pulitzer: A Life.* John J. Wiley, 2001.

Burrows, Edwin G. and Mike Wallace. *Gotham: A History of New York City to 1898.* Oxford University Press, 2000.

Daly, Christopher B. *Covering America: A Narrative History of a Nation's Journalism.* University of Massachusetts Press, 2012.

Douglas, George H. *The Golden Age of the Newspaper.* Greenwood, 1999.

Ellis, Edward Robb. *The Epic of New York City: A Narrative History.* Basic Books, 2004.

Kroeger, Brooke. *Nellie Bly: Daredevil, Feminist, Reporter.* Three Rivers Press, 1995.

Morris, James McGrath. *Pulitzer: A Life in Politics, Print and Power.* Harper, 2010.

Okker, Patricia. *Our Sister Editors: Sarah J. Hale and the Tradition of Nineteenth-Century American Women Editors.* University of Georgia Press, 2008.

Riis, Jacob. *How the Other Half Lives: Studies Among the Tenements of New York.* Dover Publications, 1971.

Roggenkamp, Karen. *Narrating The News: New Journalism And Literary Genre In Late Nineteenth-Century American Newspapers And Fiction.* Kent State University Press, 2005.

Sachsman. David B. and David W. Bulla (eds.) *Sensationalism: Murder, Mayhem, Mudslinging, Scandals and Disasters in 19th Century Journalism.* Transaction Publishers, 2013.

Schudson, Michael. *Discovering The News: A Social History Of American Newspapers.* Basic Books, 1981.

Serrin, Judith and William (eds.) *Muckraking in America.* The New Press, 2002.

Sloan, William David. *Media in America: A History.* Vision Press, 2011.

Online Collections

Chronicling America: Historic American Newspapers
http://chroniclingamerica.loc.gov/

HathiTrust Digital Library
http://www.hathitrust.org/

Internet Archive
https://archive.org/

Project Gutenberg
http://www.gutenberg.org/

Unz.org
http://www.unz.org/Home/Introduction

from The Archive

The Archive of American Journalism is a new, independent publisher of historic journalism by major authors, including Mark Twain, Nellie Bly, Lincoln Steffens, Theodore Roosevelt, Ambrose Bierce, Stephen Crane, Jack London, Ida Tarbell, and Ernest Hemingway. The collection will provide the complete, original, and unabridged newspaper and magazine work of these notable writers and offer students, teachers, researchers and librarians a comprehensive reference source for their investigations into American history.

Lincoln Steffens: The System
ISBN: 978-0-9907137-3-9
List Price: $24.95
The "muckraker" Lincoln Steffens dug deep into business criminality and political corruption in a powerful series of articles written for *McClure's* magazine. Establishment newspapers and "System" politicians dismissed his work as just another example of the decrepit modern journalism that could never pass for genuine writing. But Steffens' dogged quest for truth and justice set the bar high for investigative journalists in print, television and the Internet who follow in his footsteps. This new collection from The Archive includes the author's detailed and dramatic pieces on the high-level civic shenaningans in Chicago, Minneapolis, St. Louis, Philadelphia, Rhode Island, Wisconsin, New Jersey, Ohio, and New York.

Theodore Roosevelt: Wilderness, Volume 1
ISBN: 978-0-9907137-1-5
List Price: S24.95
In the western states and territories a young Theodore Roosevelt found inspiring loneliness and a hunter's paradise. The mountains and prairies still posed a tough, dangerous physical challenge for a vigorous sportsman; out here TR also enjoyed a pleasing distance from the half-formed men of the East, who grasped so desperately for their money, prestige, and political influence. Roosevelt earned the nation's admiration through his military exploits during the Spanish-American War and from his exploits as a hunter, rancher and western explorer. As "open season" on buffalo, antelope, mountain goat and white-tailed deer brought these species close to extinction, however, he began to understand the meaning

and value of conservation—a progression expressed eloquently in the articles he penned for *Century*, *The Outlook* and other popular journals.

Richard Harding Davis: Star Reporter
ISBN: 978-0-9907137-4-6
List Price: $24.95

The year was 1897, and the place was the front page of Hearst's *New York Journal*. With "The Death of Adolfo Rodriguez," Richard Harding Davis created a sensation -- and public outrage that helped bring about the Spanish-American War. The strapping, square-jawed Davis became a media star, the very image of the intrepid foreign correspondent. He covered the revolution in Cuba and the Boer War in South Africa; he was admitted to the inner sanctum of the Kremlin; he described the brutal German occupation of Belgium and expressed outrage over the ruthless colonial exploitation in the Congo. This collection of 25 original newspaper and magazine stories, complete and unabridged, offers the reader a front page seat to compelling events all over the globe, and newspaper reporting as it was once done with social conscience and a flair for the dramatic.

Notes

www.ingramcontent.com/pod-product-compliance
Lightning Source LLC
Chambersburg PA
CBHW031408290426
44110CB00011B/305